HENBURY

History of a Village

Researched, written and published by members
of the Henbury Society

Published March 2003 by The Henbury Society.
Old School House, Henbury, Macclesfield SK11 9PH

Telephone 01625 612657. Email fgsegs@ukonline.co.uk

ISBN 0-9544600-0-6 (paper cover)
ISBN 0-9544600-1-4 (hard cover)

All rights reserved. No part of this publication may be reproduced, stored in a retrieval system, or transmitted, in any form or by any means, electronic, mechanical, photocopying, recording, or otherwise, without the prior permission of the publisher and the copyright holder

Ordnance Survey maps are reproduced from Ordnance Survey mapping on behalf of the Controller of Her Majesty's Stationery Office © Crown Copyright licence no. MC100040261

Printed by Cambrian Printers, Llanbadarn Road, Aberystwyth SY23 3TN

The Authors

In 1999 John Mead, then Chairman of the Henbury Society, assembled a team of Society members to research and write this History. He was able to call on a history teacher (Sally Walker), and a primary school teacher (Carol Hallett) and he recruited various retired professionals who happily turned their energies in this new direction. A consultant psychiatrist (Peter Wells) had already been working on the history of Henbury farms since 1994, and John added a biochemist (Roger Bowling), an electronic engineer (Peter Casswell), and a radio astronomer (Francis Graham-Smith). Not surprisingly, they needed help, which was provided by the former Parish Clerk (Arthur Marshall) and by Iain Glidewell (Appeal Court Judge) and Hilary Glidewell (sometime Mayor of Knutsford). Peter Wells acted as chairman of this diverse group. Many other Henbury residents contributed invaluable photographs and helped with recorded interviews.

We acknowledge the help of Chester Record Office and the John Rylands Library, both of which contain a seemingly inexhaustible collection of Deeds and Wills relating to Henbury farms. We were also shown some remarkably extensive local collections, particularly the archives held by Henbury Hall; we hope the kindness of the owners is repaid by what light we have shone on the early history of their houses. Our thanks are also due to the Grosvenor Museum, the County Archaeology Department and the Archeology Department of the University of Manchester.

The production of this book has been greatly helped by the computer skills of David Walker (not yet retired) and by Hilary Glidewell, who drew on her early experience as a journalist to act as Picture Editor.

Sadly we have to record that John Mead died in 2001, before he could see the result of his initiative. Without him there would have been no History of Henbury, and we dedicate this book to his memory.

We gratefully acknowledge financial help from Groundwork (Macclesfield & Vale Royal), and the de Ferranti Trust; and to everyone who has loaned photographs or who has allowed the team to interview them and has permitted photographs to be taken. Where possible, photographs have been attributed.

Contents

All the pleasure and the truth lie in the details. Stendhal.

Preface

1	The First Farmers	1
2	Domesday Book	7
3	Place Names and Boundaries	15
4	The Farming Community	21
5	Farms, Farmhouses and Cottages	39
6	More Farms and Smallholdings	71
7	Old Houses in Henbury	81
8	Henbury Hall	105
9	Birtles	123
10	The School	133
11	St Thomas's Church	141
12	Roads, Pubs and Shops	149
13	The Mills at Birtles and Henbury Hall	159
14	The Great Damburst	169
15	The Parish Council	177
16	The Henbury Society and the Millennium Green	185

Contents

17	People, Places and Happenings	193
18	The Population: People and Movement	205
19	Looking Ahead	211
20	The Henbury Archive	213
	Index	223

Preface

In the Domesday Survey of 1086 there was already a township called HAMITEBERIE which had half a hide of cultivated land (about 60 acres) and one hide (about 120 acres) which paid taxes. We now call Henbury a village, a word which brings to mind a traditional village centre, with ancient church, duckpond, pub, manor house and thatched cottages. But wandering round the ancient village of Henbury you will find nothing like this. You will find instead a wide spread of farms and an estate, all centuries old; some old houses and a contrasting development of houses only half a century old. There is no ancient Henbury parish church with stained glass windows, commemorating long-dead lords of the manor and vicars, and an ancient circular churchyard with misshapen yew trees and centuries-old gravestones with almost illegible inscriptions.

Where are the open fields holding the long narrow strips of land that according to tradition each villager owned, before these small patches of land were taken away from them by enclosure? Henbury has existed for a millennium or more, but where is its history?

Henbury has no ancient church. It was not a parish but a township, one of many in the great and ancient parish of Prestbury. The township was, over a large part of the country, the smallest unit of local government, or to be more exact self-government. Two officers were elected, usually annually: the constable, responsible for law and order, and the surveyor, responsible for maintenance of the roads. In general, elections for these posts were not hotly contested.

Where parishes were large, the township replaced the parish organisation, and this was the case over much of the country especially in the North. Henbury is a typical northern agricultural village, like hundreds of others.

What sort of village is Henbury, with no village centre? Historians call it a dispersed settlement, as opposed to a nucleated settlement. A better term also used by historians is a Scottish term a 'ferm toun', a farm town, which really describes a pattern seen at

Henbury

several locations in Henbury of two or three farms and a cottage or two clustered together in their fields, a small hamlet. The term does appear nearby, Vardon Town, Fitton Town in Over Alderley, and Butley Town. The main focus of the early village was in the area of Henbury Moss, down Fanshawe Lane; it was not until the 19th century, when the Church, Henbury School and the main Knutsford Road were built that the village centre moved north to where it is today.

There are two Henbury Parishes: civil and ecclesiastical. Our History covers the civil parish, and therefore includes Birtles which is part of a different ecclesiastical parish including Over Alderley. At the other end of Henbury the ecclesiastical parish extends to beyond Broken Cross, while the civil parish ends where the Bag Brook crosses the Chelford Road near the Cock Inn. A map will be found in Chapter 3.

The small group commissioned by the Henbury Society to write a local history started by tapping into the wealth of local reminiscence, stretching back more than half a century. We soon amassed far more than would fit into a book, and started a local archive of papers and tape recordings which gives a picture of the rapidly evolving community in which we live today. We then turned to documents preserved both locally and in the Cheshire Record Office, the John Rylands Library in Manchester, and other repositories; here we found hundreds of wills, conveyances and mortgages which contain a remarkably detailed history of the last four or five centuries. But there is no simple key to unravelling this history. There are very few early maps; there is for example no Henbury enclosure map, and the tithe map of 1849 provides no detail for about two-thirds of the village. Before the earliest detailed Ordnance Survey map (1871) the only generally available map is Burdett's map of Cheshire (1777). Fortunately three early Henbury Hall estate maps, of 1727, 1796, and 1842 have been preserved, with farm and field names which give us some idea of the evolution of farming and ownership.

Wills are unusual among old documents in that the thoughts, feelings, ideas and wishes of the writer are expressed in their own words, as it was written by the testator or dictated to a friend who

Preface

could write. Thus when in the record office, with maybe the real four century old will in your hand, you are as close as you can get to a person of Elizabethan times. In a will of 1845 the testator is dividing his very small estate among his several children, but he also instructs: *but not to Abraham.* What on earth had poor Abraham done to upset his father? Some wills also include an inventory, listing and valuing all the deceased's property. Henbury and Birtles, compared with other townships or parishes in Cheshire have a large collection of wills, and with over sixty inventories between them it is indeed a rich collection. A list of the wills we have consulted is in an Appendix to this book.

Wills have been used extensively to produce this book, but the most productive source is a vast bulk of conveyances and leases, which we today would refer to as title deeds. The biggest problem has been to find exactly the location of the property, house or other farms or land described in these deeds. Usually all we are given is *my messuage and land lying in Henbury,* and maybe some field names, but field names change quite quickly and lacking a contemporary map it is difficult to place the messuage, tenement or farm. With tenant farmers instead of owners the problems are greater.

From this scattered information we have attempted to piece together the History of a Village.

Chapter 1

The First Farmers

The Bronze Age urn from Bearhurst Farm (Grosvenor Museum, Chester)

Our village has been a farming community from time immemorial. Long before William of Normandy and his Domesday Book, long before the Roman occupation and the construction of the mighty walls at Chester, Henbury and Pexhill were settled and farmed by people whose organised and sophisticated ways of life we now can only understand in part[1]. Our first farmers lived here around 1500 B.C.

There are no deeds or written records for these farms, no evidence of fields, houses, barns or roads. Their records, remarkably, are not so much of the earthly things but of their spiritual life, the honour they paid the dead and their concern for the life to come. Their records now are the tombs of their dead; the round barrows, of which we have at least three, and another destroyed by sand quarrying in the recent past. It is possible that there are others but they may be hard to distinguish in the bumpy and banky fields round here.

Our knowledge of these things is largely due to the work of Gordon Rowley, the Bollington postman, who took a lifelong interest in the prehistory of the area. In 1975, at the age of 55, he

---

[1] *Cheshire Before the Romans.* W.J. Varley   pub. Cheshire Community Council

Henbury

was awarded a degree in Archaeology and Anthropology at Cambridge. It is largely on his book[2] *"Macclesfield in Prehistory. The first and only definitive record of events and places in the Macclesfield area from the end of the Great Ice Age to the coming of the Romans"* that this chapter is based. Rowley concluded in 1982, that there were probably a dozen and a half genuine examples of the standard round tombs of the Bronze Age within a few miles of Macclesfield indicating that the area was well populated at that time, for the burials would have been in fairly close proximity to the settlements.

It was an odd sensation, exciting and humbling at the same time, to see at close quarters, the remains of the funerary urn that Rowley discovered when he excavated the barrow at Bearhurst Farm with David Bethell in 1965-6. Nowadays the extremely fragile urn lives in a very ordinary looking wooden cupboard, safe in the vaults of the Grosvenor Museum in Chester[3]. In fact only the top part of the urn remains - a wide collar decorated before firing with a lozenge pattern of tiny holes probably made with a pointed stick or bone implement. It was larger than might be expected and originally had an almost vertical centre section and an incurving lower third leading to a very narrow flat base. When found it was covered by another round based vessel and inside were the cremated remains of a small boned male aged around 18 years, which are now at Keele University.

Another round barrow at a site near Thorneycroft Lodge Farm was excavated in 1965 by Bethell, in advance of quarrying. At least five other in-urned cremations were found here and taken to Keele University.

Who was the young man of Bearhurst Farm and indeed the others? And why were they honoured so much in death? It seems unlikely that every one would have had such a burial. With the tools at their disposal it must have been a colossal labour and distracted everyone from their normal routine for a long time. Were they heroes, or perhaps members of the chieftain's family?

---

[2] *Macclesfield in Prehistory.* G.Rowley pub. by the author August 1982.
[3] We are grateful for help and information from D. Robinson, Keeper of Archaeology, Grosvenor Museum Chester.

The First Farmers

Perhaps you know the wonderful series of books written some time ago by Marjorie and C.H.B. Quennell[4], *"Everyday Life in the ... Age"*? In a marvellous leap of imagination they link the Bronze Age burials, especially the spectacular ones of North Wales and Ireland, with the writing of Homer, which is entirely reasonable for, after all, Homer wrote down the oral tradition of centuries before, and the archaeological sites associated with these stories are Bronze Age. Purists may point out that this is Macclesfield and not the Aegean but the vision is irresistible!

In the twenty-fourth book of the "Iliad", Homer described the burial of Hector, the Trojan warrior prince and famous tamer of horses:

"So nine days they gathered great store of wood. But when the tenth morn rose with light for men, then they bare forth brave Hector, weeping tears, and on a lofty pyre they laid the dead man, and thereon cast fire.

But when the young dawn shone forth, rosy fingered Morning, then the people gathered round Glorious Hector's pyre. Assembling, they first of all quenched the flames of the pyre with wine, even as far as the might of the flames had reached, and thereupon his brethren and his friends gathered his white bones mourning him with big tears coursing down their cheeks. The bones they took and laid away in a golden urn, wrapping them in soft purple robes and quickly set the urn in a hollow grave, and heaped above great stones, closely placed. Then hastily they piled a barrow. And when the barrow was duly piled they went back, and assembling, feasted well..."

Coming down to earth again, a great deal can be learned from the pottery urns and shards, or broken pieces which were found. Since they were too fragile to be carried far by traders they can be related to a particular group of people by their characteristic styles and decorations. These pots were made by the coil method and

---

[4] *Everyday Life in Prehistoric Times.* Marjorie and C.H.B. Quennell. pub Transworld Publishers Ltd.

Henbury

fired in the ordinary cooking fire. Probably it was something the women did in the beginning but as the community became more prosperous craftsmen-potters would perhaps have taken over the work.

Our first farmers were herdsmen who kept sheep and cattle on the land of the Macclesfield shelf, which is still so good for stock rearing. It seems likely that they moved about as the pasture was used up and that their dwellings were little more than temporary shelters. This, as well as the building of the burial mounds, implies quite a lot of organisation and co-operative labour and a systematic social structure that we can only guess.

The area was not particularly good for growing crops but we can imagine that the women had small plots of garden in which they experimented with plants and herbs. The men would certainly have hunted and fished from time to time still making use of the flint arrow heads and stone knives of their ancestors. In fact Rowley discovered a very fine arrow head at the Bearhurst excavation and he found a flint knife at Siddington, not associated with a burial but in a roadside bank, seemingly casually discarded, which he dated to the early Bronze Age.

It is possible that there were farmers in Henbury long before the Bronze Age. In the spring of 1971 a field was ploughed at New Farm[5], for only the second time in its known history. The operation revealed two large globular erratics, 0.3- 0.4 metres in diameter. Similar stones were found in the field boundaries and some had been built into a stile. Subsequent excavation in autumn 1971 by Rowley revealed thirteen pits of which eleven formed an ovoid feature surrounding a central pit. The pits were a maximum of 0.53 metres deep and some contained a circular arrangement of cobbles, others showed signs of great heat and charcoal residues. Rowley dated this possible prehistoric henge[6] to the beginning or the middle of the second millennium B.C. The County Sites and Monuments Record however dates this as Neolithic (4000 B.C. to 2351 B.C.). The purpose of the structure is not known but some alignments show the first view of the winter sun rising over Sutton

---
[5] Grid ref SJ 887728
[6] Cheshire Archaeological Bulletin; No. 3, 1975.

The First Farmers

Common, perhaps implying the calculation of the arrival of seed sowing time.

What happened to these first settlers in Henbury? Gradually over time new settlers came with different ways and ideas but although there must have been disruption, in general the older populations were not wiped out and displaced but were absorbed and their culture overlaid by a new more vigorous one. And so it is intriguing to suppose that perhaps some of the very old Cheshire farming families, who have never moved far from their roots are the direct descendants of the first farmers of Henbury.

Chapter 2

Henbury in the Domesday Book

On Christmas Day 1085 King William I announced to his Council that he wanted a complete record made of the whole kingdom - his property! The reasons for this were taxation, the allocation of holdings and the settling of disputes involving land. The Domesday Survey was set up and completed the following year. Commissioners visited most parts of the country and jurors were summoned before them to make a sworn return. The clergy were drafted in to act as scribes as very few people including the king himself were literate. Why "Domesday"? No doubt the villagers of England thought that Domesday or the Judgement Day had arrived! Questions were asked such as:

What is the name of the manor?
Who held (owned) it in the time of King Edward (The Confessor)? (abbreviated as T.R.E.)
Who holds it now?
How many hides is it rated at? (a hide was not a specific area but enough land to feed one family)
How many plough teams?
How many people, of what class?
How much woodland[1], meadow, pasture, livestock, mills, fisheries?
What was it worth, at the time of King Edward, when the present owner took over, and now?

---

[1] The woodland was extremely valuable. Wood was the raw material for houses, carts, implements, ships and fuel. This estimation was probably on the conservative side. The commissioners would not have had the time to measure it accurately.

Henbury

Facsimile[2] of the page in the Domesday Book relating to Henbury. Chester County Council Libraries supply the following transcription and translation[3].

Transcription:

Ipse comes tenet HAMETEBERIE de dimidia hida.
COPESTOR de dimidia hida et HAMEDEBERIE de i. Hida geldabili
Et HOFINCHEL de i. Hida . et TENGESTVISIE de i. Virgata terrae
Et HOLISURDE de i. Virgata et WARNET de i. Virgata et RUMELIE
de i. Virgata et LAITONE de I. Virgata terrae. Omnes geldabant.
Has terras tenuerunt viii homines pro maneriis. Terra est xvi. carucatae inter totos.
Wasta fuit et est tota.
In HOFINGEL est silva ii. Leuvis longa et ii. Lata. In TENGESTVISIE silva est
iiii. leuvis longa et ii. Lata.

---

[2] Township Pack No 58, Henbury cum Pexall. Published by Cheshire County Council Libraries and Archives 1996

[3] *Virgate* - a quarter of a hide.

Carucate - same as hide (this does not add up: there seems to have been much more arable land available than they had been paying tax for)

Hundred - a Saxon subdivision of the county which had its own assembly of notables and village representatives.

Henbury in the Domesday Book

Tempore regis EDWARDI valebat istud hundredum xl. Solidos. Modo x. solidos.

Translation:
The Earl himself holds HAMATEBERIE (Henbury with Pexhall) *for half a hide,* COPESTOR (Capesthorne) *for half a hide, and* HAMEDEBERIE *for half a hide, rateable to the gelt, and* HOFINCHEL (Henshaw) *for i. Hide, and* TENGESTVISIE (Tintwistle) *for a virgate, and* HOLISURDE (Holingworth) *for a virgate, and* WARNET (Werneth) *for a virgate, and* RUMELIE (Romiley) *for a virgate, and* LAITONE (?) *for a virgate. All rateable to the gelt. Eight free men held these lands for [viii] manors. The land is xvi. carucates among all. The whole is and was waste. In HOFINGEL is a wood ii. leagues long, and two broad. In TENGESTVISIE there is a wood iv. leagues long, and ii. broad. In WARNET, a wood iii. leagues long, and ii. Broad. In King EDWARD'S time this hundred was worth xl. Shillings, now x. shillings.*

The entry for Henbury tells a stark and terrible story. Henbury, along with many other settlements in Cheshire, had been destroyed: laid waste by the forces of the new Norman king, William I in 1069/70 as a punishment for most serious rebellion. For this reason *"the whole was and is waste."* It was waste in 1070 when the new earl *"the earl himself"* took over and it was still waste in 1086 when the Domesday survey was made. Previous to this, in the time of King Edward, Henbury had considerable ploughlands - one and a half hides - and paid taxes on them, *"rateable to the gelt".*

This part of Cheshire was sparsely populated, perhaps no more than four people to the square mile. It was poor and backward compared to the south and east of England. Forests and wild country on the western slopes of the Pennines had made settlement difficult. Henbury has fertile soil and a good water supply, however, and was probably a well favoured if scattered settlement. As a result of the Norman punitive strikes the people had gone and the fields, so painfully cleared from the forest, were returning to a

Henbury

wilderness of bramble, bracken and scrub. It was devastated and remained so for many years.

Before the Norman Conquest of 1066, Cheshire was part of Mercia, once a separate kingdom but now a vast and powerful Saxon earldom. Earl Edwin of Mercia and Earl Morcar of Northumbria had not entirely accepted the Saxon defeat at the battle of Hastings. They were remote from London and when William was away in Normandy raised rebellions against him. Their armies, supplies and other resources were provided by their domains. Initially William on his return defeated them and pardoned them but in 1069 after a second rising and their support of the Welsh, the king carried out the notorious harrying of the North.

The counties of Yorkshire, Durham and later Cheshire were laid waste by fire and sword, leaving a trail of destruction and death. William meant business. This was calculated to ruin the affected districts by destroying their population and livelihoods and it succeeded.

It seems likely that the Norman forces crossed the Pennines from Yorkshire into the north east corner of Cheshire. They advanced on Stockport along the old Roman road. Tintwhistle, Hollingworth, Werneth and Romily, lying only a mile or so from the road were wasted at this time. They moved south and attacked Macclesfield, which was also thoroughly devastated. Bollington and Prestbury were on this route and duly suffered. From Macclesfield raiding parties looted and destroyed most of the settlements in this part of Cheshire. Afterwards they divided their forces in three, sweeping across the county and regrouping at Chester which held out for some time. In 1086 Chester was described as *"greatly ruined"* and nearly half its houses were in ruin. Some places of use to the Normans, however, like Neston and Sandbach went unscathed and prospered[4].

Apart from Yorkshire no other part of the country suffered as badly as Cheshire. Nearly two thirds of all the Cheshire manors mentioned in Domesday were wholly or partly waste, others had

---

[4] *Cheshire under the Norman Earls*, B.M.C.Hudson. Cheshire Community Council.

Henbury in the Domesday Book

fallen dramatically in value: Macclesfield, for example *"it was worth 8 pounds in the time of King Edward, now 20 shillings, it was waste."* Others simply did not appear.

Apart from the need to punish the duplicity of Earl Edwin, William needed to control Cheshire because of its strategic importance. It bordered Wales which continually caused problems and he had ambitions to subdue the Welsh. It was also the main route to Ireland. To be sure of Cheshire's subservience he allocated the land to his Norman followers and most of it, including Henbury, to his nephew Hugh of Avranches, better known as Hugh Lupus - the Wolf.

Hugh, the first Norman earl of Chester, was loyal to the king and an effective and energetic keeper of the borders with the Welsh. He is described in a monastic chronicle thus:

"This man with the help of many cruel barons, shed much Welsh blood He was not so much lavish as prodigal. His retinue was more like an army than a household and in giving and receiving he kept no account. Each day he devastated his own land and preferred falconers and huntsmen to the cultivators of the soil and ministers of heaven. He was so much a slave to the gluttony of his belly that weighed down by his fat he could hardly move. From harlots he had many children of both sexes, who almost all came to an unfortunate end"

Henbury was one of eight local manors held by free men. What had happened to the freemen who previously held these eight manors, and their families? The stewards of Adlington, Prestbury, and Butley carried on after William I; the others may have been killed in the raids on the villages or maybe they had escaped to the forest to live out their lives as outlaws. The Saxon inhabitants of Cheshire had been decimated and reduced to a subclass. The Normans took firm grip of the manors and ran them in a very authoritarian way. Their administration became more efficient, communication and transport improved and they introduced new agricultural practices making the land more profitable.

Henbury

At this time each community had to be self sufficient and produced most of the bare necessities of life. Every manor grew wheat, barley, oats and peas. Sheep, cattle and pigs would have been reared. Sheep were important for their wool, and cattle for their hides as well as meat. The pigs would have been turned out into the extensive woodland to feast on acorns. Cattle or oxen would draw ploughs and carts. Corn was cut by hand with sickles and the whole village would work together to bring in the hay and corn harvests. The corn was threshed over the autumn and winter, in a barn by hand using flails, and the grain milled at the local water mill.

Ridge and furrow traces in the field behind Old School House

In this part of Cheshire the ploughed fields were small, irregular and enclosed to keep back the relentless wilderness. Perhaps some are as they always were. Pasture and meadow would have been near the streams. There was also some considerable common land for grazing. Macclesfield for example had a very large common to the east of the town, and it is likely that Henbury villagers would have used Whirley Common and Long Moss (in the Broken Cross vicinity). Some fields in Henbury still show signs of the early plough lands. Look around the village for ridge and furrow; this is where the ploughed land can still be seen through present pasture. A good example of this is in the fields across the main road from the church.

It seems certain that Henbury was always a scattered farming community, and it is unlikely that the open field system of agriculture was ever practised here. The scattered nature of the settlement eventually gave rise to the establishment of hall, parkland, mill and possibly a chapel, all within the old Saxon boundaries. For, over time, Henbury did recover as agriculture revived and populations increased generally in the twelfth and thirteenth centuries; but there can be no doubt that there had been tragedy and economic catastrophe in the early Norman period.

Chapter 3

Place names and Boundaries

There are two Henbury parishes, civil and diocesan. As can be seen on the map, the Henbury St Thomas Parish extends into Broken Cross, but not into the Birtles and Whirley Lane area. Birtles was a township in Prestbury Parish, Macclesfield Hundred, which was added to Henbury civil parish in 1894. The Parish of St Catherine, Birtles includes the township of Over Alderley, and has been a separate parish since 1890.

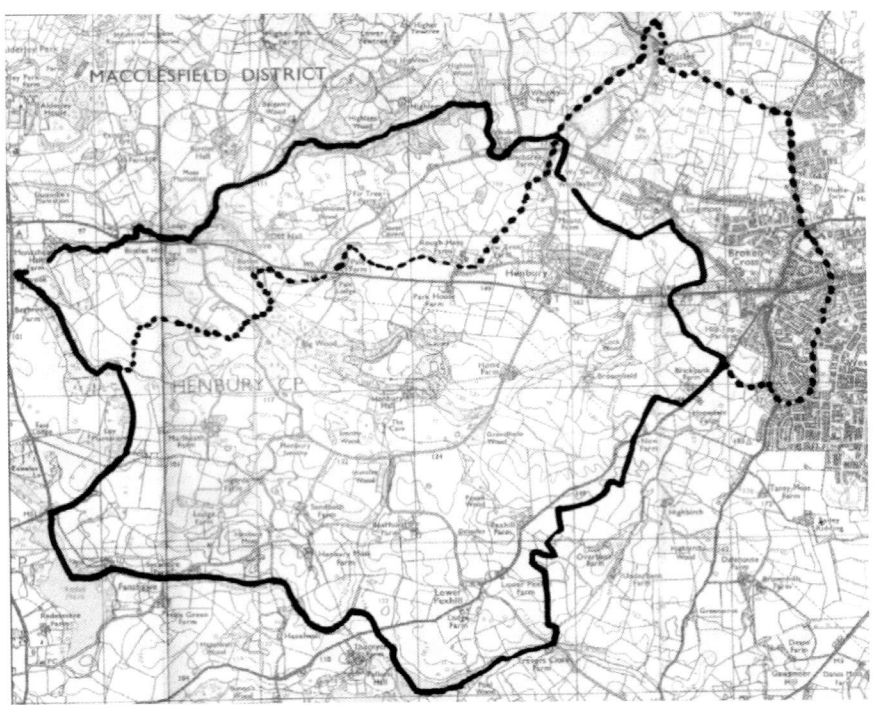

The full line shows the civil parish, and the broken line shows the diocesan parish

From about 1350, and probably earlier, the Henbury Hall Estate has dominated the land holdings in Henbury. It presently occupies about 500 acres, that is about one fifth of the township of Henbury. Until recently the estate was larger, extending to over 1000 acres,

Henbury

including many of the surrounding farms, with a compact core around the hall. Land and farms around this core changed ownership and tenancies frequently. Some properties passed into or out of the estate more than once, such as Pale Farm (see Chapters 4 & 5). Henbury was probably not a manor in the full sense, but the Davenports, whose lordship extended from mediaeval times to the end of the 17th century, seem to have run it as though it were.

In its heyday the Davenport estate probably extended to the eastern boundary of Henbury, almost to Broken Cross; and the northern boundary crossed the present Andertons Lane. Conveyances of the property by George Lucy, son and heir of the last Davenport, Isabella, reserve to himself the mediaeval dues of chief farm rent, chief rent and quit rent although he had sold the whole estate to Sir William Meredith. This sale was in 1693, when Lucy moved back to his family estate at Charlecote in Warwickshire, but a long list of these dues, still payable, (some on properties no longer owned by the estate) appeared with the conveyance of the estate from John Ryle to Thomas Marsland in 1842. From this list we can be sure that the estate was much larger under the Davenports than it was under the Merediths in the eighteenth century.

The first detailed map, drawn for Meredith in 1727, therefore shows a diminished estate of about 1000 acres, similar in size to the estate as it was in the later 20th century.

The second Sir William Meredith sold to John Bower Jodrell, and his map of 1796 shows little change. There does appear to have been expansion of the estate during the Brocklehursts' stewardship, 1874 to1956. Their lands extended in 1920 to include Unsworth Fold Farm on Whirley Road, (opposite Henbury High School), Whirley Barn Farm which was partly in Whirley and partly in Henbury, and land to the north of Church Lane and at Brickbank Farm on Pexhill Road.

Hameteberie is the name of the village as it was recorded in Domesday Book in 1086. In 1288 the name appears as *Hendebiry*, and except for small variations has not changed much for the last 700 years.

Place Names and Boundaries

All place names are descriptive, sometimes describing the geography of the area such as situated on a hilltop or a wooded place, sometimes the origin of the village such as a Roman camp, a river crossing or a castle, and sometimes telling the names of the first settlers.

There are three rules in the study of place names. The first is never to guess, for you are almost certain to be wrong, and the second is to seek out the earliest record of the name, for that will be nearer to the original version, less corrupted by all the spelling and copying mistakes over the centuries. The third rule is to leave the study to the experts of the English Place Names Society, a group of mainly academics well versed in all the many ancient languages that make up modern English[1,2].

Take the example of Whirley. The area of Whirley near to Broken Cross was in 1347 Qwellegh, and a century later Whelley, meaning a "wheel clearing" which could be taken to refer to something circular such as an assart or a field. However at Whirley Hall the name is quite different, Wirleye in 1362 meaning "the clearing where bog myrtle grows". This tells us that the land was wet and poor; bog myrtle still grows on Danes Moss. The names were so similar that sometime after 1500 they became the same. Birtles is easier, it means "little birches."

What about Hameteberie? The name is like the vast majority of English place names, originating in Saxon times[3]. The *berie* part is easy, it derives from *burh* meaning a defended settlement, sometimes a castle but here more likely a farmstead or very small hamlet defended by a ditch or fence. Sometimes *burh* means the manor or manor house, as Prestbury, "the manor of the priests", but this is probably not so for Henbury.

Dodgson (op. cit.) proposes that Henbury derives from *hæmed* and *burh* 'the manor house or stronghold where people live

---

[1] The Place Names of Cheshire.Part 1. EPNS Vol. 44 J.McN.Dodgson. Ed. CUP 1970
[2] Concise Oxford Dictionary of English Place Names. E.Ekwall. OUP 1960
[3] Potter S. Cheshire Place-names THLSC 106 1-22 1955 "Cheshire names are prehistorically Celtic, substantially Anglian, partially Scandinavian, sporadically Norman-French"

Henbury

together; where the community lives'. He comments "since the word *hæmed* is recorded in Old English only with the meaning *cohabitation*, there may be indelicate connotations.' An alternative suggestion is the combination of a personal name, perhaps *Hamet*, and *burh* making Henbury *'the stronghold of Hamet'* (or *'of Hamet's people')*.

Endesbyre et Pexhille was first recorded in 1295, and of course the use of the two linked names Henbury cum Pexall persists today. *Pexhull* occurs in1274 and is little different from the modern spelling, but even today on the latest OS maps two spellings appear, *Pexall* for the general area, and *Pexhill* for three farms. As with Henbury, the name is of Saxon origin and means "the hill of the Peacs", probably referring to the Pecsaetan, a tribe who inhabited the area we now call The Peak. Occasionally in documents the name Gawsworth Pexall is recorded which may be the western side of Gawsworth bordering onto Henbury Pexall. The name Pexhill is also found in North Rode. All this could suggest that Pexall was a settlement never becoming a township in its own right but was divided between Henbury and Gawsworth.

There are many records in conveyances and mortgages of field names, only some of which persist over the centuries. Where for example are Flax Halflond and Small Furlong, mentioned by Ormerod? The earliest map of the "Manour of Henbury" showing field names was made for Meredith in 1727; it is preserved in delicate condition in the Chester Record Office. A more complete map attached to the Conveyance of 1842 (Assignees of Ryle to Marsland) gives names to all fields in the whole Henbury Hall estate: for example, the editor of this book now knows that he is looking out over Meadow and Cordwood Field of Hulme's Tenement[4]. Closer to the Hall, Pool Field was probably the site of the old pool which fed Henbury Mill in the 17th century (see Chapter 11); a field alongside the present Upper Pool was named Mill Field.

A search for roughly similar field names in the Henbury estate to those which appeared in a 1675 indenture revealed that many

---

[4] In 1957, when these fields were part of Ruewood Farm, they were called School Meadow and Wood Croft.

Place Names and Boundaries

had survived over a 50 year period, but after over a century had passed, about two thirds had already disappeared.

ANCIENT FIELDNAMES IN HENBURY ESTATE
Fieldnames change over time, although some survive. The earliest lists we could find appeared in an indenture dated 1675 and another dated 1682.

Field Names 1675	Acres 1675	Tenant/occupier	1727 map	Field Book 1796	Estate Map 1842
Maddox House		Thomas Maddocks	+		
Henbury Park	120	Sir Fulk Lucy	+	+	+
Moore Fields, Two Marled Huntleys & Shepherd's Croft	32	Thomas Birtleys, Thos Cooper, John Heath, John Ward	+	+	+
The Moore Field	6	Sir Fulk Lucy			
Brickhills meadow	7	Sir Fulk Lucy	+		
Hallcroft Meadow	5	Sir Fulk Lucy	+		
Milnefield	14	Sir Fulk Lucy			
Ox Hey	20	Sir Fulk Lucy	+	+	+
New Closes	9	John Harding			
Birchwood Field & Coate Meadow	12	Thomas Cooper	+		
Marled Earth & Six Day Math	15	Thomas Cooper	+		
Mossfield	2	Thomas Cooper	+		
Lower Pasture	12	Ralph Phinney, Lawrence Hancock, Thos Henshaw, John (Stretton?)	+		
Wood Ground called Maddocks Birchwood	5	Thomas Cooper	+		
Maddocks Lower Ground	9	Peter Whalley	+		
Pool Field & Pool Head	20	Sir Fulk Lucy		+	
Pinching Reaves	8	William Barlow	+		+
Tadmans Croft	8	John Harding	+	+	+
Great Huntley	8	John Harding	+		+
Annis Croft Meadow	6	Sir Fulk Lacy	+		
Bromyhall Croft Field	25	John Harding	+	+	+
Butty Bearhurst	24	William Walton			
Lower Bearhurst	19	William Walton		+	+

Henbury

Field boundaries too had changed, and although some names survived, a number occupied a slightly different location, for example Tadmans Croft, which lay on the eastern side of Bearhurst Lane, crossed the road to the western side and became Padmans Croft.

Farm names also changed, usually assuming the names of long term tenants. Lingards Farm was named after John Lingard, tenant from 1713 until 1737, but a map in the Capesthorne Museum dated 1827 shows the farm as Simpson's, named after Jacob Simpson, tenant from 1795 at least until 1831. Sandbach Farm named after three generations of the Sandbach family, was previously known as Hulme's Tenement.

The 1727 Meredith map shows Sprinks Farm on the present-day Pepper Street; this became Spinks Farm, now the Geldart Studio. The name Sprinks also appears to the west of Henbury Hall; possibly he was an owner or tenant with an outlying field, but we are still looking for another meaning to this name. It may derive from 'spring'.

It is disappointing that only few names are of considerable antiquity, but common usage occasioned by change of tenure, land use, dialect and idiosyncratic spelling inevitably introduce changes.

Chapter 4

The Farming Community

The Massey family at Ruewood, 1896 (courtesy Henbury Hall Estate)

For many centuries Henbury was a stable and increasingly prosperous farming community, whose origins can be traced back to mediaeval times. In the 20th century, however, almost everything changed; many farmhouses became private residences, and many new houses were built north of the main Chelford Road. Farming itself survived only by huge changes from the traditional pattern. In this chapter we trace some of the development of farming in Henbury, starting with the older farms at Henbury Moss. The chapter ends with the story of one farm, Rough Heys, whose recent history typifies the transformation of farming and the demographic changes which are still happening in Henbury.

The present-day outlines of farms and their patterns of fields are often very ancient in origin. This is probably the case for Henbury, which seems to have been little affected by the enclosure

Henbury

movements of the 18th and 19th centuries. The Henbury Hall estate, and the adjacent estates of Capesthorne, Alderley, and Thorneycroft were already dominating the land usage in the 16th century, and the layout of farms within the estates was established by then. The farms were known as tenements and often carried the name of the farmer. For instance, Broomfield Farm was owned by John Broomfield and was referred to as Broomfield Tenement, and later when acquired by the estate in 1779 as Broomfield Farm. Sandbach farm was farmed by John Sandbach in the 17th century. Hulmes Tenement appears as the former name both of Sandbach Farm and of the farm which became Henbury school and the Millennium Green.

The growing prosperity of Cheshire farming is set out in an article 'Cheshire Farming 1500-1900' by Fussell[1]. The county was already largely enclosed in the 16th century, mainly with small fields of a few acres only. There was no three-field system. Shared open ploughed fields ("co-aration") were widely used[2], but disappeared piecemeal, probably by private unrecorded agreements. Individual ownership, or tenancy, encouraged farmers to improve the soil, and fields were extensively fertilised by marling. Marl pits, from which a rich mixture of clay and lime was taken and spread, can still be seen in many fields as ponds, although many were filled in from the beginning of the 19th century as other fertilisers became available. Dairy farming was already the pattern in the 17th century, with large quantities of cheese shipped to London via Chester and Liverpool.

As always in farming, there were setbacks. The early 19th century included bad years in which overseas competition hit the markets, with Dutch and Irish cheese arriving by sea. Improved transport inland was more helpful, and milk production became a more practical enterprise. The recent BSE and foot and mouth epidemics had their forerunners: in an 1865-6 epidemic of rinderpest more than 35,000 cattle were lost. However, Henbury

---

[1] Fussell G.E. Trans. History Soc. Lancs. and Cheshire (THLSC) **106**, 57, 1955.
[2] Sylvester, D. *The Open Fields of Cheshire*. THLSC **108**, 1, 1957.

The Farming Community

seems to have prospered; a list of outstanding dairy farms[3] in 1877 included George Millington's Horseshoe Farm (now Home Farm).

Home Farm at the time of the farm sale, 1987 (courtesy of W Hatton)

Throughout the district, water was drawn from wells and springs until quite late in the 20th century. Tom Gould of Park House Farm recalled that when he was a lad, he, Phillip Coleman and Arthur Goodall used to indulge in various pranks. A stout character called Mrs Phillips who lived on Dark Lane used to draw water from a well by Broome Cottage. The three lads were hidden behind a hedge and she doused them with her pail of water. Quite what provoked this attack is not clear. Years later when Mrs Phillips died, Tom helped to bear her coffin up Dark Lane to the Church, "A mighty burden". Making amends, perhaps?

Until mains water was laid on at Park House Farm just before World War II, they drew water from a spring via a 40 foot high wind pump, at the rate of 300 gallons an hour. Jean Gould reported that the quality and taste of the spring water was superior to mains water, and "it made a good cup of tea".

---

[3] Samuel Sherriff *Report of Liverpool Prize Farms*. J.R.A.S.E., see Fussell above.

Henbury

Parkhouse farm in the 1950's (courtesy Mr & Mrs T Gould)

People living on the western side of the Parish, including Lodge Farm, used to draw their water from a pump at Lingards Farm. Mains water only reached this part of the village in the 1960s.

Springbank cottage (previously known as Wood Farm) pumped its water from Fanshawe Brook in the valley below to a tank on the ridge above, which also fed Moss Farm and Moss Cottage. Mains water was eventually laid on after the Henbury Estate intervened on their behalf.

Fanshawe Brook before the culvert was built in 1938 (original kindly loaned by Jess Ford)

The Farming Community

Electricity did not reach many of the farms until the middle of the last century and oil lamps were in use well within living memory. Mains electricity reached Park House Farm in 1954. Mrs Ethel Heathcote, who occupied Lodge Farm from 1940 until 1970 reported that for most of their tenure there was no electricity: "there were no mod cons".

Cheese making in Cheshire has been an industry for many hundreds of years, but it was only from 1650 that it began to be sold in any quantity beyond the county[4]. Cheese factors used to collect cheeses from farms, and transport them to Liverpool, from where they were taken by sea to retailers in London. We found evidence for cheese making in Henbury; for example, part of a cheese press may be seen at Bearhurst farm and at Glebe Cottage, and at Sandbach they told us that there had once been an abandoned cheese press in their farmyard.

Mr and Mrs Ralph Hatton and their family farmed Home Farm for 47 years from 1940. They bought their first tractor, a Fordson Standard in 1942. It had no self starter, but had to be cranked by handle. In 1987, they donated it to the Wirral Country Park Museum, still in working order.

The Hatton brothers with their 1942 Fordson Standard tractor, in 1987 (courtesy W Hatton)

---

[4] Charles Foster: *Cheshire Cheese & Farming in the North West in the 17th and 18th Centuries.* Arley Hall Press, 1998.

Henbury

Ploughing with horses continued on some farms until after the war. George Heathcote of Lodge Farm, who died in 1970, worked the land with a horse and never used a tractor. Tom Gould still ploughed with horses in the 1950's. Harold Bayley of Sandbach Farm told us how difficult it was to cut corn using three horses abreast, because when they turned they tended to trip on each other's hooves. The shoes were liable to be wrenched off exposing their nails, with the risk of injury and infection.

Tom Gould ploughing (courtesy Mr & Mrs T Gould)

As was the case nationally, the start of the 1939 war imposed much change on village life. Many farmers' sons and other young men joined up; sadly some never returned as is testified by the war memorial in St Thomas Churchyard. Others undertook the duties of Air Raid Precaution wardens, mainly to ensure that no stray light functioned as a beacon to guide enemy bombers on their way to bomb Manchester. A Henbury Home Guard platoon was based at Broken Cross, but there are no defensive pill boxes in this area. Evacuee children from Manchester were placed on farms and

The Farming Community

homes in the district, and used to walk to Henbury School, carrying their obligatory gas masks.

Home Farm potato harvest, 1944, Pale Lodge behind
(courtesy W Hatton)

People tended to get about on bicycles as public transport was largely commandeered for military use and petrol rationing restricted the use of cars. Later in the war there were frequent convoys of American troops on the main road, and a Prisoner of War camp was established near Knutsford. Both German and Italian prisoners of war were brought in daily by lorry to help on

Henbury

farms, and were accepted and well behaved. Elsie Knight recalled how Italians enjoyed congregating at the Smithy for a chat, and one of them taught her mother how to make ice cream. A Czech who had been compelled to join the German army worked for Tom and Jean Gould at Park House Farm, and wrote to them for three years after the war. The letters suddenly stopped, and they worry over what might have happened to him when the Russians took over his home country.

During the war, the Ministry of Agriculture employed inspectors to check that farms were running efficiently, and complying with wartime regulations. They possessed draconian powers to evict and replace an inefficient farmer. When everything depended on the maximum production of food, a field growing full of thistles, for example, implied neglect and was hastily cleared before an inspector arrived. Ralph Hatton of Home Farm would not allow his sons Walter and Charlie to clear thistles with a mowing machine, as he believed that they grew more profusely afterwards - they had to use a scythe.

Farming left little time for socialising. Ernest Kennerley who worked at Pexhill Farm from 1942 told us that as a young man he had to rise at 5.30, and on some days had to keep going until midnight. "There was always pressure to finish essential tasks before weather held things up". He had one day off in 7 years. When he started at Pexhill he told us that the wage for an 80 hour week was £2.10s. (£2.50), and rent was £47 an acre (now around £160 an acre). Milk made 1s. (5p) a gallon in 1942. He remembered using horse hair mortar for repair jobs on the farm. He used to plough with three horses, and harvested the corn with a scythe: "I doubt if anyone could use one these days" he commented. Pexhill was a mixed farm on 160 acres with cattle, sheep, pigs and crops of barley, oats, wheat, potatoes, turnips and mangles, employing two men. He encouraged parties to visit from local schools to teach them about farming; " Some of them had never seen a cow before!"

Opportunity to meet the opposite sex was limited in the early 20th century. Many of the women only met their future partner after starting work at one of the mills in Macclesfield. For those

The Farming Community

who had the time and were not too exhausted by working long hours, there was considerable social activity as reported in Henbury Parish Magazine, for example between 1904 and 1911. It reported dances held in the school, harvest festivals, sales of work, evening classes, a Parish drive in a wagonette, Sunday School field trips, old people's teas (43 present in 1908, 56 in 1910), and trips to Blackpool. In 1911 there were celebrations at the time of the coronation of King George Vth, although the marquee collapsed in the wind. Coronation mugs were distributed among schoolchildren.

Jean Tatton (Ethel Heathcote's daughter) and her husband talked of courtship in the mid twentieth century. After a day's work, he would cycle 5 miles to Lodge farm, and they would ride back together to the Blacksmith's Arms, where they would leave their bikes and catch a bus to the Institute at Broken Cross where a dance was held. They took a bus back to the Blacksmith's Arms, cycled from there to Lodge Farm, and he would then cycle back to Macclesfield - a real test of devotion!

Here is an account of village life given by a 75 year old lady called Joan Foschtinsky, (nee Birtles) of Birtles Farm, Hocker Lane. Although she lives in a neighbouring Parish, her description of life in the country in the 1920's and 30's is just as relevant for Henbury, and is a delightful recollection of life in a very different world.

'You might think that the district has not changed much apart from the fact that many farms in those days are now dwellings for commuters. Apart from Hare Hill, Birtles Old Hall and Birtles Hall all dwellings were farms, small holdings or cottages for farm workers, gardeners or estate workers. Most people were born and bred in Over Alderley or adjoining Parishes. The great difference from today was that everybody knew everybody. I have been in every house, either because school friends lived there or with my father visiting his friends or selling and buying eggs, vegetables or rabbits etc. Virtually everyone was related in some way. There w ere the three Oakes families; Maggie Oakes was a Read from Baguley Farm in Hocker Lane, where Sam and Lizzie lived and

Henbury

they were brother and sister. Another sister was Florrie Foden at High Yew Tree whose Mother-in-law lived at Varden Town and was related to the many Barbers who were related to the Postles at Hare Barrow laundry at Varden Town - nearly everybody was related.

Life was very simple and uncomplicated and safe. Only Mr Nash the vicar and one or two farmers had cars, so there was hardly any traffic. Practically all the time was spent in Over Alderley. People did not need or have the time to go out of the parish except perhaps to go to Macclesfield or Alderley. Tradesmen came round. There was Mr Hallworth the grocer - and... there was Mr Partington the butcher who came on Tuesdays and Fridays, Handkinson the breadman called twice a week and Ted Wright's father called every Wednesday afternoon, selling candles, matches, paraffin, soap, brushes etc. He had a black horse and a lorry with a tarpaulin cover.

There was no electricity until 1940, and no mains water until the fifties. When I got married in '51, we had no mains water then, so it must have reached us later. Only the vicar had a telephone in the vicinity. If anyone was ill, someone had to run across fields or cycle to the vicarage to phone for a doctor.

Dad tells a tale - there was a terrible accident down here. A lot of people used to come out from Manchester and I think some boys used to come and stay at the farms to make a bit of money for the occupiers. Some lads were sitting on the five barred gate and they must have been flicking sticks at the horse. The horse lashed out and took a piece of one lad's forehead bone right out. He managed to walk to the house holding his cap to his head because his brain itself was not damaged. Now the ambulance would be here in half an hour. Can you imagine someone going to the doctor and his coming out so slowly? The lad survived - I think he had a plate put on his skull.

Passers by were mainly farmers going to fields with horse drawn carts or machinery, such as Mr Cheetham from Acton Farm with Charlie his grey horse taking produce to Broken Cross. No one had riding horses except the two riding schools, one in Mottram, one in Henbury - Mr Evans and Mr Goddard. We used to run out to see them ride by - they used to come on a Saturday morning.

I remember running out to see an aeroplane, a biplane flying very low compared with today's flight. Leisure time was spent in Parish whist drives, and dances in the Reading Rooms were well attended by locals as were concerts there, which consisted mainly of local talent'.

Joan told us that when her father was a young boy they used to go to Birtles Church through the rhododendron bushes in a little garden via Birtles New Hall in a crocodile file. The vicar walked at the head of the procession and the vicar's wife was stationed at the rear. One of the boys would dive into the bushes and then a second would make his escape, to the cry from the vicar's wife, "another one gone Henry !". Jos adapted this cry for use around the farm. He took a dislike to the vicar, so changed to chapel for a time before coming back to Birtles Church as a chorister. He was a sidesman for many years.

Families had very few outings, so the once a year charabanc trip was greatly enjoyed, organised by the Sunday School Choir. Trips started very early at 7am, so they had to get up at 5.30 in the morning to finish the milking in time. Going over the swing bridge at Warrington excited much interest, and later there was competition to be the first to catch a glimpse of the sea.

We could probably count on our fingers the number of meals we had away from home, not counting packed lunches at school, so it was lovely to be served by smart waitresses in black dresses and pretty white aprons, black caps and a plateful of fancy cakes to choose from at teatime, with icing of different colours.

Most mothers were good cooks, but mostly made scones or 'cut and come again' cake. We set off home about 7 or 7.30. Unlike today, it took about three hours. I can remember the choir singing favourite hymns for most of the way home.'

I must mention the tearooms - Davenport's at Lower Yew Tree - that's above the Church. They had a large wooden shed where teas were served to the cyclists who rode our lanes at weekends from places like Stockport and Manchester. Peg Read's sister-in-law Lizzy served refreshments at Baguley Farm.

Henbury

There were various craftsmen and shops in the Parish. The house at the top of Hocker Lane was a cobbler's shop. I used to love watching shoes and boots being cobbled, and John Holt who lodged at Baguley Farm ran a wheelwright business from there and was kept busy. I remember in a heat wave having to hose our cart wheels because the wood tended to shrink in very hot weather and the iron rims expanded. Hosing them tended to tighten the rims.

Mrs Rimmer at Church Cottage had only one door opening to a tiny parlour, where she had a bookcase displaying chocolate - Domino and Five Boys - the latter illustrated faces showing expectation, realisation etc, from glum to smiling. We always called the shed at Birtles Farm 'the shop' - we sold home grown vegetables, fruit, chicken, eggs, various meats etc. As well as farming, my uncles and father each learned a different trade. They had to - one was a butcher, one did carpentry and so on.

Many cottages and houses were thatched in those days, and Mr Dingle at Piper Hill Cottages (called Shawcross now) was the local thatcher. He rethatched our old house. My great uncle Hugh who lived at Varden Town was a blacksmith at the Black Greyhound - that used to be a farriery, not just a smithy. When I was very little, it was no longer a smithy, and I often used to go with Dad to the Nether Alderley smithy opposite Nether Alderley School.

I once had to take the horse to the smithy when I was 14 or 15. Dad was terribly busy, but I had a confirmation class at Church that summer evening. It took over half an hour to walk down. Then I had to walk back, then to Birtles Church for the class, then down to pick up the horse. I got down about 9.30, but the smith was on war work in Manchester; he hadn't even come home. Eventually, I had to leave the horse at the smithy and return home empty handed. Dad wasn't too pleased, until he understood why. When the Alderley smithy had closed, I took the horse to be shod at Mottram St Andrew smithy. It was a three hour task: an hour's walk each way and an hour for shoeing.'

The Farming Community

Rough Heys Farm extended from its present location to the Mount and Davenport Heyes. The Census returns enable us to learn who lived at and farmed the house and 60 acres of land which was later to be named Rough Heys from 1841 onwards. They were: from 1841, Cyrus Slater and his wife Ann, with their three children, two farmworkers and a maid; from a date between 1857 and 1861, John Whitty and his wife Rachel, their son, a retired farm bailiff, two farm workers and a household servant;from before 1881 the farm was held by Thomas Whitty, presumably John's son, who was then 26. His mother Rachel Holmes (twice widowed?) kept house for him. Also in the house were Herbert Deaville aged 20, a boarder and farmer, a farm worker and a maid.

In 1883 William and Mary Worthington came to live at Rough Heys Farm as tenants and started a family connection with the farm which lasted for over a century. The farm then had about 60 acres of land, mostly pasture for dairy cattle but with the usual mixture of some arable land, a few pigs and chickens. Until then the farm itself seems not to have had a name - "Rough Heys" was the name of several fields at the eastern end of the 60 acres. William and Mary had four children, daughters Charlotte and Annie, a son Ephraim and a younger daughter. They must have been fairly successful, because by 1891 they had two male farmworkers and a maid in the house. By 1901 the maid had gone, presumably because Annie was by then 19 and still at home

Two years later, when Ephraim was only 18, Mary died and the children were on their own. Ephraim and his oldest sister Charlotte took over the tenancy and proceeded to run the farm in partnership. Mary's brother Simeon Massey was the tenant of Birtles Old Hall Farm, which adjoined Rough Heys, so presumably he could guide the youngsters, but it must have been very hard for them. However, when both Charlotte and Ephraim married, they were able to dissolve the partnership and Ephraim took over sole responsibility for the farm.

Ephraim must have been not only very hard working but a remarkable character. Certainly he had some ideas ahead of his time. For instance, like all the other farms in the area, there was no

Henbury

mains water supply to Rough Heys until 1940. The only supply of drinking water was from a well. However, Ephraim made a diversion from a stream above the farmyard to supply a cattle drinking trough, and constructed a dam in another stream, away from the yard, which supplied water to the house for washing through a pipe across a field. In the 1930s it was his proud boast that his was the only local farmhouse which had hot and cold running water on tap.

In the 1930s Ephraim bought a car. The farm not only supplied most of the family's food, but had some produce in addition to milk available for sale - eggs, vegetables and poultry. Ephraim for some years made a weekly run to a market in south Manchester to sell his produce. However, when the war started in 1939 this was no longer necessary. With the restrictions on shipping there was need for all the food British farms could produce, and they had no difficulty in selling it.

Before the war Ephraim had taken his next major step. Rough Heys was then part of the Alderley Park Estate. In October 1938 the estate was put up for sale by auction, and the tenant farmers were encouraged to buy their farms. Many were reluctant to do so, but Ephraim took his courage in both hands and bought Rough Heys Farm with its 60 acres. It was a wise move. Since about 1925 he had also leased a detached plot of about 12 acres behind Davenport Heyes, the large house in Church Lane. In the early 1940s Ephraim was able to buy this plot also.

Until then all the cows were milked by hand in their shippons. However, an electricity supply reached the farm in 1940, and it was possible to install milking machinery. Throughout the war all the agricultural machinery and carts were drawn by horses. In 1951 there were seven horses in all. In that year the farm acquired its first tractor. The impetus for this change no doubt came from John Worthington, who worked the farm with his father. With his enthusiasm for shire horses, he must have been sad to see the horses go.

Also in 1951 Ephraim had the opportunity to expand the farm substantially. The owner of Birch Tree Farm, which adjoined Rough Heys to the north, offered its 60 acres and house for sale.

Ephraim bought Birch Tree Farm, added the land to Rough Heys but resold the house.

In 1952 Ephraim retired and went to live in a house nearby. John took over the running of the farm. By this time with the detached 12 acres he had about 130 acres and was milking about 40 cows.

Ephraim died in 1962. The development of the houses on Henbury Rise and Hightree Drive had recently started. As a result, the 12 acres behind Davenport Hayes were valued for probate purposes as building land. This added considerably to the estate duty payable on Ephraim's estate, and his executors were obliged to sell the 12 acres in order to pay the duty. It was on this land that the final part of the development was constructed from 1967 onwards, and was named Worthington Close. John later replaced the 12 acres by buying a plot of about the same size, adjoining his own land, from Peter Swain the owner of Mount Farm in 1970.

In John's time, Rough Heys remained essentially a dairy farm, with a few pigs, poultry and some arable fields growing wheat or oats. The cows (about 50 of them eventually) were milked by machinery, the milk was sold in bulk to the Milk Marketing Board and tractors had replaced the horses, but the pattern of the farming was much as it had been a century earlier.

In 1982 John and his wife Mary decided to retire from farming. They moved a short distance to live at Lime Tree Cottage. They retained two fields and a connecting strip of land known as "the Dumbah" on which they kept John's precious shire mare. The remainder of the farm, 112 acres with the house and buildings, they sold to David ("Jim") Fletcher, who farmed Marl Heath Farm, part of the Capesthorne Estate.

David Fletcher and his son Andrew farmed Rough Heys as an intensive dairy farm. They constructed a large steel framed building in which the cattle were kept during the winter, being turned out to grass in the spring of each year.

In 1989 David Fletcher sold the farm house, a former stable and shippon and a 7 acre field (formerly part of Big Dial Field) to Duncan Collins, who substantially extended the house by incorporating two shippons and a hay store into the main building.

Henbury

Rough Heys farm sale, 1982 (courtesy D Fletcher)

In 1992 Anthony Dale started an agricultural contracting business from the yard of Rough Heys farm. At first he had only one tractor, but in ten years, as a result of his energy and hard work, this became a large enterprise. Anthony has a wide variety of farm machinery which he sends out with operators to farms throughout east Cheshire to carry out almost all farming operations such as ploughing, seeding, fertilising, harvesting, drainage. At any one time up to twenty people, mostly men, are engaged in the business. Many of them are not residents of Henbury but this new kind of farming activity almost certainly involves more people than any other in the Parish.

In 1997 Andrew Fletcher ceased to use the land at Rough Heys as pasture for milking cattle. The quantity of milk allowed in the quota could be produced at Marl Heath. Since that date, the fields at Rough Heys have been sown each year with cereal crops, mainly wheat and maize. Anthony Dale now farms the land under a tenancy from Andrew. Much of the cereal produced on the farm is supplied to Andrew Fletcher for cattle-fodder.

The Farming Community

Rough Heys is thus now a busy and productive agricultural unit. The changes in the past twenty years have resulted in the agricultural activities being very different from what used to be regarded as the traditional pattern of agriculture on a Cheshire farm. Perhaps instead they typify modern progressive farming.

Chapter 5

Farms, Farmhouses and Cottages

Pale Farm 2002 (courtesy Mr & Mrs Tuckman, photograph P G Wells)

The township of Henbury has a number of old buildings, many of them remnants of an earlier busy farming community which evolved into the present agricultural landscape. In this chapter we describe some of the farmhouses, all of which were at some time part of the Henbury Hall estate. Much of their history is in the archives of Henbury Hall, but there are also ancient title deeds in the Chester Record Office and the John Rylands Library, Manchester. Many are in the form of indentures; these are documents consisting of two parts cut with a wavy line allowing them to be matched together, although often only one of the parts now exists. The secretarial hand with which early deeds were written and the legal terminology make them hard to read, and deeds often failed to identify the precise whereabouts of properties or the names of their occupants.

Material for this chapter derives from visits to present and former farms, and interviews with local residents who are or were farmers or who have lived in Henbury for all or most of their lives.

Henbury

In addition, historical archives were consulted at the County Record Office. These included all the available Henbury censuses (from 1841 to 1901), the Land tax records from 1784 to 1831, the Hearth Tax record for Henbury (1663, 1664, 1673 and 1674), Prestbury Parish Registers, Tithe Apportionments for Henbury, Maps, Henbury Wills and Title Deeds.

Many local farms are of considerable antiquity; Sandbach, Marl Heath, Lingards, Lodge Farm, Pale Farm and Sycamore Farm all display timber frames and some show evidence of wattle and daub infilling. Pale Farm in particular, a beautiful black and white yeoman's house on Chelford Road dates back at least to the 15th century, and possibly earlier.

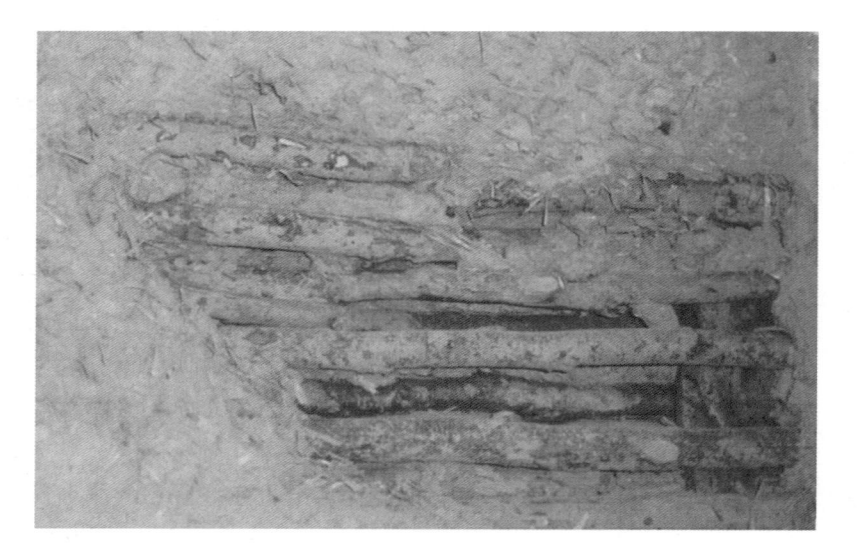

Pale Farm, wattle and daub (courtesy Mr & Mrs Tuckman, photograph P G Wells)

There are a number of cottages too, some thatched, in the Fanshawe Lane area probably dating from the medieval period. Moss Cottage was known to have a 1561 date stone, now concealed under render. Sandbach Farm bears a 1641 date, just before the Civil War.

Broomfield Farm has a date of 1868 over the front door, but there is evidence to the rear of an earlier structure. Land tax

Farms, Farmhouses and Cottages

records for this farm go back to 1784. On Church Lane, Davenport Heyes carries the date 1733 on what was the stable, and High Trees, a cottage on Andertons Lane is dated 1765. Manchester University Department of Archaeology have agreed to carry out a three year historical survey of Henbury Farm Buildings, including dendrochronological surveys, which will considerably enhance the detailed work we have already completed.

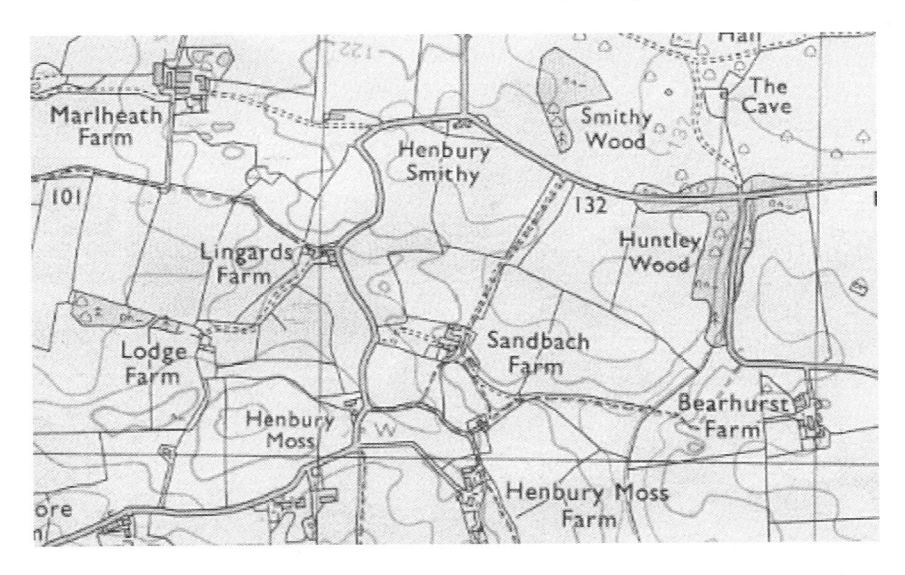

The Farms on Henbury Moss (OS 1979)

A small area around **Henbury Moss** contains a remarkable concentration of small farms. Seven - Bearhurst, Sandbach, Henbury Moss, Lodge, Lingards, Marlheath and Henbury Smithy - are all within a radius of less than half a mile. There are also many cottages, which may have been attached to the farms but may also have had their own smallholdings. Good farmland, a reliable water supply, and proximity to ancient roadways all contributed to the development of this nucleus.

Every settlement in its earliest beginnings had to have access to water in some form or other. Henbury Moss was no exception; it had ample supply from Fanshawe Brook, on its way to Redesmere, and wells were easily dug. Within living memory farms would

Henbury

mechanically pump their water supply into storage tanks for domestic purposes. Even as late as 1936 the Blacksmith's Arms relied on water from a pump in the yard behind the public house. Henbury is blessed with an underground source of water which appears to have never failed its population right up to modern times.

The first two cottages described may represent the original village centre. They lie on a lane leading off Fanshawe Lane.

Moss Cottage has an inscription recording renovation in 1884, but a plate which is now not visible gave the date 1561. The roof is stone flagged. Inside there are timber beams, including a huge bressumer over a fireplace.

Timber framing and beams, Moss Cottage (courtesy Mr & Mrs Kerr, photograph P G Wells)

The Barber family are recorded as living there in 1794, 1835 and 1842. Henbury Estate Rent Book lists in 1915 'late Aaron Ward', Henry Brown 1920-34, and Edward Vaughan 1940-57.

Lily Cottage, opposite Moss Cottage used to be called Sandbach Cottage. A Henbury Estate Field Notebook for 1794 lists 'late Rathbone', and Joseph Rathbone was there in 1838 and 1842. The Henbury Estate Rent Book lists in 1915 Mr Wright, 1922 Mrs Mary Nixon, 1921-52 Edward Prince and 1957 Mr Norman.

Florence Bayley who lived at the Smithy has some watercolours of Henbury and of the Smithy done by a local artist, Ralph Wright, who lived at Lily Cottage with his wife and two adopted sons. The boys were in the army during World War II, and she says that if

Farms, Farmhouses and Cottages

they returned on leave too early or too late in the day, rather than incur parental wrath, they sought shelter at the smithy until a more appropriate time to go home!

Before 1970 Harold Bayley had **Henbury Moss Farm**, 35 acres on the Henbury Estate. During his tenure he remodelled the shippon into a milking parlour, but the farm was not economically viable, and he moved to Sandbach Farm. Prior to this the house was three separate cottages, and a family called Southworth lived in one.

Mrs Ward outside Henbury Moss Farm cottages, 1890 (courtesy Mrs Y Pugh)

The appearance of the house with its flagged roof and rustic brickwork suggests a late 18th century date although there may have been an earlier dwelling. In 1796 the Henbury map and its accompanying tenants' list shows Widow Rathbone as the occupant.

Springbank Cottage was another small farm, which was part of the concentration on Henbury Moss. At one time it was called Klondyke, and earlier it was known as Wood House Farm or Woods Tenement. The present owner, Duncan Boddington, believes that the farm once housed a gamekeeper, who worked on the Thorneycroft Estate.

Henbury

There are a number of indentures dating from 1691 relating to Woods Tenement, leased to James Wood by George Lucy of Henbury Hall, and later to George Wood, James's son. This might have been the one later known as Wood House Farm, which came into the possession of the Willot family, and is listed in the Land Tax records from 1784 until 1831, during which time the tenants were: William Thorley 1784-87, Widow Thorley 1789-1807, and Isaac Slater from 1809, who is also in the 1841 census returns. In 1857 the farm was sold by William Cooper, the surviving devisee of David Willot (deceased) to Samuel Bullock of 'Gawesworth' for £1500. The occupant was Hugh Coppock, and he is again shown as tenant on a map dated 1860.

Fanshawe Cottage and **Apostle Cottage** on Fanshawe Lane were collectively known as Moss Cottages, but the Post Office felt this was too imprecise, and insisted on a change. Apostle Cottage once housed a Sunday School and the yard was dubbed Halleluya Square. Fanshawe may once have been a smallholding; it still has an old pigsty in the grounds, and a large orchard.

Fanshawe Cottage, 1950s
(courtesy Miss Betty Blackhurst)

Mr and Mrs Main now own Fanshawe cottage. It has no timber frame, but there are huge beams under the roof. Some of the windows are bricked up, probably to avoid the window tax. An ivy covered date stone above the front door, is inscribed *BWS 1760*. The house seems to have been extended from a small central core, older than the date stone; the unusual dimensions of bricks from the central part suggest a much earlier date.

Betty Blackhurst's family lived at Fanshawe Cottage for over 70 years. Her paternal grandfather was a wagoner, who moved there from Capesthorne Lodge in 1909. Her father, George Blackhurst, bought it from the Capesthorne Estate for £300 in the 1950s. They sold the cottage in 1987, after George died aged 83. Subsequent inhabitants include Sir Christopher Rose and the Wigglesworth family

Fanshawe Cottage is associated with a tragedy. Maria Rathbone, a child aged 8, was dispatched by her parents John and Frances on an errand in December 1822 to buy bacon from a farm believed to have been near the present Cock Inn. On her journey home she lost her way, and was seen passing through Chelford. She asked for help, but nobody took her in. Her parents were frantic, and searched far and wide, unable to find her. Eventually a search party led by Robert Hibbert was set up in January. George Dooley, who had never met her, reported a dream, in which he saw a child lying under a willow tree, surrounded by water.

Maria was eventually found after several hours' search, lying in a field in Lower Peover, under a willow, having died of exhaustion, hunger and hypothermia. At the coroner's inquest, held at the Crown Inn, Lower Peover, John Hollis the coroner was reduced to tears, and awarded the father a guinea. Her grave is in Prestbury Churchyard.

Glebe Cottage lies on the lane leading to Fanshawe Vicarage from Fanshawe Lane which was once known as Fanshawe Brook Lane. Fanshawe Lane was then called Redesmere Lane. Capesthorne Estate sold off Glebe Cottage in the 1970s. As the name implies, Glebe Cottage must at one time have belonged to Siddington Church; produce from glebe lands together with tithes once provided income for the incumbent. Fanshawe Vicarage was originally the vicarage for Siddington church, built by the Davenports of Capesthorne on the Henbury part of their estate. Glebe cottage is a thatched and timber framed dwelling, believed to be 17th century.

Henbury

Jess and Arthur Ford bought Glebe Cottage in 1982 and extended it at both ends. The previous accommodation consisted of two up and two down rooms. The Bailey family lived there before the Fords, and the Heaths before that. Patience Hadfield of Sycamore Farm recalls that Mr Reeves originally lived at Glebe Cottage before moving to Sycamore Farm in 1931. Thomas Taylor was recorded there at the time of the 1849 Tithes Map.

Glebe cottage before restoration in 1982 (courtesy Mr & Mrs A Ford)

At the eastern end of Fanshawe Lane, Sycamore Cottage, formerly **Sycamore Farm**, is thatched like its counterpart at the opposite end, Glebe Cottage. By the gatepost is a disused well, and some outbuildings are across the lane alongside the brook. Indoors there is a wealth of timber beams and evidence of a timber frame. The roof truss consists of a crown post and two queen posts. A Mr Reeves lived there from 1931 and the cottage was renovated by Mr & Mrs Hadfield from 1981 onwards. Mr Reeves told the Hadfields that, there being no midden, he had an economical means of nurturing his vegetables; an early eco-enthusiast. He had previously occupied the other two cottages on the lane, and had persuaded the Capesthorne estate to connect Sycamore Cottage to mains water and electricity earlier than many other local dwellings. There is reference to the Coppock family previously occupying the cottage.

A map at Capesthorne lists Thomas Taylor as tenant in 1827, and Stephen Curtis was there at the time of the tithes

Farms, Farmhouses and Cottages

apportionment in 1849. At that time, Thomas Taylor had moved to Glebe Cottage.

Sandbach Farm (map ref. SJ863722) now farmed by the Bayley family, has a date stone from 1641. The farm was originally mixed, but is now a dairy farm. The building consists of two wings with a mid section built in brick, but on both sides, part of the structure is in well dressed stone, suggesting that there have been modifications or possibly an earlier building.

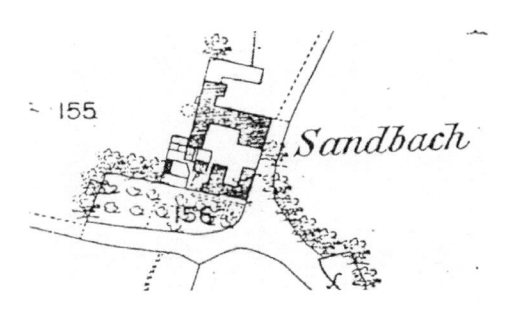

Sandbach Farm (OS 1872)

There is a stone framed window without mullions on the west side, and also evidence for a stone base or sill. In the present living room the timber frame on a stone sill is now open, but was once filled in and divided the space. This room was originally used for making cheese. There was a cheese press in the yard when Harold Bayley took over the farm. There are two wells in the farmyard. One of the ground floor rooms was said by Harold's maternal great-grandfather, Mr Brown, to have been used for Non Conformist religious services, during the 19th century.

According to an Abstract of Title, an indenture of lease was made in 1667 between Sir Fulk Lucy and Peter Walley as tenant, of what was then called Hulmes Tenement (there was later a different Hulmes Tenement at the site of Henbury School).

By a lease and release dated 1699, George Lucy, son of Sir Fulk Lucy conveyed to William Walley of Henbury, husbandman, the *"messe* (messuage, usually a dwelling) *in Henbury then in the possession of William Walley and also several pieces of arable land and pasture"* which were named the Carr, the Knowle, the

Henbury

Mosse (16 acres) Black Meadow and Bearhurst Meadow (8 acres), Old Marl Field and Huntleys Thorns (12 acres), the Two Acres, the Barn Fields and the Rye Fields (12 acres). These field names show that Hulmes Tenement was the property which is now known as Sandbach Farm. George Lucy reserved the right of turbary (cutting turf for fuel) from the Moss.

Timber framing at Sandbach Farm (courtesy P Bayley, photograph P G Wells

In 1700 the premises were taken by John Sandbach of Snelson, Richard Sandbach of Duckinfield, yeoman, and Mary his wife. Richard's Will dated December 1720 directed that his estate should be inherited by his wife, then his son Nathaniel. As Nathaniel did not survive long enough to inherit the farm, it went to his brother, Samuel Sandbach. Richard's will shows that he was a tanner. He left *"his stock in the tanner's trade, and his stock in bark and leather"*, which Samuel his son, also a tanner inherited. His brother in law, Nathaniel Wright of Plumley who witnessed the Will was also a tanner. One of the fields attached to Sandbach farm was named in the 1909 O/S Map as Tan Yard Meadow.

Farms, Farmhouses and Cottages

Samuel and his son, Richard, mortgaged the property in 1747 to Thomas Vawdrey, *'gent. of Cranage'*. There were further mortgages in 1757 and 1767 made by Richard Sandbach before he finally conveyed the farm to Sir William Meredith in 1771.

Sandbach Farm remained the property of Henbury Hall until recently, and was the only surviving working farm belonging to the estate. It occupies about 450 acres (174 acres in 1881).

With the aid of the Land Tax, censuses, directories and estate records it has been possible to identify most of the tenants since Richard Sandbach sold up in 1771: Thomas Rowlinson 1784-94, Joab Simpson 1795, Job Simpson 1797-1831, Jabez Wright 1851 and 1861, Edwin Stubbs 1871 and 1881, Henry Brown 1905, Walter Bough 1919-29, Wilfred Bayley and Daisy 1929, Harold Bayley 1972, and since 2000 his son, Paul Bayley. One of the conditions when Harold Bayley took the tenancy in April 1972 was *"not to put a bull in the Park"*.

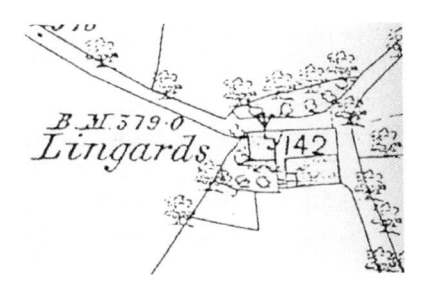

Lingards Farm (OS 1872)

We obtained background information about **Lingards Farm** (map ref. SJ860724) from Miss Edith Windsor, Mrs Jean Jodrell, widow of Herbert Jodrell, and Mr and Mrs A. Snape, all of whose families were tenants of the Capesthorne Estate at different times since 1938. Edith told us that the rough track running past the farm towards Capesthorne Lodge, was once the main carriageway to Fanshawe Lane and School lane by which the occupants of Capesthorne Hall travelled to Macclesfield. Another old track leads to the neighbouring Lodge farm.

Henbury

Lingards Farm in the 1940s (courtesy Miss E Windsor)

The farmhouse is brick built, with evidence of various extensions. Jean Jodrell recalled a wattle and daub panel in one of the ground floor rooms, which collapsed after their cellar was flooded, and there are some exposed timber frames in the walls and ceiling beams. There is a substantial structural beam, or bressumer, over a fireplace, and. a huge chimney with a broad base occupies one wall. One external brick wall is supported by two buttresses. A yard pump was once used by several neighbouring properties until mains water was laid on in the early fifties.

Herbert Jodrell, the son of the farmer at Whirley Barn, took over from Mrs Mary Blackshaw in 1938. The Jodrells farmed 20 acres, which were gradually increased to 50. Herbert used to drive his cattle along the lanes to Chelford market in the days when traffic was much less hazardous.

The earliest record of the farm is a lease by Sir Fulk Lucy and Dame Isabella his wife, of Henbury Hall, to John Harrop in the 19th year of Charles II (1667). John Harrop is listed in the Henbury Hearth Tax returns for 1663, 1664 and 1674 as owning one hearth. An inventory made in 1686 after his death lists the contents of each room in the farmhouse, consisting of *"the carte House, the parlor, the buttery, the chamber over the house, and the chamber over the parlor"*, which usefully conveys an idea of its size.

By indenture dated 20th May 1713 George Lucy conveyed the premises to John Lingard of Monks Heath, blacksmith, *"late in the tenure of John Harrop, late of Henbury, husbandman, and now in*

Farms, Farmhouses and Cottages

the possession of Thomas Harrop, son of the said John". Useful for identification, it listed the names of surrounding fields, including *"the Underfield, adjoining to Richard Sandbache's"*, who as we have seen, was a tanner occupying neighbouring Sandbach Farm.

John Lingard made a will in 1730 leaving his estate to his son John and daughter Mary by his first wife, and to his wife Sarah and their five daughters. An Inventory of his possessions made on August 16th 1737 also named the rooms in the house: *"ye house place, the parlor, the kitchen, the buttery, the chamber over house, and chamber over parlor"*. If they all still lived at home, nine people were sharing six beds. There were no tools of the blacksmith's trade listed, except perhaps a pair of bellows.

Subsequent tenants were Hannah Bradbury, Charles Bradbury, Thomas Rowlinson (1785), Job Simpson and Jacob Simpson (Land Tax records 1792-1831), Jonathan Walkley (censuses 1851, 61 and 71) Sarah Wallsey (sic) 1881, and Joel Blackshaw in 1891 and after. Farmers then (and until recently) had multiple skills - John Lingard was a blacksmith, and Joel Blackshaw was a wheelwright.

Illustrating the custom of naming farms after long term tenants, a map of the district dated 1827 names the farm as Simpson's. In 1794 the farm was conveyed by Peter Rowlinson to John Bower Jodrell of Henbury Hall, and at some as yet undetermined time, it was sold to the Capesthorne Estate.

Michael and Penny Mottram kindly showed us round the converted farmhouse at **Lodge Farm**. Mr and Mrs George Heathcote and their son Henry were tenants of the working farm from 1940 until 1970. Terry and Norah Hargreaves farmed there until 2000, latterly purchasing the farm from the estate.

Ethel Heathcote told us that an interior wall had been timber framed, and a panel of wattle and daub had been concealed behind plaster. A clue to the farm's antiquity is the stone sill which supported the brick structure. The chimney markings suggested an earlier and steeper roof, possibly of flags or thatch. There is a legend that Henbury Estate lost the farm to the Bromley Davenports over a game of cards. There being no well, they had to use the pump at neighbouring Lingards Farm. They could draw

Henbury

water from a land drain, but it dried up in summer. Mains water only reached them in 1962, and for most of their tenure there was no electricity. Henry recalled an open fireplace in the kitchen, over which was hung a large cooking pot. He believed the house was a gamekeeper's cottage at one time, because of its name, the small acreage and its proximity to a wood. George Heathcote farmed 10 acres, and worked the land with a horse, never using a tractor. He died in 1970.

Lodge Farm timber framing (courtesy Mr & Mrs M Mottram, photograph P G Wells)

The tenant before the Heathcotes was a Mr Lomas, one of whose daughters married Mr Bayley, the blacksmith at Henbury Smithy. The Hargreaves, who succeeded the Heathcotes wrote us an account of their tenure at Lodge farm. Apparently until they showed an interest, the property had been scheduled for demolition, the land to be added to neighbouring farms. Before they moved in, the Capesthorne Estate put in a damp course, and the stone sill was removed.

An early problem was the very uneven track past Lingards farm which was their main access. There was however an ancient track leading from Fanshawe Lane past Knoll Cottage (now called Holly Bank), which had been a farm manager's cottage. When they

Farms, Farmhouses and Cottages

bought Lodge Farm from the Capesthorne Estate in 1979, they decided to establish a right of way for this more convenient route. This involved proving that the track had been in use before 1970 with the help of an earlier tenant Mr Lomas, who reported *"when my family lived there the only entrance had been our track and not the Lingard one. When my grandmother died they had to physically carry the coffin down to Fanshawe lane because the track was waterlogged and the horses could not get up. There was a natural spring at the top of the track and this caused flooding in winter, making the track almost impassable. It was after this episode that my brother and I reopened the Lingard entrance"*. Apparently before School Lane and Fanshawe Lane joined and became one, the only route to Siddington was along this ancient track.

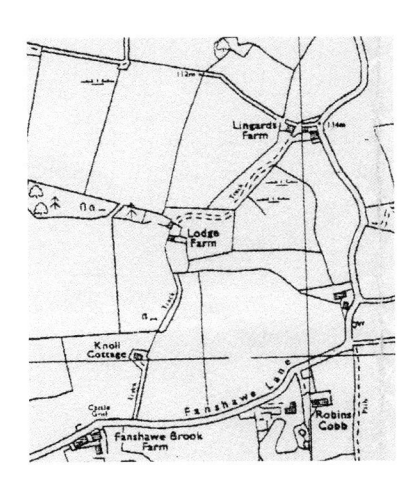

Lodge Farm, showing the old access from Lingards Farm (Ordnance Survey)

After the Mottrams bought the property in 2000, they undertook extensive renovation using traditional methods of building and timber framing, and provided additional accommodation; when the Lomas family lived there, Lodge Farm comprised a kitchen and pantry, a living room and tiny parlour on the ground floor, and two bedrooms and a landing bedroom upstairs, accommodating at least 8 people.

Records of earlier tenants are scarce. The Land Tax records show Joseph Slater as tenant from at least 1784 until 1786,

Henbury

Thomas Barber from 1787 until 1800, then a gap until 1826 when Samuel Hulse took over; he was still there in 1831. He is listed in the 1841 census as a gamekeeper. When John Ryle sold Henbury Estate to Edward Marsland in 1842, Joshua Barber was listed as tenant at Lodge Farm. The Capesthorne Drainage Book lists Henry Lomas there in 1889, and William Lomas in 1913. He was still there in 1923.

We met 3 members of families who had been tenants of **Broomfield Farm** (map ref SJ881730). Joyce Bostock's parents, Samuel and Elsie occupied the farm from 1923. The death of her brother aged 38, and her father only a year later precipitated their move in 1963. Joyce told us that the farm was mixed arable and dairy and they also made cheese during the war. Her father, Samuel was born in Marton about 1888, and had 2 brothers, Harold who farmed Pexall farm, and Frank who worked Birtles Hill Farm after his father. The family were at Birtles Hill Farm for about 100 years.

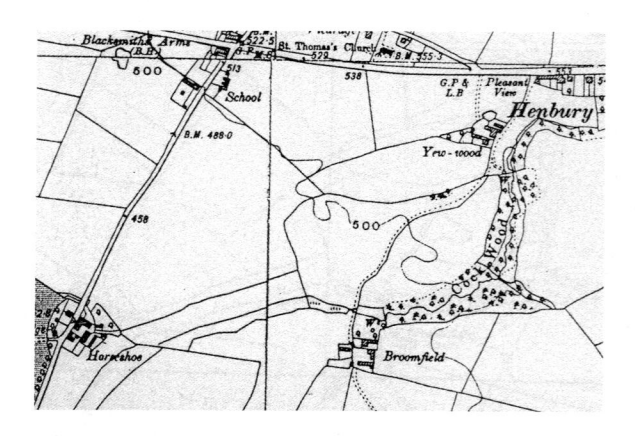

Broomfield Farm showing access from Ruewood (then known as Yewwood). OS 1910

Mrs Kathleen Massey and her sister Marjorie were members of the family which took over Broomfield after the Bostocks left in 1963. Kathleen met her husband John when she was working as a land girl during the war, on a milk round. John at that time was farming at Ruewood Farm.

The Masseys were at Broomfield for about 36 years and continued to deliver milk locally as did many local small farmers until the early 1980s. The farmhouse has 6 bedrooms, and

Farms, Farmhouses and Cottages

considerable outbuildings were added during the Massey's time there, including a milking parlour and shippon for 250 cows. As neighbouring farms became empty, John agreed to cultivate their land extending to about 800 acres in total. They lost a lot of poultry and game birds from foxes in spite of the activities of the local hunt.

We obtained permission from the present owner, Colin Hooley, to look round the farm, where a herdsman was in residence. Although there is a date plaque of 1868 on the present building there is evidence of an earlier building in the orchard to the rear, confirmed by maps and early records. From the orchard looking north there is a stream, Bag Brook, across which you can see the spire of Henbury Church. There is a curious cavity there with a concave brick lined roof which may have been part of a cellar, or a place for storing cheese.

Broomfield Farm 2002 (Photograph P G Wells)

The track leading to the farm runs in a westerly direction to gain School Lane via Home Farm, as it did according to 1796 and 1820 maps, but an estate map dated 1842 shows the track running south

Henbury

east towards the Pexhill road. A small farmstead, Fitchett's, lying on the line of the new track was demolished possibly at that time.

The origins of the farm are unknown, although it is shown on the 1727 Henbury field map with its surrounding field names. This has assisted the identification of the location of the farm in a number of early indentures. The earliest record is a release by George Lucy of Henbury Hall to Philip Bromfield of Somerford Booths in 1691 of the *'messuage late in the occupation of Elizabeth Birtles, widow, late wife of Thomas Birtles deceased'*. The farm covered over 45 acres consisting of 6 named fields. Philip Bromfield had moved to Danebank in Congleton at the time he made his will in 1710, and both his son and heir, John Bromfield, and grandson, also John were concerned in a number of transactions involving the farm. It is likely that the present name of the farm originates in this family name.

John Bromfield leased the farm to George Bayley in 1720 for a rent of £76 per annum[1], and a surviving tenancy agreement includes certain conditions: *'John Bromfield shall bear, pay, discharge all lays as well as parish duties and Parliamentary taxes which shall be charged on as become due or payable for said premises during the said term, the tax on duty on windows, watching, warding and working on the highways only excepted'*. John also agreed to maintain the property *'in good tenantable repair'*. George was to be allowed 6s 8d yearly out of his rent *'in lieu of satisfaction of plowboot, cartboot and other husbandry boot on the said premises, and shall not fell any timber (except hedge wood) without the consent of John Bromfield first had'*. (The ancient term *boot* implied a right, e.g. to take out timber for firing or repair work from the landlord's land).

George was forbidden to plough or sow more than 14 acres yearly *'upon the penalty of paying five pounds an acre for every acre ploughed or sowed above that quantity and also rateably for a lesser quantity than one acre'*.

By 1722, the field names had increased from 6 to 15, and the farm extended to 75 acres. George is mentioned in indentures at

---

[1] Chester Record Office D/5678/6

Farms, Farmhouses and Cottages

least up to 1730. In 1779 Sir William Meredith purchased the property 'late in the occupation of George Bayley'.

The Land Tax record lists 'late Jacksons' from 1784 to 1787. Peter Bullock was tenant from 1789 to 1797, followed by Thomas Walley to 1806, then Nathaniel Walley at least to 1831. Mary Whalley, widow was there in 1835. Following a gap, Jacob Bowers was listed there in the 1841, 1851 and 1861 censuses, then Hugh Coppock and John, followed by Thomas Stanhope circa 1908, and Samuel Bostock in 1923, followed by the tenants mentioned above.

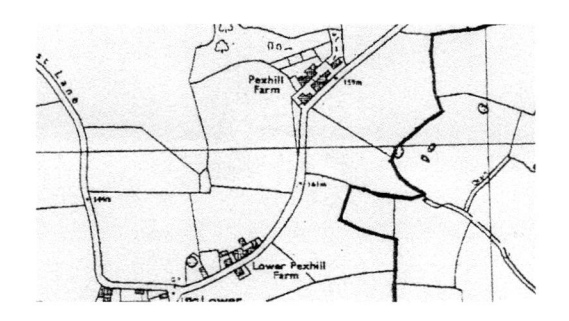

Pexhill Farm (OS 1910)

Pexhill (or Pexall) Farm was a mixed farm on 160 acres with cattle, sheep, pigs and crops of barley, oats, wheat, potatoes, turnips and mangles, employing two men. The land drew on a good supply of well water locally; there were wind pumps at both Pexhill and neighbouring Brick Bank Farm.

We interviewed Ernest Kennerley, who died in 2002, one of the last tenants of Pexhill Farm before it was demolished in the 1980's. He was born at Broad Oak Farm, Siddington, went to Pexhill in 1942, and married Enid Bostock, the daughter of the previous tenant, Harold Bostock, at Siddington Church.

Ernest was a well known and respected figure in Henbury, with a wide knowledge of local people and the surrounding countryside. He often spoke approvingly of the neighbourliness he experienced in the past, when others would freely offer help when loading the hay at harvest time, or if someone was ill, but he felt that generous

Henbury

spirit had practically disappeared. He spoke warmly of the care given to the tenants by the Henbury Estate. After retiring, Ernest and his wife Enid moved to Horseshoe Lodge and used to supply beautifully dressed game around the village.

Pexhill Farm 1970s (courtesy Alan Kennerly)

The farmhouse had 21 rooms, and contained a magnificent three storey oak staircase, which may have been installed from an older building, perhaps the "Old Hall". After the farm was demolished the staircase was preserved, and installed in a cottage in Blandford Forum, Dorset. The farm must have been about 200 years old; it was replaced by a modern house, although the barns remain, and are being converted into dwellings. An earlier farm may have existed on the site since White's 1860 Directory states that the farm was once the seat of the Davenport family: *'It is supposed that the house was of much larger dimensions than at present, as foundations are often dug up'*.

The earliest record found so far is a deed listing leases at the Chester Record Office[2] showing John Gatley with a 14 year lease in 1700. The Land Tax record gives details of tenants as follows:

---

[2] CRO ref D/5678/34

Farms, Farmhouses and Cottages

1784-97 John Gatley, 1798-1806 Thomas Warburton, 1810-30 Isaac Simpson.

Pexhill Farm, Jacobean staircase before removal

Samuel Atkinson was there at the 1851 and 1861 censuses, John Bostock in the 1881 census and Jane Bloom, widow, at the 1901 census. Kelly's Directory for 1902 names John Broom. The Henbury estate Rent Book named John Brooke as handing over to Harold Bostock in 1918, who in turn handed over to Ernest Kennerley.

The present owner of **Brick Bank Farm** (now known as Henbury House, map ref. SJ888730), Mr Woodward, thought the house was built around 1788. It was not possible to identify it from the Land Tax records, and the first tenants we have found were listed in the 1841 census as James Norbury and his wife Ann. The 1849 tithe map for Henbury names the proprietor as Peter Higginbotham, and James Norbury is listed again in the 1861 census. Following him, Thomas Robinson was there in 1871, Thomas Bradley in 1881, and Henry Leech in 1891 and 1901, although the census names the farm as Brick Kiln Farm. Henbury

Henbury

Rent Book names Herbert Joshua Priest in 1908, and Charles Bridle in 1925. Kelly's Directory names Herbert Joshua Priest at Brick Bank Farm in 1923. C.R. Mitchell farmed there in 1939 and 1944 (rent book).

We were shown round **Bearhurst** farmhouse by a recent tenant, Mrs Linda Reid. There is a flagged floor in the kitchen, folding window shutters, and cellar steps lead down to a stone slab table on which was engraved a circle divided into quadrants, part of a cheese press. A heavy studded batten door leads out from the kitchen, and may have been part of the original building.

The front door faces east and according to a 1727 estate map the drive at that time ran in an easterly direction towards Bearhurst Lane, rather than its present course northwards to the same lane. Brickwork is English bond and the roof is stone-flagged.

A large barn, three stories high has a central opening, roof high, which was probably for winnowing. The roof is supported by a king post timber frame. The second storey windows have horizontal sliding shutters. To one side are pigsties and a cow shed or shippon.

In a hollow to one side of the main drive near a small pool there is a brick lined cavity below ground, with an arching brick roof (very similar to the partially collapsed one found at Broomfield Farm). Its function is unclear; it may have been a cool chamber for storing cheeses. During the war when the house gave shelter to evacuees, it was used as an air raid shelter.

Although the farm was shown on the 1727 map, the earliest tenants found so far were listed in the Land Tax Records. Thomas Rowlinson was tenant to the Jodrell family from 1784 to 1816, followed by Philip Bracegirdle from 1818 to 1826. Cyrus Slater was listed from 1829 to 1831, and again in the 1835 and 1842 lists of tenants. The 1849 Tithes Map does not include Bearhurst. The censuses give more details: 1851 Andrew Hannay, 1861 Joseph Hough, 1871 and 1881 Thomas Knott, 1891 Margaret Knott, widow, 1901 John James Bayley. The latter obtained a lease in 1896. Harold Bayley took over in 1923 until 1937, and was followed by Harry Lomas in 1937.

Farms, Farmhouses and Cottages

Walter Hatton's father, Ralph, his mother Rose and their children moved to **Home Farm** (map ref. SJ876731) in 1940, and the family were there until 1987. They had sheep, pigs, cattle, grew potatoes and corn on 15 acres, and their fields were dispersed at some distance from their farmhouse. They employed two men. Walter said they *'tried their hand at anything, including rearing turkeys'*.

They sold their corn to a merchant rather than using Birtles Mill, and sold their cattle at Chelford or Congleton Markets. Walter described how he took 3 or 4 calves in his Hillman car with the back seat tipped up. To restrain them, they were put in sacks, with their heads protruding.

Walter thinks that the part of the building which fronts the road is more recent than the house, which is some 200 years old. A huge sycamore tree opposite the farmhouse has a girth of 238 inches, giving an age of about 238 years, contemporaneous with the house.

The farm is shown on a 1796 map of Henbury estate, but not on the 1727 map. Its earliest name is shown in an 1820 field notebook as New House, which continued to be used at least until 1842. It later became known as Horseshoe Farm, (the lane past the farm was called Horseshoe Lane before it became School Lane after 1846), and at a later date it became Home Farm.

In 1794, Isaac Mellors was tenant of the surrounding fields, and then Jonathan Lane in 1796. Jonathan Lane was tenant until around 1820, and then Thomas Dawson. Dawson was followed by Thomas Wood in 1845. The early census returns do not identify the farm clearly until 1871, when Abraham Unsworth aged 70 is listed followed by George Millington 1881, Sarah Millington, widow 1891, and Thomas Millington in 1901. In 1906 the farm was leased to William Stanner at a rent of £295 until 1918. George Hollinshead took over from 1927 until the Hattons took over in 1940 and the present occupant is Mr Bernt Vietor.

The last tenants to farm at **Park House Farm** (map ref. SJ873737), Tom and Jean Gould, retired in 1997. Tom's grandfather, Abraham, who had farmed a hill farm at Taddington, moved to Macclesfield to manage a smallholding near the present

Henbury

Fire Station. He cultivated grapes under glass, which he sold in Manchester. After serving in the police force, he moved to Park House farm in the 1880s (1891 census for Henbury, and Henbury Rent Book records a lease in 1895).

The family farmed 79 acres, and Tom's father William kept and sold horses. Tom ploughed with horses until about 1970, when he bought his first Ferguson tractor, costing some £600. William suffered a serious accident, so Tom had to leave school when he was 13 to help his father. They kept cattle, grew kale and turnips, and ground their grain to feed the cows. They also ran a milk round, which was heavy work; milk churns held 18 gallons, and weighed 180lbs.

The original farmhouse was smaller, and Tom believed it dated back to the 16th century, although there was no evidence of a timber frame. Some of the windows had been bricked up, probably to avoid window tax, levied from 1696 until 1851. After the Goulds retired, the farmhouse was replaced by a mock Tudor mansion, and sadly very little remains of the original buildings.

The earliest known tenant was both owner and occupier, Charles Bradbury; and Charles Jr from 1784 to 1810, listed in the Land Tax returns. In 1810, Charles in his Will left the farm to his wife, Jane, although Thomas Priest was in occupation at that time. Johnathan Morton was tenant from 1813 to 1816 under the management of David Shaw and Joshua Sidderley, the executors of Charles Bradbury's estate, followed by James Wylde tenant in 1818.

Another Charles Bradbury occupied the farm from 1821 to 1826 under the proprietorship of Mrs Jane Bradbury and Cyrus Bullock. Cyrus had married Elizabeth, daughter of Charles and Jane Bradbury in 1808.

David Powell was tenant in1829 and 1830, followed by James Taylor and Cyrus Bullock in 1831. James Taylor was a son-in-law of Cyrus and Elizabeth.

Later census returns record the following: 1841 D.M. Shaw, 1851 Thomas Knott, 1861 Charles Bullock, 1871 Charles Bradbury Bullock, 1881 Charles Bullock, 1901 Abraham Gould.

Farms, Farmhouses and Cottages

Peter and Beryl Casswell have lived at **Ruewood**, once called **Yew Wood** and then **Ruewood Farm**, (map ref. SJ882734) since 1986. An earlier tenant was Edgar Harrison, whose wife was Arthur Marshall's sister, Arthur being steward of the Henbury Hall estate until he retired.

Before Edgar Harrison, Ruewood was farmed by Samuel Massey and his son, John. John's son, Samuel had a son, also called John and he and the family moved to Broomfield Farm in 1963.

Ruewood is not mentioned by name in the Land tax records 1784-1831. The census however lists the following: 1841 Joseph Priest, 1851, 1861 and 1871 Henry Taylor, 1881 Jane Broome, 1901 John T. Massey.

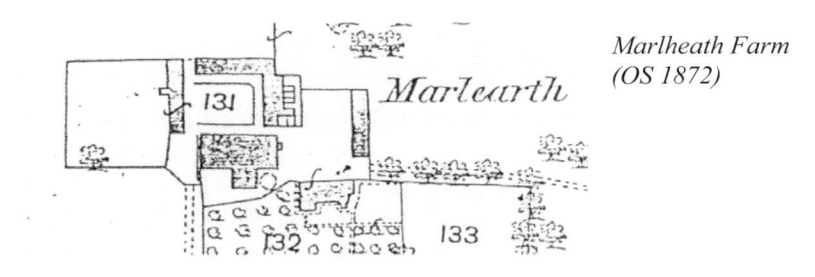

Marlheath Farm (OS 1872)

Marl Heath farmhouse (map ref. SJ857728) is L shaped with a lean-to extension to the east. It has an early, timber framed core, and there have been several brick built extensions over the years. Jim Fletcher, the present farmer, recalled that that the north facing wall, now pebble dashed, once displayed a massive timber frame with brick infilling. Some alterations to the bathroom revealed a timber structure with brick infilling beneath the plaster.

The farmhouse is situated on the south side of the farmyard, with surrounding buildings including a shippon. One barn was recently demolished, and one of the bricks, probably made on the premises had scratched on it that it had been laid on the date that the King died in 1910 (Edward VII, 6 May 1910).

As an illustration of how a place name can change over time, Marl Heath farm appears in the Land Tax as Marlyorth from 1785 until 1796, then as Marl Earth in 1797 and 1798, Marl Hearth from 1799 to 1802, and Marl Earth in 1831 (also Marl Earth in

Henbury

Bryant's 1831 Map of Henbury). In the 1875 OS Map, it is still listed as Marlearth, but is now known as Marl Heath. Marl is a mixture of clay and lime dug from marl pits, and spread on the land to improve the fertility of the soil, particularly where it is acid.

Timber framing, Marlheath Farmhouse (photograph P G Wells)

One of the oldest outbuildings, known as the Drift House was used for winnowing (separating the grain from the chaff by tossing it in a draught of air) and two sets of doors are sited to utilise the prevailing wind to best advantage. Marl Heath is now a dairy farm on 300 acres, part of the Bromley Davenport Estate.

Its earliest origins are obscure. By an Indenture dated 1667 Sir Fulk Lucy and Isabella his wife, of Henbury Hall had let a messuage by lifehold, an agreement which let a property for three lives, to Randle Cragg late of Siddington. It passed to Randle's son Edward, Margaret his wife and Joseph Cragg. The property previously had been occupied by John Heath earlier in the 17th century. The dwelling became known as Cragg's tenement. In 1693, Edward Cragg and his wife Margaret sold to John Ward of Capesthorne a messuage in Henbury for £400, occupied by John Heath, then by Randle Cragg, and later Edward Cragg his son. The sale also included '*a little house called Radcliffe's House and one orchard garden and meadow belonging to the same little house and also all that mossroom (?boggy field)...bordering on one side to that close known as Corne Pasture in Henbury*'. John

Farms, Farmhouses and Cottages

Ward had the right to take out marl from a close then belonging to George Lucy Esq *'commonly called the marled earth which is the most near to the premises aforesaid...adjoining to Thomas Harrup's tenement'*. This must refer to what is now called Lingards Farm, and so clearly identifies the locality.

The map of Henbury Estate in 1727 shows a little house to the east of Marl Heath Farm; it is no longer standing, but there are field contours which may indicate its site. The field names mentioned in various indentures identify Craggs Tenement as what later became known as Marl Heath Farm. The 1727 map shows Well Croft between the little house and the road. John Ward also had the right to draw water from a well sited in the field called Marled Earth and had the right of passage on a lane to take out marl *'wide enough for two carts to meete'* and *'hee and they being at one half of the charge in making thereof'*.

An indenture dated 1700 conveyed Coate meadow, Great Sprink Wood and Little Sprink Wood to Sir William Meredith, all of which are shown on the 1727 map as lying in the vicinity of Marl Heath farm.

The Land Tax record 1785-1831 gives Davies Davenport of Capesthorne as the owner, with tenants as follows: Thomas Jackson 1785-1806, Joshua Lear 1810, James Nixon 1813-1816, Joseph Dale 1818-1826, Joseph Dale senior 1829-1831. Joseph Dunn's 1827 survey of the Capesthorne estate confirms Joseph Dale as tenant in 1827, and a rent book names Samuel Ridgeway as tenant in 1840. Charles Hannay is listed in the 1849 Tithes Apportionments and in the 1851 census, and William Shufflebotham was at Marl Heath for the 1861 and 1871 censuses. William Shufflebotham junior had taken over by 1881. John Bostock was listed in the 1891 census and still occupied the farm in 1889, but his widow, Sarah was listed in the 1901 census.

The Slater family worked the farm from before the First World War until about 1935. They were held in high regard as being very skilful in tending the land. One huge field called The Bank is on a steep gradient, which few would wish to tackle with a plough, but Slater did so with a team of horses, and grew potatoes during World War I. They sold produce from a stall in Stockport Market.

Henbury

A farmer called Kennerley was then at Marl Heath for about 3 years, before the Baker family took over in 1939. John Baker's father had been a butcher in Mobberley. They were there for 14 years, and Mr Baker senior died suddenly whilst haymaking.

Herbert Meyer farmed there from 1953, followed by David (Jim) Fletcher and his son Andrew in 1962. Andrew took over from his father in 2000. Jim told us that an epidemic of rinderpest struck the area in the 19th century, believed to have been introduced by drovers; the area was on the cattle route from the south to market at Manchester. Many of the carcasses of the affected cattle are thought to have been buried in the meadows east of the farmhouse, and also at Sandbach and Park House Farms.

Pale Farm (map ref. SJ865739), now separated from the Henbury estate by the A537 road, was twice part of the estate. It was known as 'Birtles o' the Pale' when it was bought in 1771 by the first Sir William Meredith from Dinah Birtles.

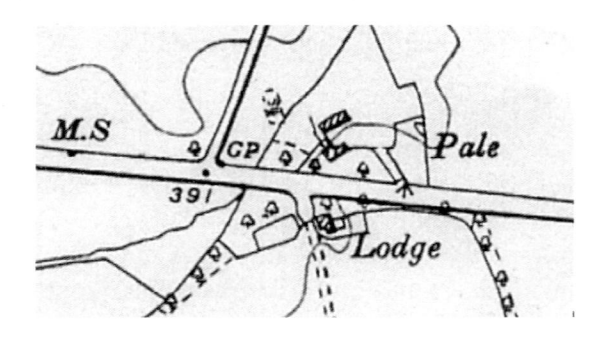

Pale Farm (OS 1954)

The early history of this beautifully preserved timber framed house on the Chelford Road is unknown, but with the interest and agreement of the current owners, Mr and Mrs D. Tuckman, we were able to persuade the Department of Archaeology at the University of Manchester to undertake a dendrochronology survey to try and determine when it was built. The survey is not yet complete, but preliminary findings suggest a date of 1366 with a possible error of 60 years, which gives at least an early 15th

Farms, Farmhouses and Cottages

century date at which the timber used in the construction of the house was felled.

Pale Farm (picture thought to be from sales brochure, date uncertain)

The windows of the main room contain some interesting stained glass. When Robert Hibbert was building Birtles Church in 1840, he imported some antique and valuable 13th century Flemish coloured glass to be used in the new Church. He stored it in Pale Farm, and what was left over went into the farmhouse. Another feature is a small niche with a triangular shaped upper part near the fireplace. Its purpose is not certain. It might have been used to display a figurine of the Virgin Mary or a crucifix, or was it a place to keep the salt dry?

The house comprises a three bay unit, standing on a sandstone base. The roof is Kerridge flagstone, and there are two carved posts, one a replica on a gable over a window, and the other probably original on the eastern gable end. The brick built outbuildings, interesting in their own right are early 18th century in part. In the dining room, the present owners have exposed wattle and daub behind a pane of glass.

The earliest Deeds held by the Henbury estate, dated March 1743, concerned the sale of Birtles of the Pale to Dinah Birtles, who had been a tenant there for a year, by Thomas Swetenham the elder and his son, also called Thomas. The latter, who was about to serve abroad as Lieutenant in the Horse Guards, authorised his attorney, John Bromfield to act in his absence. The Swetenhams

Henbury

from Somerford Booths, Cheshire were a distinguished landed family. An earlier Thomas Swetenham married Mary Birtles in 1602 at Swetenham Hall, after which they moved with her father, John Birtles to live at Birtles Manor Hall. It is possible that this hall was later replaced by what is now known as Birtles Old Hall.

The Hearth Tax record for Henbury includes the names of two Birtles. In 1663, Ralph Birtles had two hearths and Roger Birtles one. In 1664, Roger still had one, and Ralph had four. In 1674, Roger again had one, but Ralph was not listed, and nobody was recorded as having 4 hearths; if these were contained in one building, it suggests quite a sizeable structure.

It is not clear into which branch of the Birtles family Dinah married; she was described in the 1743 indenture as a widow from Mobberley, who borrowed several sums of money to make the purchase of Birtles of the Pale. Her eldest son and heir, John, also of Mobberley, stood surety for her debts and took possession of the house. They borrowed further sums in 1768 to pay off the original loans, but in 1771 they sold the property to Sir William Meredith of Henbury Hall, including a cottage 'lately erected' by Dinah Birtles for £1270. The sale included a pew in the Tytherington Chapel of Prestbury Church.

By 1784, the Pale had been taken over by William Booth. After William's death, his widow, Alice, married John Cooper, and they sold the Pale to John Bower Jodrell in 1796. It was still part of the Henbury Hall estate at the time of the sale by John Ryle to Edward Marsland in 1842. After Dinah Birtle's time, the farm was tenanted by members of the Pimlott family. Thomas Wood lived there in 1851 and 1861, followed by Ernest Dooley and George Dooley. Ernest was tenant at the time of the Stanley sale in 1938.

One 17th century member of the Birtles family is of interest. A book published in 1678, 'Wonders of the Little World' by Nathan Wanley, Vicar of Coventry relates: *'While I was writing of this book* (that is, in December 1671) *there came to the City of Coventry one, Mr Thomas Birtles, a Cheshire man, living near unto Maxfield; he had been in London, where, and in his journey homewards, he made publick shew of himself, for his extraordinary stature; his just height, as himself told me, was somewhat above*

Farms, Farmhouses and Cottages

seven foot, although upon trial it appears to want something. His father he said was a man of moderate stature, his mother was near two yards high: and he himself hath a daughter, who being but about sixteen years of age, is yet already arrived to the height of six foot complete'. Thomas would have had painful problems had he lived in Pale Farm, given its limited headroom.

The name Pale Farm suggests that it lies on a border. The Estate and Prestbury Parish boundaries run close, but another explanation is possible. The term 'pale' and the proximity of Park House Farm may suggest a deer park nearby. Apart from a description[3] of Henbury Hall in 1558, there is little direct evidence for a deer park in Henbury, although there were 3200 deer parks in England by 1300. The perimeter embankment or fencing of a former deer park was not uncommonly coterminous with a parish boundary[4]. Another name for a fence or enclosure, particularly one within a park, is a 'hay'; Rough Heys Farm, and Davenport Heyes[5] lie quite near and it is possible that Henbury Hall was originally the centre of a deer park.

---

[3] See Chapter 8.
[4] The History of the Countryside. Oliver Rackham. 1987 J.M. Dent, London.
[5] Batsford Companion to Local History. Stephen Friar. 1991 Batsford London.

Chapter 6

More farms and cottages

There are several ancient **cottages on Dark Lane.** Dark Lane is one of the oldest thoroughfares in Henbury, and was once the main route to Knutsford and Chester from Macclesfield. It used to run from Broken Cross on a ridge just south of the now A537, which was opened as a turnpike in 1808, and then behind what is now Putty Row.

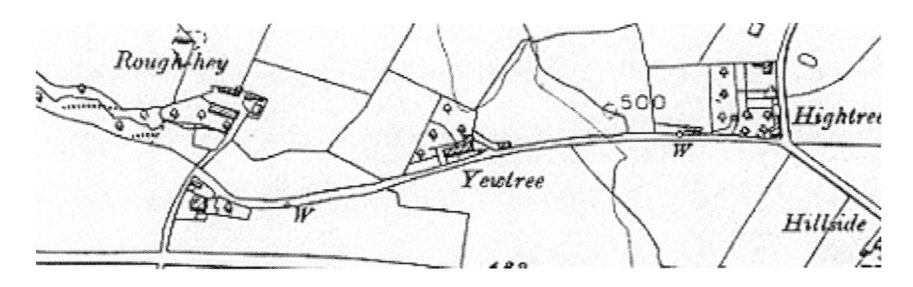

Dark Lane, from High Trees to Lime Cottage and Rosemary Cottage, nearRough Heys. OS 1954

Characteristically for a lane of great antiquity, Dark Lane is sunken with high banks on either side. In the meadow at the top of the lane, there are indentations surrounding a small plateau, that might be of archaeological interest – perhaps the *burgh*. An aerial photograph seems to confirm this conjecture.

The cottages on the lane are grouped around **High Trees** at the upper end, Yewtree in the middle, and **Lime Tree** and **Rosemary** Cottages at the lower end. High Trees was once a small holding with four dwellings, including a cottage of the same name close by on Andertons Lane, and also **Broome Cottage** on Dark Lane. Part of the latter was probably originally a barn. The three contiguous dwellings were sold off separately early in the 20th century.

The other **High Trees,** on Andertons Lane has a datestone *WJH 1760*. Prestbury Marriage Register records the marriage between John Wainwright of Prestbury, chapman, and Hannah Bibby of the same parish, widow, by licence on November 3rd, 1763. It is likely that the initials on the datestone refer to this couple. A

Henbury

chapman was a door to door salesman, and in Macclesfield was usually connected to the silk manufacturing industry. 1760 was not necessarily the date on which the cottage was built.

Among the Deeds for High Trees, Dark Lane and for Broome Cottage are papers referring to the John Day charity. John Day by his Will dated 1729 left annuities of 20 shillings, including to the poor of Prestbury. In 1732, his brother Richard Day, and Joseph and Martha Day put this on a legal footing with the Overseers of the Poor in Prestbury. It was agreed to charge John Day's land in Henbury with the payment of the annuities for ever. His land consisted of *'a close of land and buildings thereupon newly erected situate in Henbury called High Trees, containing by estimation one acre of Cheshire measure'*.

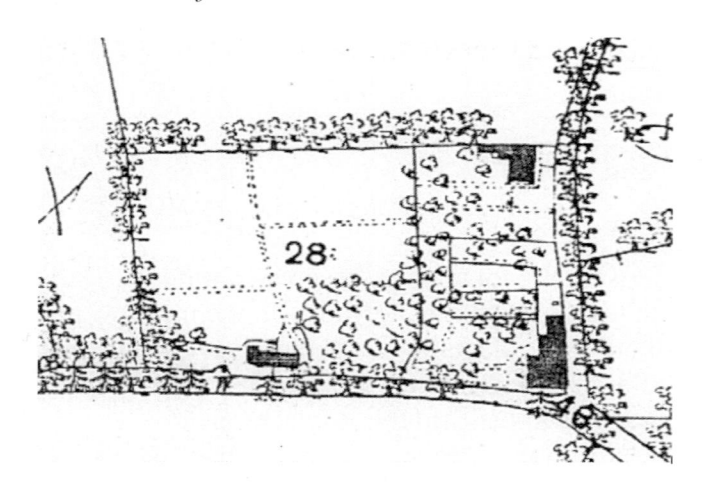

High Trees, including High Trees Andertons Lane and Broome Cottage. OS 1872

A later note states: *'High Trees contains one Cheshire acre, a house, stable, cowhouse, garden and meadow land'*. This suggests that only one house was built circa 1732, and the others were built later, perhaps to house agricultural labourers for the smallholding. The land tax lists Mrs Wainwright as both proprietor and occupant of the Andertons Lane High Trees, 1788-92, followed by A. Brownhill in 1794 (variously spelt). He continued as proprietor until 1830, but the tenants changed. In her Will dated 1788,

More farms and cottages

Hannah Wainwright left *'the house in which I now live'* and most of the furniture, to Anthony Brownhead of Henbury, weaver *'who now lives with me'*. Martha, the wife of Thomas Goodwin *'who also lives with me'* got twenty pounds and *'my best bed'*. Anthony Brownhead who lived at High Trees, is probably the Anthony Brownhill listed in the Land Tax.

The tenants were: 1793 A.Brownill, 1794 and 1795 Jeremiah Worthington (late Lathams), 1796-1811, Martha Goodwin 1812-24, Joseph Leigh 1829-30. In 1831, Joseph Leigh was proprietor and shared tenancy with Ann Gibson. Ann died in 1848 leaving the premises to James Shepherd.

The censuses listed James (sic) Leigh aged 50, joiner, High Trees in 1841, and Joseph Leigh age 63 joiner High Trees in 1851. In the 1849 tithes Joseph Lee was shown living at High Trees, Andertons Lane and James Shepherd with others was listed at High Trees and Broome Cottage, Dark Lane.

James Shepherd died in 1899, leaving High Trees to S E Newton and Mary Agnes Poole. Mrs Newton was later certified by the Masters in Lunacy, and her husband was authorised to sell *'5 freehold dwellings situate on Dark Lane and Andertons Lane'*. The property then came into the hands of the Poole family.

In 1901 Thomas Jenkin was listed living at Hendon House with Ann his wife and his daughters Jane and Annie. He leased High Trees Dark Lane in 1902, and appears in the 1914 Kelly's Directory as still living at High Trees. Some years ago a Jenkin descendant from New Zealand called bearing an old photograph of the house circa 1902, showing Mrs Jenkin standing in the now vanished porch. In 1910, the tenants Jenkin, Taylor and Heathcote lived at the Dark Lane High Trees cottages and France at the other one. An indenture at that time gave the right to use the well belonging to John Broome Coterill on Dark Lane.

In August 1902 an auction was held at the Macclesfield Arms Hotel and Broome Cottage was sold for £170 to John Broome Cotterill (was the name a coincidence?). Alfred Ernest Poole bought the two High Trees properties for £530 and £245 respectively; they were subsequently sold separately in 1910. Alice Walker lived in the end of the row of High Tree cottages in

Henbury

1940, and Philip Coleman in the end two in 1944. His mother taught at the Henbury Church School.

Broome Cottage, which is first referred to in a deed of 1732, has many large old beams in the two older parts and an exposed stone wall at the south-west corner. It seems likely that there was a barn attached to, or part of, the house. **Yew Tree Farm**, also known as Yew Tree House, halfway down Dark Lane, has a handsome Georgian frontage which may conceal earlier structures. Land tax records show that in 1784, Yew Tree House, Cottages and surrounding land (*7a.1r.34p.*) was owned by Wm. Carless. He did not occupy the property until 1821. Between 1823 and 1826 the property was purchased by John Bratt but Wm. Carless continued to live there.

The 1841 census shows that Richard Keyt Bratt (son of John Bratt?) and his wife Ellen were living at Yew Tree Cottage but by 1851 had moved to Yew Tree House with Mary Locket (house servant).

In the kitchen of Yew Tree House, in an alcove beside the fireplace, a door (now hidden by a cupboard) leads through to the sitting room of Yew Tree Cottage. Beneath the kitchen is a brick built vaulted cellar.

On 5th November 1880 Richard Keyt Bratt - now of Hall Bank, Buxton - died, leaving all the real estate he owned to his friends George Chapman, James Watts and Thomas Chapman. The real estate was to be sold *'as soon as conveniently might be after his decease'*. On 25th June 1881 Thomas Chapman declined to administer to the estate and renounced all rights to it. In September 1881 Yew Tree House, cottages and land were sold to Thomas Unett Brocklehurst of Henbury Park, for the sum of £2,030. It was described as four messuages or dwelling houses and tenements and six parcels of land.

When Ernest Thompstone purchased Yew Tree Farm (but not the cottages) from the Brocklehursts in 1921 the price was £1455.00. He obtained a mortgage of £1500.00 from Charles & Edward Howard Brocklehurst. Interest was to be paid at the rate of £6 5s per cent per annum. The cottages were purchased by Samuel Wright in 1948.

More farms and cottages

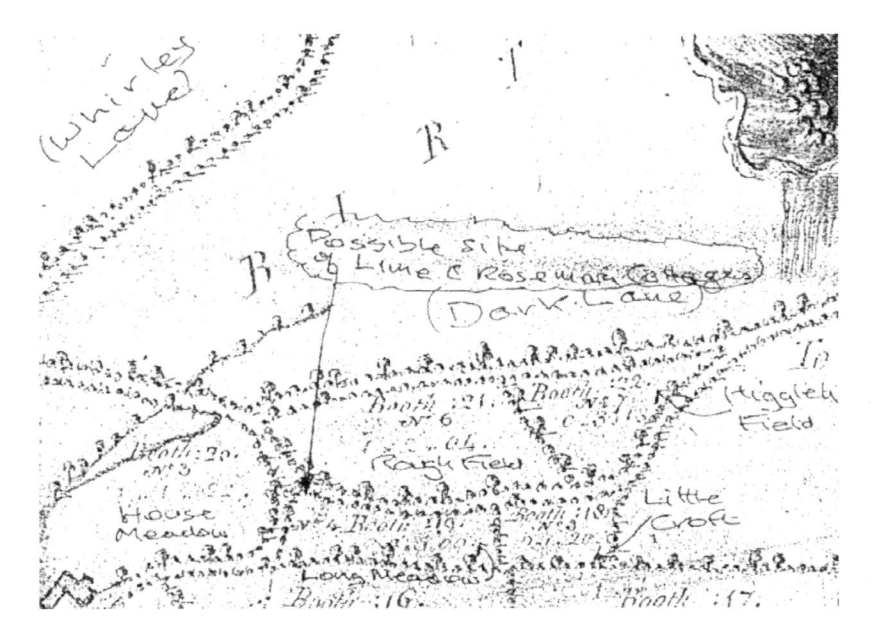

Dark Lane on the 1796 map. This map shows a lane – no longer visible – like a short loop running parallel to and south of Dark Lane, which may be the road for carriages and horses.

Old Chapter, the end cottage at Yew Tree, was sold on, with Fred Barber as sitting tenant, in 1949 for £200 to John William Weedall, and in 1950 for £385 to Samuel Woodman, and again in 1955 for £1000 to Mrs Gladys Taylor, who lived there until 1994. She renamed the cottage and trebled its size. She was a keen gardener and a very practical person; at the age of 90 she was still climbing ladders to clean out the gutters. The Taylor family ran a delicatessen shop in Mill Street, Macclesfield for many years, and her two daughters ran a millinery business from the same shop.

Old Chapter's owners, John and Mavis Halligan believe that the cottage's change of name in 1955 was based on Gladys Taylor's religious beliefs, for which there was ample evidence when they first viewed the property in 1994.

Lime Tree Cottage and **Rosemary Cottage** at the western end of Dark Lane also have a long history, not yet fully explored. At Lime Tree Cottage live John and Mary Worthington who are very

Henbury

knowledgeable about the village. John's paternal great grandparents retired from Whirley Barn Farm to live at High Trees, Andertons Lane, which then belonged to the Henbury Estate. John's maternal grandparents farmed Ruewood Farm off Chelford Road. His grandmother's maiden name was Massey.

John's grandparents William and Mary tenanted Rough Heys Farm from 1883, and the family were there for nearly 100 years. When the Stanley estate was sold in 1938, John's father Ephraim took the opportunity to buy the farm (see Chapter 4).

Ephraim, John and Mary and their children all attended the Church School. John attended from 1923 until 1928, when Mrs Coleman (who lived at High Trees middle cottage) was headmistress. Mrs Swindells was head mistress when the later Worthington children were there. The room in which we talked to the Worthingtons was timber framed, with massive timbers.

Lime Tree Cottage was once occupied by Mr Scragg, a gardener, whose son then lived next door at Rosemary Cottage. Both worked on the Henbury Estate. Earlier tenants are difficult to find. The 1843 map of Henbury held at the CRO and a list of fields and tenants relating to an auction of tithes held at the same date show William Lockett at Lime Tree Cottage and James Hulse at Rosemary Cottage. A Henbury Estate Field Notebook dated about 1820 shows a sketch of a cottage near the new turnpike occupied by William Hall, then William Savage, which is probably the right location. Pencilled in is *'part of Lowndes'* and also written on it are the names Pimlott and Lockett. According to the 1842 Henbury estate sale particulars, William Lockett occupied what is now Lime Tree Cottage, and 1835 he and Sarah Pimlott occupied the two cottages.

Lowndes Tenement was shown on the 1849 tithes map as consisting of several meadows south of what is now Blacksmiths Arms, and opposite the school, but indentures going back to 1692 mention Edward Lowndes, husbandman and subsequent members of the Lowndes family owning this property. The property included what was called the Sprink, or Spring. Ann Whitworth was an early tenant of a messuage mentioned in an indenture dated 1763. It is possible that either Rosemary cottage or Lilley Cottage

More farms and cottages

is the one identified in these indentures. If so, it was probably built between 1743 and 1771.

Rosemary Cottage and Lime Tree Cottage are typical of a number of cottages locally, in that they consist of a very old central core which has been added to and altered over time. The oldest parts of Rosemary Cottage are the four central rooms, two up and two down. The walls are oak framed with an infill which would have been wattle and daub originally. The wattle and daub infill was still there in the 1960s when the house was renovated though most of it was in a very decayed state. This was replaced by a modern material, but some of the original infill remains in the roof space.

The early staircase rose from the present dining room, the nearest room to the other cottage. It is probable that the roof was thatched when the cottages were built, perhaps as early as the 16th century. It retains the 18th century slate roof and there are some early and fragile panes of glass, now set in a new window, which probably belong to the same period.

Of interest is the remnant of a sandstone sill at the base of the wall dividing the dining room and the other early room, the present sitting room, which may mean that this was originally an outside wall; in which case the building may originally have been one main room with a loft above and possibly a wooden lean-to outside.

At one time Rosemary Cottage was known as Scragg's Fowd (fold). Did a notable shepherd live here? It seems likely that these cottages housed families who worked on the nearby farms of the Henbury estate.

A vanished cottage is referred to in an Indenture dated 1771, occupied by Alice Bradburn, *'lately erected by Dinah Birtles and a close opposite thereto called the Meadow next to Lowndes of about half an acre'*. The meadow is probably Long Meadow identified in the Birtles Estate map of 1837 as east of Pale farm. An Indenture dated 1795 states *'Mr Jodrell to have the cottage and gardens late Bradburn's on the south west side of the lane, and also a corner of Pale Croft on the south side of the rivulet'* (Pale

Henbury

Croft is identified on the 1837 map as lying east of Long Meadow and immediately south of the old Dark Lane).

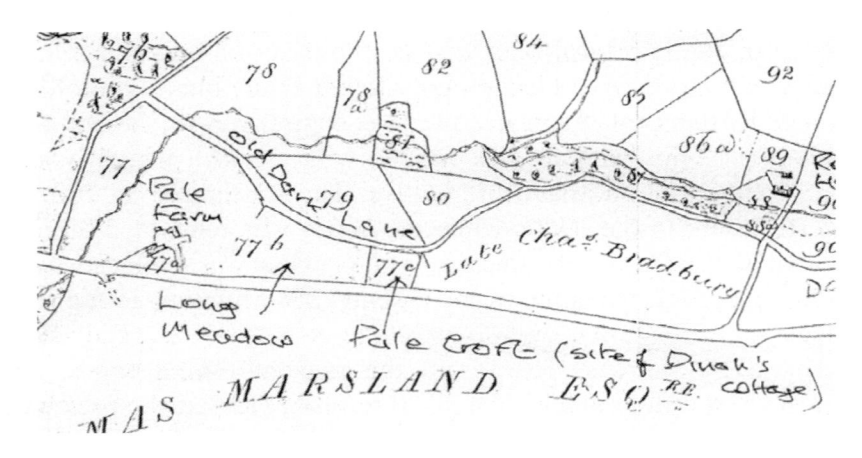

Pale Croft, on the 1837 Birtles Estate map

'He is to have the privilege of a road for horses and carriages over the Pale Croft to the gate on the Turnpike Road, the new fence to be made and maintained at their joint expense'. The turnpike at that time was what is now Whirley Lane. The rivulet referred to is probably the one running through Rough Heys Farm into Bag Brook

From **Henbury Smithy,** School Lane we met Miss Florence Bayley and her sister Mrs Elsie Knight, two of four children of Frank and Miriam Bayley. Elsie's grandfather, Henry Bayley came to live at the Smithy in 1882, and Henry Bayley his grandson was the last blacksmith to work there before it closed around 1955. They also had a smallholding of 24 acres, and a pinfold.

Frank Bayley used to walk twice on Sundays to Gawsworth to ring the church bells. He occupied the smithy from 1888 until he died in 1950, after shoeing a horse. A boil on the horse burst in his face, and sadly he developed meningitis. Elsie Knight told us that one of his particular skills was shoeing shire horses which required a special type of shoe. Henry Bayley, Elsie's brother, used to farm the 24 acres attached to the Smithy and continued to work as

More farms and cottages

farrier there until the work declined in the 1950's. The Smithy since then has been converted into a private residence.

Opposite the smithy is a pinfold which was used for holding stray animals. Custom provided that if they were not claimed within a set time, they became the property of the blacksmith. The grindstone, used for sharpening the blacksmith's tools, is thought to be one of the largest in existence, and is now situated in the Henbury Hall grounds. Colonel Geoffrey Sparrow remembers leading ponies to be shod there from Birtles Old Hall when he was a boy in the thirties.

Florence Bayley remembers their resident owl, probably a tawny. Once when returning from a dance with her boy friend, he mistook the owl's hoot for her mother, and took to his heels. An owl once alighted on her father's shoulder when he was cycling through Bluebell Wood.

We have not been able to determine when the smithy was built. It is not shown on the 1727 map, but a building at the right location is shown on the map dated 1796. Joseph Lancaster, blacksmith of Henbury married Mary Warrington, widow, of Gawsworth at Prestbury in 1811.

The 1841 census lists Joseph and Hannah Lancaster and their children, together with John Thompson and Charles Bradbury (aged 20), both also blacksmiths. In 1851 Hannah Lancaster, widow, was at the Smithy. George Lancaster, blacksmith, his wife Mary and their children were listed at the Poor House. George was blacksmith at Siddington in 1861, so his fortunes must have changed.

The blacksmiths following in Henbury were: 1861 William Henshall and Thomas his assistant, 1871 William Henshall and an assistant (Charles Bradbury, blacksmith is also listed, probably at the Blacksmiths Arms), 1881 William Henshall, 1891 and 1901 Henry Bayley whose son Frank and grandson Henry followed him at the smithy.

High Lodge[1], Whirley Lane occupies a commanding vantage

---

[1] We are indebted to Mr and Mrs H. Rosenthal for information on High Lodge.

Henbury

point, secluded behind its walls. High Lodge is one of the most unusual houses in Henbury. It was once a hunting lodge of the Stanleys of Alderley.

The property has been altered many times over the years but in the mid 19th century there were three related buildings: a small but comfortable pavilion for members of the family and guests who wanted to view the progress of the hunt, a stable block, and a service suite. A green carriage way can be clearly seen leading from the lodge across the fields towards High Lees Wood and thence to Birtles Hall and Alderley Park.

What was being hunted? We are not sure, but certainly foxes latterly, and in the wilder parts of Cheshire, deer, as they were at Lyme Park. Looking out from the lodge the spectacle could have been followed for miles, while the onlookers remained warm and cosy with every attendant comfort.

Chapter 7

Old houses in Henbury

There is enough history in Henbury houses to fill several books. We concentrated on some with particular associations: Arthur Marshall lived in Parkfield House which no longer exists, and Roger Bowling has made a detailed study of the Firs, in which he has lived for many years.

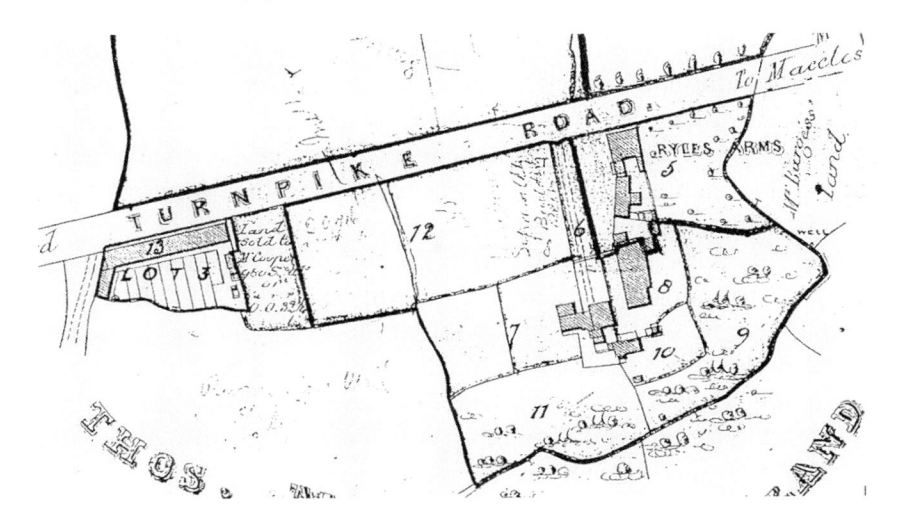

The Firs and the Cock Inn *A section of the 1860 map of the Henbury estate of the late David Willott who died in 1837. The map shows the Ryles Arms with farm buildings and an orchard where the car park is now, The Firs (centre), and lot 3 which is Putty Row. The map was prepared for his daughters when they sought advice for the first time from the court at Chester as both the original executors had died.*

A Tale of Two Houses[1]**.** In 1604 less than one year after the death of Queen Elizabeth 1, John Mottram, yeoman of Henbury Pexall died. He lived at Mottrams Tenement. In his will he leaves some treasured items to his daughter Margaret. The will also details some of his business affairs, land let to various persons, the rents owed and to be paid, and details of leases with years yet to run.

---

[1] We are indebted to Sheila Gordon and Mary Barber for information and Ron Frost for the loan of a document concerning this section.

Henbury

After his death four men produced an inventory and valuation of all his goods and chattels, but not the buildings or land. We can follow the tracks of the appraisers through the farm and house.

The inventory shows a large, well equipped farm. The animals included 4 oxen, 4 horses, 12 cows, calves, stirks, sheep, swine and poultry. There were all kinds of implements, 5 harrows, 4 ploughs, carts, traps, wains and tumbrels and a large collection of small tools. The collection of cooking and eating utensils was very large and of the best quality; pewter plates, many brass vessels, wooden plates called trenchers, treen, glassware, trinket dishes table linen and napkins. There was plenty of furniture, cupboards, dish boards, that is shelves, chairs and forms. In the house were 16 beds, and bed linen in sufficient quantity to furnish them, feather mattresses, cushions, pillows and pillow beres, that is pillow cases. John Mottram's goods and chattels were valued at over £150; the equivalent today is £22000. It is likely that only the Hall could surpass Mottrams Tenement for wealth, comfort and luxury, but what was it all for? Is it possible that the tenement was a hostelry and provider of accommodation? This might not be too strange an idea when we realise that Mottrams Tenement was on the site that 400 years later we know as the Cock Inn, at one time also called Jodrells Arms and later Ryles Arms.

The tenement was situated at the side of the old road that ran from Broken Cross to Henbury; it crossed the river just at the rear of the Cock Inn. On the other side of the road lived John's neighbours, the Harding family, just 50 yards to the south at Hardings Tenement. The will and inventory of Elizabeth Harding, widow, who died in 1683 shows a large dairy farm with 29 milking cows and a bull, 8 twinters (a cow of two winters), 12 stirks, 5 horses, 5 pigs and 12 calves. In store she had 10 hundredweight of cheese, value £9. Even by Cheshire standards, famed for its dairy products, this was a very large farm. The household goods, though not as numerous as those of their neighbours, showed a very comfortable standard of living, but only 5 beds. The total valuation was £181, equivalent today to at least £18000. She left many small bequests to members of the family; to her daughter furniture, bed and bedstead and to her eldest son John all the

Old houses

husbandry ware. John succeeded to the farm, and was probably running it already, but died 7 years later. Hardings Tenement, later named Old Cock and Sycamore Cottage is now The Firs and Cockwood.

The Firs, Cockwood, and Ivydale Farm

Is there any thing left today of these two farmhouses? Both houses have brick arch vaulted cellars and in The Firs and Cockwood there is internal timber framing, dated by dendrochronology to about 1640, an early staircase and, dug up in the garden, stone window mullions, a stone carved face and a medieval quern (a hand powered corn grinder). The cheese press mentioned in Elizabeth Harding's will also remains.

How did these two farms, well away from most of the other old farms in Henbury, come to be so successful? The term tenement probably gives us a clue, for in this context it probably means that they were founded by the person named in the title. Mottrams Tenement was probably taken from previously unused land by John Mottram or his father, sometime in the 16th century, by

Henbury

enclosure. The land he enclosed was between Whirley Road and the A537, that is the western end of Long Moss. The owners of the Moss could have been the burgesses of Macclesfield, the Grammar School or St. Michaels Church. The latter two both held land here in later times. Enclosure at these times was by agreement. Both parties were quite happy. The encloser got land for a farm and the owners had their land improved and received a rent. Some of the land of Mottrams Tenement 400 years later is still held by the Cock Inn, but in the name of Robinsons the brewers, while that of Hardings Tenement passed to the farm that succeeded it, Ivydale Farm where George Dooley and his sister Nellie farmed for over 40 years, until the 1990's.

Long Moss adjoins Whirley Common which was shared by Henbury, Over Alderley and Macclesfield. As late as the early 17th century there were no boundaries between the three townships in this area. John Mottram probably also enclosed some of the common, since a field to the north of Church Lane has been called Mottrams Meadow and Mottrams Moss.

Parliamentary Enclosure, that is enclosure by act of parliament came to Macclesfield in 1804 and the map of this date shows the enclosures on the Macclesfield part of Long Moss, but on the Henbury side the moss is named *"old enclosure"*; no act of parliament was needed, as all the land was already enclosed. One of these old enclosures can still be seen quite clearly, that is if the light is right with a low sun in the early morning. A small patch of ridge and furrow, undulations on the ground, betraying ancient ploughland, ploughed for very many years. Suspecting it might be less ancient than I thought, while helping George Dooley to cross the cows over the road, I asked him if it was any of his doing. "No" said George "it isn't, them's butts," using a term several centuries old.

Both farms appear on the hearth tax returns, John Mottram in 1663, and Thomas Harding in 1673, each assessed at one hearth. Both were clearly doing what most others were doing - evading the tax.

Two more John Mottrams carried on farming at their tenement. One died in 1674 and the other in 1724. These were presumably

Old houses

son and grandson of the John who died in 1604. The Hardings' tenure ended in 1715, at the death of Felicia and her daughter Jane, both in the same year. Most of the Hardings died without leaving a will and so family relationships can only known from the grants of administration given to a near relative. The inventories that do exist show much less detail.

Luckily for us, the last John Mottram dying in 1724 left a very interesting will. He bequeathed *"all my husbandry ware such is part and parcel of plowes, harrows, horse geers, saddles and all my husbandry ware whatsoever to William Rowbotham of Henbury Pexall, chapman"*, also *"all the rest of my personal estate whatsoever unto my hoore Sarah Bayley of Henbury Pexall aforesaid spinster who now lives with me to her own particular use forever"*. The inventory is not large but lists the contents of the farm, the buttery, parlour and two chambers over the house. John seems to have had no family, his wife had died some years earlier and so he left it seemingly to an unrelated friend. It is possible that he and William Rowbotham were neighbours, that is if William were already tenant or owner of the neighbouring property, Hardings Tenement. There is also circumstantial evidence that they may have been related through William's first wife who died soon after her marriage, but this has not yet been proved. Whatever the reason, five generations of the Rowbothams remained in Henbury for 120 years.

In the will William was described as a chapman. This usually means an itinerant hawker of smallware. However in Macclesfield it means something quite different. Chapmen were the organisers of the early silk industry, especially silk button making. They purchased the raw materials, distributed them to the out workers, collected the finished goods and marketed them. There were more men named as chapmen in Macclesfield than anywhere else. Some became wealthy and were the founders of the silk factories in Macclesfield. William may have had enough money to purchase one or both of the two farms. The will which was signed in 1719 says he was living in Henbury Pexall so he could have been living with John Mottram or he could, after his marriage, have purchased Hardings Tenement, if it became vacant after the death in 1715 of

Henbury

the two Harding ladies. Whatever the case, in 1727 William Rowbotham with eleven others appears in the list of Henbury freeholders, so he certainly owned one, or more likely both properties. After all what is the point of John Mottram bequeathing "all my husbandry ware" if William had no farm to use it?

One of the houses, probably the one in which William lived, Hardings Tenement, was altered in 1753, and probably in the early summer. The east end of the present Firs and Cockwood building is in the Georgian style both externally and internally. This style in a yeoman farmers house, in rural Cheshire, at so early a date seems unusual, but it does show that William Rowbotham had a taste for polite architecture and the money with which to carry it out. But how do we know so accurately when this was done? In more recent refurbishment, a piece of rolled up newspaper with old plaster attached was found filling a gap between window frame and plaster, just like any handyman does today. The newspaper was "Adams Weekly Courant" published in Chester, and dated June 26th to July 3rd, 1753.

As early as 1744 ale was being sold in Henbury by John Oliver, but we are not told where; and in 1753 are recorded three premises selling alcohol. No more details are given, but we think one could be the Hall, and the other Mottrams Tenement, which became the Cock Inn. In 1758 in the ale house registers, two are recorded in Henbury, Timothy Worthington, yeoman and Joseph Bradburn, maltster. Not until 1774 were more complete records made. The list of ale house keepers with their sureties for Henbury commences in 1774 and finishes in 1811 with some years missing. Only occasionally does the name of the pub appear, and none are listed for Henbury. There appears to be only one pub but from recognisable names this was the Cock Inn. The Rowbothams never until 1809 appear to have been the licencees. They must therefore have leased it to others along with about 15 acres, while farming and living at Hardings Tenement.

Three generations, William Rowbotham dying in 1772, aged 88, his son John dying in 1803, and the grandsons William and John, farmed the tenements until both were sold. The land tax

Charlie Hatton ploughing with three horse team (courtesy Bill Geldart)

George Heathcote and Tommy, Lodge Farm probably 1950s (courtesy Mrs E Heathcote)

George Dooley crossing the cows to Ivydale Farm over the A537, 1992 (courtesy R Bowling)

Reaping at Home Farm (Mr W Hatton)

Loading corn, Rough Heys (Mr J Fletcher)

Moss Cottage, 2002 (PG Wells)

Lily cottage, 2002 showing original timber framing (PG Wells)

Henbury and Broken Cross Schools' Victory Treat, 1945

Home Farm, Hatton brothers with mare and foal (courtesy Mr W Hatton)

Broken Cross, Edwardian postcard

Dukinfield Cyclists' Club meeting at the Cock Inn, 1 September 1889, for their first ever 25 mile road race (courtesy Mrs G Hallworth)

Bluebell Valley, Edwardian postcard

Flemish stained glass, Pale Farm (photograph P G Wells)

Old houses

assessments record land owners and occupiers in Henbury from 1784, with only one year missing, to 1831. The Rowbothams appear in every year, nearly always the same tax to pay, except for just an acre or so, bought or sold.

When John died in 1803 it was his wish that the two sons, John and William would carry on the Rowbotham business of farming and owning a public house. His intentions, probably due to a badly planned will, were not fulfilled; he left Mottrams Tenement, then the Jodrells Arms, to the younger son John, who was then not 21 years old, and left Hardings Tenement to the elder son by a previous marriage, with £200 to top up an earlier loan of £200. Both gifts included all the husbandry ware and land. The five other surviving children each received £400. For John's wife he left "sufficient to furnish a room in my tenement called Mottrams Tenement" and "use of kitchen as long as she is a widow", also, "the tenement to be charged yearly the sum of £25 to be paid to my wife, and all the coals for the said room".

Probably another error John makes is to divide a property, which had for almost 80 years provided a comfortable life for one family, into two, for clearly soon after his death both sons were in financial trouble. Indeed the loan of £200 to William suggests something was wrong before his father's death.

This error was compounded by another probably more serious one. John instructed that his two executors were to be paid by a charge on Mottrams Tenement of £500, within 12 months of his death. Although seemingly well off .John appears not to have the money to simply be given to the executors, so the gift of the tenement was immediately blighted by a debt of £500. The present day equivalent of this sum is £19000. What on earth was this payment for?

John when he received his legacy was young and inexperienced at farming, innkeeping and managing his own money, or rather his debts. He did pay off the £500, but not within the time limit, with £200 of his own and the rest borrowed. This was only one of a long series of debts.

Between 1806 and 1808 the Jodrells Arms was closed, but for the following three years until 1811 John is listed as licensee, so it

Henbury

appears he was trying to make a go of it. It is very likely that the two brothers ran the farms as one concern. They were not helped by the fact that the pub until after 1808 had no access suitable for wheeled traffic, and that due to the Napoleonic wars inflation was rampant; the value of money from 1799 to 1800 fell more than 30% and did not recover until 1820. Things just got worse and in 1816 *"John Rowbotham of Rainow, eldest son,* (that was not correct)*, and heir at law of will of father John Rowbotham, late of Henbury, John Rowbotham owes money to Henry Barlow and William Pauldon (partners in trade) and to diverse other persons in considerable sums of money and being unable to pay had agreed to grant release and convey the several hereditaments and premises to John Mellor and Thomas Gaskell, to be sold to pay off and discharge such debts"*. Mellor and Gaskell were then in possession.

Both properties, the Jodrells Arms and brother Williams farm Hardings Tenement with all the fields, and *"Mottrams Moss, being six Cheshire acres of moss ground"* were included in the sale. One big field was not included in the sale. This was the Great Patch, being *"2½ acres of Cheshire measure"*, once one of Williams fields. This was sold back to William for him to keep a patch of his own farm, purchased for him by his trustee William Brocklehurst, Gent. Reading between the lines there did seem to be goodwill and help for the brothers during these trials.

That was the end of the sad story, the end of Rowbothams, yeoman farmers of Henbury for over 90 years and the end of owner and occupier farmers in the two properties. For at least the previous 210 years, three families, Mottrams. Hardings and Rowbothams had farmed the land of the two tenements.

John went to Rainow where he had family and maybe founded or joined the family business of wheelwrights, which survived into living memory. Tragedy still followed them, for between 1820 and 1825, four children of John and his wife Amy died, aged 3 weeks, 6, 12 and 20 years. The elder two were born in Henbury.

William remained in Henbury as a farm labourer, probably on the farm which was once his own. He moved just a few yards next door to Moss House, which is now Ivydale Farm. For himself he

Old houses

must have farmed his own small patch, the "Great Patch". He died in 1846. His will was an inferior will, meaning his estate was less than £40, but the executors swore that his estate was valued less than £20.

The purchaser of the estate, the Jodrells Arms and Hardings Tenement, for the sum of £2726, was a Macclesfield businessman and property speculator, whose family had for very many years owned a small farm, Woodhouse Farm, now called Springbank on Henbury Moss. His name was David Willott, plumber and glazier of Duke Street, Macclesfield. If it could then be expected that order would return to the two properties, expectations were foiled; for 50 more years nothing improved.

In addition to his small farm in Henbury, Willott owned property in Macclesfield, shops, cottages and his business premises in Duke Street, and the Green Dragon public house, and once property on Danes Moss. He never lived in any of his Henbury houses but leased them. He did leave us one well known Henbury landmark, Putty Row, now known as Pleasant View. When the new turnpike road was constructed soon after 1808 a small piece of waste ground was left where the new road crossed the old road at the end of Church Lane. This narrow strip of land was once the end of one of the fields called the House Meadow, belonging to Hardings Tenement. Upon it Willott built ten cottages; one had a schoolroom and another a weaving shed. Only a property developer could think of doing this. Why Putty Row? Because it was built by the plumber and glazier, the putty man. It was named Putty Row in the 1841 census, and probably ever since it was built. David Willott died in 1837. He had a large family including seventeen grandchildren, and complicated business affairs. The will was straightforward; his three children to get all the property, a natural son Thomas Owen £40 each year for life, and there was provision for the grandchildren. He appointed two executors, one being William Cooper, his son-in-law.

To cut a very long story short it then took until 1902 to complete the instructions in his will, that is 65 years after his death (Henbury's own Bleak House!). To be correct the disposal of the Henbury property was completed fairly quickly, in only·thirty two

Henbury

years. Just one month after probate was granted, one of the executors died leaving William Cooper on his own. David Willott's son, also David, was invited to be an executor but declined, also refusing to have anything to do with his father's business; he must have known something. William Cooper, due to his difficulty in selling any property, agreed verbally with three of his married daughters to divide amongst them the proceeds at valuation, making provision for all the grandchildren.

The first property to be sold was Woodhouse Farm to Samuel Bullock of Gawsworth in 1858 for £1500, and in the same year Putty Row to Thomas Cooper, all ten cottages for £450 the lot. At an unknown date, but probably also in 1858 Hardings Tenement, now called Old Cock, and including the cottage that later became Ivydale Farm was sold to John Booth, yeoman of Park Lane. He died in 1860, and by provision in his will, Old Cock passed to his grandson Edward Arthur Clarke; in fact Booth purchased Old Cock specially for his grandson.

In 1858 Ann Shaw, who had married one of the sons of the Shaw family of Park House Farm, and was one of William Cooper's daughters acquired the Cock Inn, *" the messuage or dwelling formerly called the Jodrells Arms, afterwards the Ryles Arms, but now called the Cock Inn, formerly in occupation of Edward Hough, later in the occupation of John Bradbury, since in the occupation of Martin Leah and now of Joseph Hague, and land as far as belong to Unsworth."* That is as far as Unsworth Fold on Whirley Road.

In 1869 Edward Arthur Clarke added to his Henbury estate by the purchase of the Cock Inn from Ann Shaw for £1950. Thus after thirty two years was David Willott's Henbury property disposed of. His Macclesfield property took a little longer. The original executor William Cooper died in 1860, leaving no executors. In 1881, in the court at Chester it was stated the personal estate of David Willott was left unadministered as executors had died. Executorship was granted to Martha Worth, widow, one of the daughters of William Cooper. That was still not the end of the matter, for in 1902, again at Chester, administration was granted to Emma Worth, spinster, one of the executors of

Old houses

Martha Worth; in other words, the last executor was the great grandchild of David Willott, which meant that many of the intended beneficiaries never received what was theirs. After sixty five years the business was finished.

Edward Arthur Clarke was one of a large family of silk manufacturers who were pillars of Macclesfield society. In 1883 as president of the Macclesfield Chamber of Commerce he visited Krefeld in Germany to see how the German manufacturers could produce silk goods far cheaper than those in Macclesfield. He was a JP and later became Alderman Clarke. In addition to the gift of The Firs from John Booth's will, he was also given grandfather Booth's own house, Park Cottage, in Park Lane. He never lived in Henbury; it was probably too far from town to attend all his society and business engagements. Maybe at one time he did intend to live in Henbury for he made large alterations and additions to The Firs and the old small cottage, which later became Ivydale Farm. To The Firs he added a new wing of bedroom, bathroom, kitchen and hall. At the rear he built a coachhouse and stable, and a larger wash house. The front of the house was rebuilt with a balustrade and a two storey bay window. The garden was laid out, and the arrangement of the paths remains today.

Until Clarke's ownership The Firs had been for at least the previous 200 years a farm, with the farm buildings and yard to the east, and access to the fields by the cow lane, which still remains today as the drive next to the Cock Inn, continuing across the main road right into the middle of the moss. He converted The Firs into a gentleman's residence, which of course it still is, and the old cottage nearby became Ivydale Farm. We rather think that the name is Clarke's choosing, as he later left Park Cottage and moved to Ivydene on Ivy Lane. The farm was recently renovated and building work revealed a small double arched window previously well hidden; its age is unknown, but it looked very old. The arrangement of John Mottram's will of 1604 suggests the possibility that he also owned a second small cottage; this could be it. But since that time the cottage, later Ivydale Farm, was always part of The Firs. They were separated on the death of Clarke in 1917 and the sale of his estate in 1920.

Henbury

Clarke made a very nice job of the two houses and I think maybe he wished to retire to his gentleman's residence, right next door to his own pub. He did leave one nice memento of his stewardship, two variegated sycamore trees at the front of The Firs. These gave the earlier name to the house, Sycamore Cottages, in the 1880's. They remain healthy and very large.

From large scale plans of 1860, 1874, 1891 and 1920 it appears that the Cock Inn was never altered, despite Clarke owning it for 50 years. A large range of farm buildings was to the rear, stables, cow houses, pig sties and a cart shed. The present car park was an orchard with a pump in the centre. The Cock Inn is built on the site of the 1604 building, but underneath the present 1960's render is not much of the 1604 farm, but a rather pleasant red brick country pub; if Clarke didn't build this, who did? It must have been built after the main road was constructed, that is after 1808, but before Clarke's ownership. That can only be in the time of David Willott, or his executors. The executors had quite enough trouble selling Willotts property, so it must have been built between Willott's arrival in 1816 and his death in 1837. .If this is correct then the Cock Inn is contemporary with Putty Row.

In Clarkes time the Cock Inn prospered, for in a public house guide of 1891 appears *"Henbury, Cock Inn. Fully licensed, owner and leasee E.Clarke Jnr. Of Ivy Lane, Macclesfield. Licensee Charles Hatton. Free house. One bed and refreshments for 20 persons. 1 stable with three stalls. Good house and accomodation."* And of course it still is. Just for interest at the same time the Blacksmith's Arms is listed as *"an old house run by a woman"*, (oh dear!). The Cock Inn, and also another public house at Monks Heath crossroads, the Iron Gates, were well known in the 1890's by the south Manchester and Stockport cycling fraternity, or as they were called the wheelmen. An issue of the Macclesfield Courier in 1894 describes the cyclists waiting at the Iron Gates while their tea is prepared, it being a temperance house. An old photo of the Cock Inn shows the wheelmen of Duckinfield outside the Cock Inn, but with beer not tea.

Ivydale Farm buildings were later altered to give a larger and more convenient yard. All the range of farm buildings of the Cock

Old houses

Inn were later swept away. Edward Arthur Clarke's Henbury estate was sold in 1920, in six lots: the Cock Inn with about 15 acres, Old Cock Farm, now Ivydale Farm with forty acres, The Firs and one field sold together, The Knoll, that is the white house on the north side of the road, and two semi-detached houses now called Brookdale. On October 19th Robinsons of Stockport became owners of the Cock Inn and the land. The first landlord was Walter Goddard who remained at the inn for 33 years, being followed by his son-in-law for a few years. Walter is still well remembered for being the owner of Goddard's Riding Stables which had buildings on the opposite side of the road. This ran for many years before the second world war but due to the shortage of animal food had to close during the war. Walter's predecessor at the inn told him many tales of times before World War I. During potato harvests it remained open all night to cater for the carters on their way to Macclesfield market, up to 17 carts being drawn up on the road outside at seven in the morning. Walter Goddard was well known in the riding world and was a judge for several societies. Robinson's land is still farmed but the inn is no longer a farm; you might however be misled on seeing all the ponies, donkeys and sometimes goats, well cared for in their field next to the car park.

The Firs was bought by Samuel Holland who was giving up farming at Hill Top Farm, Pexhill. He was also the proprietor of S & W Holland, Agricultural Engineers of Broken Cross, the concern founded by his father William Holland, one time licensee of the Bull's Head and a blacksmith. William's excellence in ironwork brought him many prizes at agricultural shows and eventually led to the engineering business founded about 1860.

Samuel Holland, his wife Ann and their three daughters moved to The Firs but by 1926 both parents had died. The three daughters Esther, Jane and Annie lived in the house for 40 years. Esther had been married and widowed by 1917, but the others never married and both were teachers. All the family were pillars of Henbury church; Samuel was a governor of Henbury school, churchwarden and sidesman.

Henbury

The agricultural engineering business lasted through four generations, and eventually was sold to Burgesses; the buildings are now a car showroom.

For forty years The Firs was a ladies' residence. The house was well looked after, the furniture especially in the large lounge was of the highest quality, and my informant well remembers visits for afternoon tea; this was quite an occasion. Esther died in 1945, Jane and Annie remained until too infirm, and then moved to Macclesfield and their home was sold.

The only other residents of note were the Hughes family. They lived at The Firs for seven years until 1970. Dr. Hughes was a doctor at Parkside Hospital. The family is best remembered for their enjoyment of life. Their four children kept pigeons and, as Mr. Dooley said a 'nowty', bad tempered donkey. The children spent much of their time at Ivydale Farm and enlivened George and Nelly Dooley's days greatly.

This story has a postscript. The will left by William Rowbotham, the last of the yeoman farmers, dying in 1845, mentioned two young brothers John and Henry, *"the executors shall retain in their hands the sum of five pounds for each of my grandchildren Henry and John Rowbotham sons of my late son Thomas Rowbotham."* Now the story moves to 2001. In June of that year while surfing the net, on the 'help sought' page of the Cheshire Family History Society website I found a Mike Rowbotham seeking information of Rowbothams of Henbury pre 1845. Mike had traced his direct ancestors back to the two brothers and their father; from later census schedules the brothers were born in Macclesfield and Embhy or Embery, Cheshire. I e-mailed Mike that I might be able to help as three generations of his family had lived in our house, The Firs from 1724 to 1845. Mike, his cousin and their wives spent a day in Henbury, studying wills in his six times great grandfather's farmhouse and having lunch in his pub, the Jodrells Arms. Mike has discovered what had happened to the brothers after their fathers death when they were both about ten years old.

Their mother remarried and the family left Henbury. No doubt John and Henry had heard the story of how the family had about twenty years previously lost their two houses, lands and pub,

Old houses

leaving grandfather a labourer on his own farm and dying almost penniless. They must have decided to leave the farming life behind, join the great exodus from the land and seek a fortune elsewhere. Only a few years later in 1845 they both married in Yarwell, Northants, working building the Nene Valley Railway, now a preserved line. We hope they received the legacy of £5 each. Henry worked on other lines while John later went building railway lines in India, notably the East India Railway. What a story he could tell, poverty in Henbury to railways in India. Mike and Roger Bowling had discussions about some of the problems in the Rowbotham story. He provided Roger with the genealogy of the family before and after they lived in Henbury, but we did not discover any single reason why the family lost their farms and land. Mike was able to trace his direct ancestry right back via the West Midlands, India, Yarwell, Henbury and Macclesfield (probably Hurdsfield) to 1682, eight generations, five of which spent some time in Henbury.

If a member of these early generations, such as William, the first Rowbotham in Henbury, in 1724, or John Mottram of Mottrams Tenement, (the Cock Inn) who died in 1604, were to return today, what would they think? Their houses would have altered, their farms, the buildings, barns, stables all gone, no oxen or even horses. The road between the two houses gone and little trace of it remaining, the road now being on the other side of the house, and they would be shocked by the traffic, just as we are. But there is one thing they would have no difficulty in recognising, their fields. A hedge or two may have gone, but they would be able to name all the fields and the crops they grew. Standing in front of the Cock Inn today, looking north across the road, except for the houses on Whirley Road, the view is much the same as it was 400 years ago, and John Mottram, his father or his grandfather could still see the results of their oxen's work, "them butts."

Henbury

Davenport Heyes, on Church Lane OS 1954

Davenport Heyes is a beautifully proportioned early Georgian style house, brick built with a white render, with tiers of sash windows and a stone flagged roof. Bernard Rhodes, who kindly showed me round, believes that the premises at the rear, where an outside flight of steps leads to an upper storey are of an earlier date than the main building. Adjoining the rear building is what used to be a pigsty, at the time the Rhodes first moved in about 32 years ago.

Bernard was told that the Bromley Davenports converted the house into a gentleman's residence circa 1846. Certainly, judging by the orientation of some tiles projecting from the chimney base at the gable end, the line extending down the gable end wall below additional brickwork, the roof has been raised sufficiently to permit the addition of an upper row of sash windows, smaller in size than the remainder. It is possible that these were the modifications introduced by the Bromley Davenports.

The gable ends support four round windows, situated below the earlier roof line. Three of them are bricked in, probably to avoid the highly unpopular window tax, imposed from 1696, and only repealed in 1851. Within the house, some of the glass panes look original, and in one of the upper rooms of the adjoining building there is a particularly old window comprising tiny leaded and fragile glass panes. There is no evidence for a timber frame, although there are a number of ceiling beams. The initials on this

Old houses

Davenport Heyes with former stables behind (photograph P G Wells)

Date stone on the house next door to Davenport Heyes, which was once the stables, giving the date 1733. The date stone is displayed with initials, over a circular window (photograph P G Wells)

Henbury

datestone probably refer to Charles and Hannah Bradbury. According to Prestbury St Peter's Church Marriage Register, Charles Bradbury, servant, married Hannah Wharmbie in 1723 at Chelford. Hannah was the daughter of William Wharmbie.

Thanks to Bernard and Carole Rhodes, the present owners, we were able to transcribe and photocopy many of the Deeds of the house - some of which were in a very fragile condition - from which we could trace its early history. In June, 1694, George Lucy (the son of Sir Fulk Lucy of Henbury Hall) and Sir Samuel Eyre sold Motterhams Moss *'late in the tenure of John Motterham'* to William Gaskell for £345. It included a messuage (a dwelling house), and allowed William Wharmby, Philip Bromfield, gent, Hugh Birtles and John Harding to dig turves and collect firewood from the site.

In 1712 William Gaskell of *Gawesworth*, yeoman, leased *'Davenport Heys or Mottram Field'* in Henbury to John Wharmby of Henbury, yeoman for £25. John Wharmby in his Will made in 1719 left land in Poynton to his brother William Wharmby and his house and land to his wife Hannah for life, and then to his sister's children.

In 1728 William Wharmby of Henbury, yeoman agreed to purchase the estate of the late John Wharmby, *'now in the occupation of Charles Bradbury'* for £88 from William Latham of Sutton, husbandman, John Latham of Henbury, yeoman, and William Salt and his wife Mary of Withington. The former were described as *'the children of John Wharmby's sister'*, mentioned in John Wharmby's Will. The subsequent Indenture included two closes in Henbury called the High Trees and Lower High Trees, and another close in Henbury *'known by the name of Davenport Heys or Motteram Field, which said premises are now in the occupation of Charles Bradbury'*.

William Wharmby died only a few months later, and his will in 1729 states *'I give and bequeath all the close, field or parcel of land lying and being in Henbury, and commonly called by the name Mottram Field and all newly erected buildings there standing with its appurtenances, now in the possession of Charles Bradbury unto my nephew William Latham of Sutton in the said County, yeoman, after the death of Hannah, Charles Bradbury's wife'*. He directed that John Latham of Henbury should have access through Mottram Field with a cart to dig marlpits *'with as little dammage as possible'*. The 'newly erected buildings' suggests a date for the foundation of the house Davenport Heyes, and so the stable building with its 1733 date was probably added a few years later.

In January 1729-30 William Latham agreed to sell *'a close in Henbury and all newly erected buildings thereon in the occupation of Charles Bradbury'* to Charles for £60 after the death of Charles's wife, as stipulated in William Wharmby's will. In spite of the fact that Charles was buried in Prestbury in 1737 and was survived by his widow, the proposed deal still went ahead whilst Hannah was still living, and Davenport Heyes was sold to Charles Bradbury for £60.

In 1776 William Careless of Henbury, tailor, and William Careless his son made a bond with a later Charles Bradbury, possibly Bradbury senior's son, in the sum of £80 to keep the covenants made in an Indenture allowing the two to take turves from the Moss Rooms, part of a close called Davenport Heys, *'now in the possession of Charles Bradbury'*. (Peat for fuel, called turf, was dug from the 'moss rooms', a name for a peat cutting area.).

The Land Tax records show names of proprietors and occupants of properties, and name Charles Bradbury in the former role, and Charles Bradbury senior as the occupants of *'house and lands'*, paying tax of 5s 9d from 1784 until 1792. In 1794, this property had changed hands, John Bradbury being both proprietor and occupant of the premises described as *'late C. Bradbury'* (Charles Bradbury senior was buried in 1793). Tax had increased to 10s, but by 1796, this had fallen again to 5s 9d, and the occupant was Mrs Partington. She was described as *'widow Partington'* in 1799, but in 1800 was joined by a second tenant, Mr Swannick, and tax went up to 10s again. The 1808 map of Henbury shows Jonathon Bradbury as the owner of Davenport Heyes at that time, which

Henbury

suggests that the unnamed premises in the land tax have been correctly identified.

John Bradbury continued to let Davenport Heyes to different tenants, including another Charles Bradbury in 1818, followed by John Gill. John Bradbury died in 1821, and his place as proprietor was taken by Thomas Wardle who was still there in 1829 paying the same tax.

Unfortunately it has not been possible to place the house in any of the censuses from 1841 to 1891, but Joseph Windows is named as the occupant in Kelly's Directory for 1892, and in the 1901 census, and William Millington was there in 1923. The house was empty for some time before the Rhodes bought it, and for a period was threatened with demolition by building contractors. The Muir family with two daughters lived there before the Rhodes, and Garside before them. The house is listed.

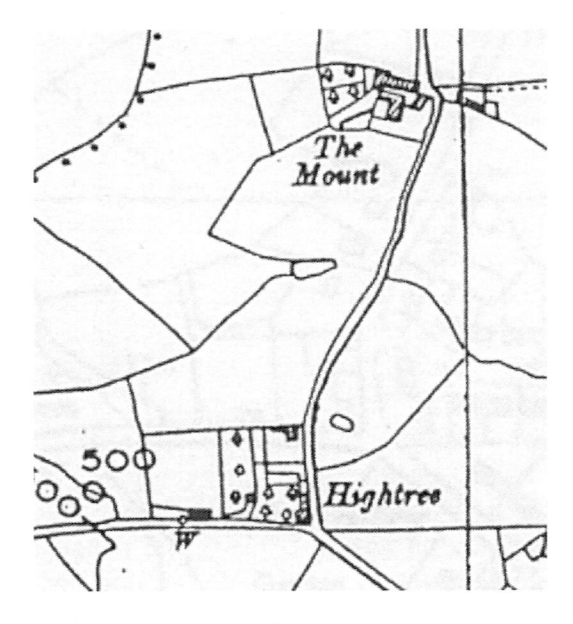

The 1909 OS map shows the fields of Mount Farm which originally extended to Hightree and were known as Latham's Tenement. The Mount, on the south side of the farm buildings, is now a separate residence.

Old houses

The Mount is an elegant house in Regency style, built in the early 19th century as part of an older farm on Anderton's Lane. The two properties were separated in 1923. The farm, which at that time comprised 24 acres of good Cheshire measure^2 extending to High Trees, was formerly known in 1764 as Latham's Tenement. The owner from 1799 to 1834 was Samuel Anderton, and the occupier was Edward Anderton. Samuel lived in Marylebone, and later in Bushey, Herts; he was described in 1799 as a baker. It may have been Samuel who brought the idea of a Regency house to Henbury. A comprehensive set of Deeds held by the present owners, Nicholas and Mona Payne, record a succession of owners since then, including a Lt. Col. Charles Harrop Beck who died of wounds in 1915 leaving an infant son born 1914. In 1923 his Trustees sold the farm to Samuel Swaine. The farm buildings are now divided into three separate residences.

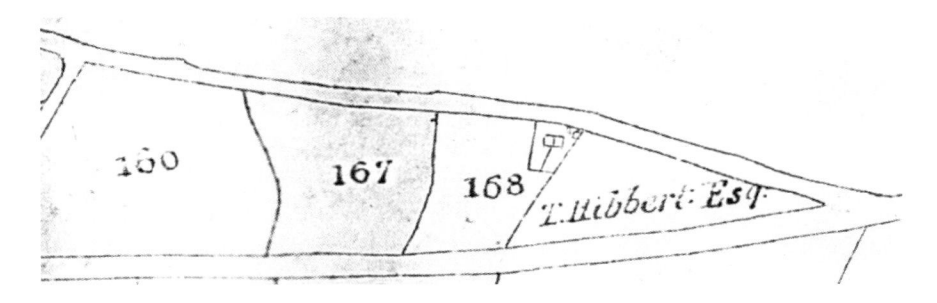

Possible location of the Poor House in field 168 on Church Lane. From Henbury Estate map 1842.

The Henbury Poor House. Before the General Workhouse Act of 1723, which empowered parishes to build workhouses, many of them had already provided poor houses to give shelter for the needy in their midst. From 1572, an Overseer of the Poor, an elected parish official, was made responsible for supervising charitable funds, and in 1597 parishes were expected to levy a poor rate, from which cash payments to the poor could be made.

---

^{2} Equivalent to about 56 statutory acres. An old Cheshire acre was not much different from a hectare.

Henbury

A map published in 1808 to show the route of the newly intended Broken Cross to Pale Farm Turnpike Road (see Chapter 10) showed the Henbury Poor House as situated on the south side of Church Lane, possibly the same site as Beech Cottage before it was demolished about 30 years ago. On the Henbury Hall Estate map of 1842, there is a building which appears to be two adjacent semi detached dwellings on the same site.

In 1734, Amos Meredith of Henbury Hall let the Birtles and Savage tenements to Samuel Sandbach and Gamaliel Carter, the Overseers of the Poor for the Township of Henbury, and their successors for one shilling a year rent *'for the proper use of the town and joint inhabitants of Henbury...and tenantly profits and advantages'*. The Overseers were expected to keep the premises in good repair. Amos appointed Charles Bradbury, yeoman, as *'his true and lawful attorney to take possession of the premises and to deliver unto Samuel Sandbach and Gamaliel Carter'*. As we have already seen, Samuel occupied Sandbach farm, and was a tanner. Another benefactor was William Wharmby of Davenport Heyes, who in 1729 bequeathed *'thirty shillings to the poor of the higher end of Henbury'* (an early distinction between the north side of the village and the Fanshawe Brook and Pexhill parts!). The poor of Henbury should still be benefitting from another bequest, from Roger Holland in 1850; this was a yearly sum of three shillings, charged on lands in Mottram.

In 1779 Sir William Meredith let the premises *'commonly called the Poor House'* previously in the possession of Edward Davenport deceased, and now in the possession of Edward Goostrey, to John Pimlott of Henbury, tailor for an annual rent of one shilling. It is not clear if John had taken on the management of the Poor House, but it certainly retained that function for a considerable time afterwards, being mentioned in the 1851 census, when William Pimblott aged 28, an agricultural labourer and his family, and George Lancaster, blacksmith aged 36, and his family of 7 children lived there.

The Poor House is not listed by name in subsequent censuses, and by 1901 it became or had been replaced by Beech Cottage, occupied by Elizabeth Bloor, *'living on her own means'*. Within

Old houses

living memory, Edward Vaughen, local roadsweeper occupied the cottage. He was sexton for several years to the Church of St Thomas, and eventually went to live at Moss Farm on Fanshaw Lane.

We have no records of the administration of the Poor House, as Henbury Township records are not deposited, and the Prestbury Parish Overseers of the Poor records are not available for the period.

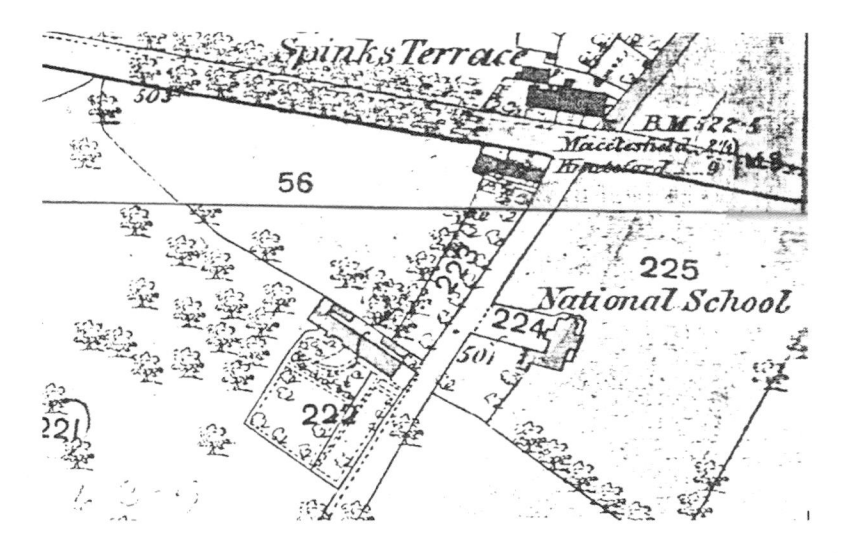

The site of Parkfield House and Cottage (field 222) OS 1872

Parkfield House. Across the road from the old school on School Lane, there is an area of land that resembles a paddock; a thorn hedge forms the perimeter of the area and daffodils flower under the hedge. In the far corner stands a tall graceful weeping ash tree. Prior to Sir Vincent de Ferranti's arrival at Henbury Hall the site consisted of an old cottage and an attractive country house. Previously it had been a small farm, but later the farm was dispensed with and it became a private house, Parkfield House.

When Sir Vincent purchased the estate, he quickly demolished Parkfield House and the cottage, at the same time as the old Henbury Hall. Arthur Marshall, Parish Clerk from 1947 to 1993, who lived there, suggests that it could have been saved; it only

Henbury

needed a damp course which could have been inserted without too much difficulty. The paddock serves as a lasting memorial to an attractive country house and an older country cottage believed to be the home of one of the early teachers at Henbury School and possibly built by Thomas Marsland for that purpose.

Henry Bayley, after he married Phyllis Nield, went to live at Parkfield Cottage. After his father, Frank, died at the smithy in 1950, Henry and his wife swapped with his sisters and moved to the smithy. Arthur Marshall's father, Lionel, had to move from the Blacksmith's Arms, where he was proprietor, to Parkfield House as he was also a policeman, and police were not permitted to run a business.

The next door neighbour at Parkfield House once told Florence Bayley's mother that she had heard mysterious footsteps in the night, and had seen a spectre dressed in taffeta by the cellar door. Florence's mother volunteered to go and see if anything hanging on the door could be mistaken for a ghost. They gingerly opened the cellar door, and were startled to find that water was lapping the top step. The cellar contained a well, which had filled up and overflowed, so the ghost had warned them in time before the rest of the house was flooded!

Chapter 8

Henbury Hall

When William the Conqueror came to the English throne in 1066, he set about dividing the country into regions for good government. Each region was controlled by either members of his family or his army commanders. Cheshire (along with two other counties, Kent and Durham) was privileged to be called Palatine, a form of self-government, and William appointed his nephew Hugh Lupus to govern this part of the kingdom.

Hugh gave this particular part of the county to the Barons of Halton, who in turn authorised the Mainwarings of Peover to supervise Henbury. It was eventually sold to the Trussell family and later by purchase to John de Davenport of Weltrough in about 1350. The Trussell family and later the Davenport family between them occupied Henbury for over 400 years. It was the Davenport family who developed the Henbury estate and played an important role in the history of Macclesfield. The Davenport line continued through Sir Fulk Lucy, who married Isabella Davenport, and it was not until 1693 that the continuity was broken by the sale to Sir William Meredith.

There is no written record of when the first Manor House was built nor how many such dwellings have been on the site of the present Henbury Hall. A typical mediaeval Manor House would probably be cruck framed with the spacing between the cruck

Henbury

framing filled with wattle and daub. One can only surmise that there would be a large hall at the centre of the Manor House, where the lord and his family had their meals, with their workers all sitting in their correct order of seniority at meal times. In the centre of the hall would be a brazier, the smoke from which would rise through a hole in the roof, creating a fire risk from sparks onto the thatched roof. Successive stages of improvement have led to the splendid Hall which was built in 1986.

A description of the house in 1558 is given in The Agrarian History of England and Wales[1], as follows:

> *The manor house was singularly well equipped, with several courts of outbuildings, including stables, barns, turfhouses, hayhouses, oxhouses, cowhouses and dovehouse. The estate also included a deerpark, fishponds, orchard and hopyard, but not apparently any permanent arable. The rest of the land consisted of woodland and pastures, with names which betrayed their condition: Little Moorfield, "not very profitable land;" Mossfield, "gorsy and heathy in many places;" other pastures and meadows were "woody," "gorsey and benty," or "full of fern." Their owner was clearly embarked upon an ambitious plan of improvement. Of three pastures of 12 acres apiece, one was full of fern, one was fenny, broomy ,and benty, and the third was sown with oats. Of two other pastures, one of 5 acres was "gorsie and bentie," the other of four acres was "this year sown with rye." Altogether five fields, amounting to 28 acres, had been ploughed, and carried crops of oats and rye.*

---

[1] The Agrarian History of England and Wales. Vol. 4, 1500-1640. Ed. Thirsk J. Gen.Ed. Finberg H.P.R., Cambridge University Press. Two references to what is probably the original are given: CRO. Cholmondeley Coll. F237 El 10 E125 E126 E127, and John Rylands Library, Charters 2047.

Henbury Hall

A report in the 'Cheshire Sheaf' of 1640, commenting on Sir Fulk Lucy's Cheshire estate, describes what may have been the next Hall on this site. It describes the Hall as "A very sumptuous house with courts, gardens, orchards well stocked with good fruits, dove house, banquetting hall, excellent stables, and other outhouses fair and convenient the building of which cost nearly £5000". This "sumptuous house" may still exist; it may be identified with a magnificent timber framed building, now used as a carriage house and stable, which is dated between 1580 and 1620[2]. A Tythe Barn is mentioned in the Land Tax Assessment 1794; possibly this is the same building. There was no mention of a water-driven corn mill, although one may already have been in operation on the dam of the lower lake.

Although Sir William Meredith bought the Hall in 1693, it was another five years before he came to live in Henbury. The hall which he built lasted until 1957. This was a classical block with a giant order of pilasters set up on high bases. It used to be said that there was more of Meredith's Hall underground than above ground. There still is an amazing series of underground passages, off which are scores of small rooms in which possibly the earlier occupants of the hall stored their wines, beer and food. There are larger cellars with beautifully vaulted ceilings which would do justice to any church crypt. In fact it is not unlikely, although there is no proof, that the largest underground room was once a place of worship, or a room in which gentry of the area gathered. We do know that Edward Brocklehurst allowed the rooms to be used as air raid shelters during World War II. It would seem from the extensive cellars that the original Meredith building was much larger than the Hall shown in photographs immediately prior to demolition. There is evidence to show that a wing of the hall was pulled down, possibly by William Meredith. Legend has it that he arrived from one of his foreign travels a day or two earlier than expected and found his staff dancing and merrymaking in the Hall. He was livid with anger and ordered the wing of the house to be pulled down.

---

[2] We are indebted to Dr Nevell of the University of Manchester for opinions on this and the water mills of Henbury Park (see Chapter 13).

Henbury

The Palladian style of house was enjoying a boom towards the end of the 17th C, becoming very popular with the new wealthy industrialists. Many sprang up throughout the shires, and it would seem appropriate that William Meredith should select this classical style of house when he bought the estate in 1693.

The interior of Meredith's Hall was described in 1874 when it was advertised for sale. It included: Entrance Hall (30ft.x 10ft 8ins.) with a handsome staircase, Drawing Room (36ft 8ins. x 16ft 8ins.), Ante Room (15ft x 13ft.) Dining Room (35ft x 21ft 8ins.), Morning Room (32ft. x 14ft 9ins.), Ante Room (14ft. x 13ft), Study (19ft.9ins. x 10ft.) and Billiard Room (22ft. x 20ft). In addition there were a Kitchen Servants' Hall, Butler's Pantry, Housekeeper's Room, 9 good Bedrooms with dressing rooms, Bath Rooms, 10 Maid/Servant Rooms, 5 Men/Servant Rooms, with extensive arched cellary, good laundry and washroom and all the usual offices required in a gentlemen's residence. Apart from the stables and harness rooms there were two coach houses, cow houses with tying for 27 cows, bakehouse, brew house, malthouse, dairy, slaughter house, a joiners shop, hayshed etc. In the gardens were a gardener's cottage, greenhouses, peach and apricot houses, a fern house, pineries, forcing pits, potting sheds etc. To complete this magnificent rural setting and to improve the corn mill, Meredith in 1717 added the upper lake by constructing the dam which carries the main entrance drive. He may also have reconstructed the middle pool, which is called Engine Pool, presumably referring to the mill. The lowest lake, which was later known as Great Pool, may be even earlier; it was held by an enormous earth bank which is probably mediaeval. Meredith's estate map of 1727 shows all three pools, with a house on the dam of the Great Pool which must have been another mill, probably the earliest in the township. The whole system collapsed in 1872, when the dam of the Great Pool was breached. The dam was never repaired but the bed of the pool is still in evidence and is known locally as the Marsh.

When Thomas Unett Brocklehurst purchased the Henbury estate in 1874, he employed a local contractor, Mr.Aspinall, of King Edward Street, Macclesfield from 1875-1878 to renovate the two remaining pools following the flood, and to rebuild the carriageway drive including renewing the ornate bridge between the two pools, using stone from Teggs Nose Quarries. The cost was £6000.

Thomas Brocklehurst was a great traveller and brought many interesting objects from foreign parts. One unique artefact was the large Japanese Bell which stands in the picturesque surroundings of the Gardener's Cottage. This Bell was obtained with much difficulty from Tokyo City in the year 1880, at a time when the temple was being restored and the priests wanted a larger bell. It had been in the temple since 1770; how Brocklehurst acquired it is not recorded but the great Bell still stands serenely in the quiet solitude of an English garden. Many of the rhododendrons in the garden were brought back from China. He also introduced the grey squirrel from North America[3]. When Thomas Brocklehurst decided to make his house ornate with mosaic floors and plaster work, he went to Italy in search of the most skilled workmen who were recognised as masters of their craft. When they arrived and settled in at the Hall, the estate workers were mystified by their occasional early morning visits to the woods, returning with large fungi which they had cut from certain trees. These they cooked for their breakfast, but despite the interest of the estate workers, they would never disclose the whereabouts of the fungus nor the trees on which they grew.

Rent day, 1960s: Ernest Kennerly, Harry Lomas, Wilfred Bayley, John Massey, Sir Vincent de Ferranti MC FRS, Tom Gould, Ralph Hatton (courtesy Mrs K Massey)

---

[3] Ellison, Norman F. "A Naturalist's Notebook: Cheshire's Grey Squirrels". *Cheshire Life*, Oct 1973, p 115. See also Chapter 17 of this History.

Henbury

It was during the Brocklehurst era that the stable block which Sir William Meredith had built in the late 1690s for his horses was converted into the Tenants' Hall and amongst its many uses was the annual rent day gathering of the tenants on the 25th March, Lady Day. This was when all the tenants would assemble to pay their rents to the squire. This was a festive occasion and a meal would be served with beer and refreshments in plentiful supply. The custom persisted into the time of Sir Vincent de Ferranti.

Local Cheshire society in the 19th century was dominated by the three stately homes at Capesthorne, Birtles and Henbury; it was said that each could hear the dinner gongs from all three!

Old Henbury Hall, from an Edwardian postcard

When Sir Vincent de Ferranti purchased the Henbury Park estate in 1957, the old Hall with its long history and many owners was riddled with dry rot; the sitting room floor had actually collapsed under Edward Brocklehurst while he was sitting in his armchair[4]. Sir Vincent demolished the Hall and converted the

---

[4] Recounted by Harry Fairhurst, who advised Sir Vincent and designed the conversion of the stable block.

adjoining stable block and Tenant's Hall into a residence. He threw himself wholeheartedly into restoring the estate and farms to something of their former glory. All the farms and cottages were brought up to a good standard and the villagers were happy that someone of Sir Vincent's standing had purchased and improved the estate. The gardens were laid out and stocked by Matthews' Nurseries from 1957 onward as one of their first major commissions. Ian Urquhart remembers taking his father-in-law Fred Matthews to see Sir Vincent every Saturday morning, when he sketched the landscaping plans on the back of a packet of Senior Service cigarettes. In the same spirit Sir Vincent's son Sebastian has restored estate cottages, built a graceful Chinese bridge and a glazed fernery housing a pool and a cascade. Sir Vincent contemplated rebuilding Henbury Hall, but it was his son Sebastian who carried the idea to fruition in 1984-86.

The English Palladian house owed its creation to Inigo Jones[5], who in 1638 built the Queen's house at Greenwich in the style of Andrea Palladio (1518-80), the Italian architect. The new Henbury Hall built by Sebastian de Ferranti on the site of its predecessor is likewise of Palladian design, following closely the pattern of Palladio's famous Villa Capra or Villa Rotonda of 1552, near Vicenza in northern Italy.

A key figure in the design[6] was the painter Felix Kelly, previously employed by Sebastian de Ferranti in 1978 to design a transformation of a gamekeeper's cottage[7] on the Henbury estate, a plain brick box, to which he added side pavilions, a trellised verandah and Gothic glazing. The result, 'The Cave', is a romantic

---

[5] Inigo Jones was a picture framer by trade in 1603, when he began to try his hand at designing royal masques for dances and balls attended by aristocracy. He became adept at producing masques and became known to King James I, who sent for him and made him Surveyor of Works in 1615 when he was 42 years of age.

[6] A full description is given by Peter de Figueiredo & Julian Treuherz: *Cheshire Country Houses*; Phillimore, 1988. The following paragraphs draw heavily from this seminal work.

[7] The Cave has a long history as a tenanted farm, using fields within the area of the present Park. There is a possibility that it was more recently used as a public house.

Henbury

eye-catcher in the tradition of 18th century garden follies. Kelly also designed the improvements to Bearhurst, where Sebastian de Ferranti lived before the new Hall was built. In discussion with Kelly, de Ferranti conceived the idea of creating a Palladian temple in which one could live. After sketching various possibilities Kelly painted a picture of how it might look; the idea of starting with a painting and then finding an architect (Julian Bicknell) to realise it has a suitably 18th century ring about it.

Henbury Hall is a small house, smaller than its Palladian ancestors and smaller than most country houses. Everything has been neatly fitted into a plan 56 feet square. Nevertheless it is not an occasional retreat, nor a rustic villa in the original Palladian sense of something close to a farm. It is an ambitious and cultivated country house. The principal room is a room of parade, a grand hard space. Comfortable rooms with sofas and cushions are arranged around it, but these are subordinate to the architectural statement. Faced in stone, with statuary, giant order, dome and saloon, Henbury marks the coming of age of the new Palladian revival.

Henbury Hall Garden 2002 (photograph Sir Francis Graham-Smith)

Henbury Hall

The Hall now stands as a centrepiece in a carefully landscaped park, with vistas to open countryside. A polo field and varied terrain provides the ideal location for annual horse trials. The gardens are spectacular, having been improved notably by the late Naomi de Ferranti (d. 2001). Irrigation is provided by a force pump operated by water from the upper lake, and there is a well-preserved ice house (probably early 19th century) of classic egg-shaped design close to the middle lake.

On 18 June 1872 a tremendous rainstorm deposited over 4 inches of rain on the catchment area of the Bag Brook within 10 hours, and an overwhelming volume of water flowed into and through the three lakes of Henbury Hall. The dams holding all three were burst, and a flood rushed down the valley, destroying everything in its path (a contemporary account is to be found in Chapter 14). Birtles Mill was spared the worst damage, as its reservoir was fed by a separate stream and it suffered only some silting of its water channels. Four bridges were swept away, and the County Council sued Mrs Marsland (widow of Major Edward Marsland) for £4000. She challenged this in the Courts. In 1875, the Court established a legal precedent under which the catastrophe was classified as *an act of God* or *vis major*, which absolved Mrs Marsland from having to pay anything at all to the Council. However, under the threat of having to pay crippling damages, Mrs Marsland had already taken the precaution of selling Henbury estate in 1874 to Thomas Brocklehurst.

Brocklehurst set about repairs to the dams and weirs of the upper two lakes (known in 1842 as the Engine and Upper Pools; see Chapter 13). His work stands today, and has been admired both as exemplary engineering and as a contribution to the landscape. The top dam cost £5000, while the second dam was constructed by 'private enterprise', which presumably means by direct labour from his own men. He did not tackle the lowest dam, which remains as an earth bank with a gaping canyon through which the Bag Brook flows.

Sir Vincent de Ferranti assessed the possibilities of repairing the dam and restoring the lower lake (the "Great Pool") to its former glory. He was mainly deterred by the necessity of felling several

Henbury

large beech trees which grow on top of the bank: he was a great tree-lover. Surveys commissioned by Sebastian de Ferranti from 1979 to 1985 revealed more serious difficulties. The dam, although substantial, is simply an earth bank using the local sand and clay, without an impervious core or facing. Although the flood had washed away the dam by actually topping the bank, there was a chance that the dam might give way even without a major flood, unless a waterproof core or facing could be added. One solution might be to accept a lower water level, but the ground contours showed that this would move the top end of the lake some distance from the new Hall, losing its value for the landscape.

We have found no record of the construction of the lower dam, or even of its instigator. If, as we believe, it is a mediaeval structure created for the water-mill, it was accidental that it provided such a extensive stretch of water which must have been a dramatic feature of the landscape. Restoration as a purely ornamental feature is an attractive prospect, but estimates of the cost of restoration are daunting. The old dam remains lost to view, covered in woodland, and there is regrettably no proposal to rebuild it.

The proprietors of Henbury Hall were also referred to as Lords of the Manor from Sir Fulk Lucy (1662) at least up to 1892. In the 14th century John de Davenport was "Lord of Hendebury"; in the 15th century Hugh was "Lord of Hennebury", and in the 16th century the estate was variously named Henburie and Henbury.

The Henbury estate was sold by the Trussell family to Sir John de Davenport of Woodford about 1350, and remained in the family for 343 years. Randle Davenport, born 1545, was appointed High Sheriff of Cheshire in 1586. An unbroken male dynasty came to an end in 1640 when Isobel Davenport became the sole daughter and heir. She married Sir Fulk Lucy of Charlecote in Warwickshire in 1656. Their sons, Davenport Lucy and George Lucy, inherited Henbury, and George sold the estate in 1693. There is a link to Capesthorne: early in the 16th century Joan Davenport of Henbury married John Ward of Capesthorne. He previously lived at Monks Heath Hall, which is now the site of a craft centre near the cross roads.

The Proprietors of Henbury Hall

MAINWARING	1086-1288
TRUSSELL	1288-1350
DAVENPORT	1350-1657
SIR FULK LUCY	1657-1682
DAVENPORT LUCY	1682-1691
GEORGE LUCY	1691-1693
SIR WILLIAM MEREDITH	1693-1752
SIR WILLIAM MEREDITH Jr	1752-1779
JOHN BOWER JODRELL	1779-1796
FRANCIS BOWER JODRELL	1796-1829
JOHN W. JODRELL	1829-1835
JOHN RYLE	1835-1842
THOMAS MARSLAND	1842-1854
EDWARD MARSLAND	1854-1867
JANE MARSLAND	1867-1874
THOMAS UNETT BROCKLEHURST	1874-1886
WILLIAM WALTER BROCKLEHURST	1886-1918
ARGYLL BROCKLEHURST	1918-1926
EDWARD H. BROCKLEHURST	1926-1956
SIR VINCENT de FERRANTI	1957-1980
SEBASTIAN de FERRANTI	1980 - date

Sir Fulk Lucy's father, Sir Thomas, was knighted in 1565 by Queen Elizabeth in his own house at Charlecote. About 1585 William Shakespeare was prosecuted by Lucy for stealing deer from his Park at Charlecote.

Fulk Lucy was knighted in 1661, and he was made MP for Cheshire in 1664. He died in 1677 leaving a family of 13 children. The eldest son, Davenport Lucy inherited Henbury in 1691; he never married and the estate passed to the second son, George. He decided to return to Charlecote, and sold the estate to Sir William Meredith in 1693.

There were two Sir William Merediths. The first was born in Ashley in Cheshire in 1665 and married Mary, daughter and heiress of Henry Whopload in Lincolnshire in 1686. He was a wealthy man, with land at Ashley Hall, Timperley Hall and Oldfield Hall, and estates at Altrincham, Holbeach in Lincolnshire and Peterborough.

Henbury

The long tenure of the first Sir William Meredith meant that the estate passed directly to the second Sir William, who was his grandson. His son Amos, who died in 1745, is seen among a group of eleven portraits of early 18th century Cheshire gentlemen on the wall of the main staircase at Tatton Hall. At the start of the Jacobite revolution of 1715 this group met to discuss whether to support the rebels. They decided not to do so, and sided with the new King George I. After the event, they celebrated their prudence, or good luck, by having their portraits painted. So there they are, looking extremely smug.

Amos married Joanna Cholmondley at Tarporley in 1718; their son, christened at the Church of St. John the Baptist in Chester in 1724, was the second Sir William Meredith, who inherited Henbury in 1752. This Meredith was MP for Wigan, and mayor of Macclesfield in 1762. In 1774 he was described as "One of His Majesty's most Privy Councillors" and was Comptroller of the Household. He appears to have lived chiefly in London. In 1779 the Prime Minister Lord North became involved in a riot in London. Sir William was at hand to save his life, and in return, Lord North gave William's brother, Theophilus, a clerical living.

Meredith was known as one who liked the high life and incurred many debts, which may have led to the sale of Henbury in 1779 He lost his seat in Parliament and found a job with the Friends of the Embassy. He died in Lyon in 1790 and left no issue.

The Meredith family were strong supporters of the Parish Church in Prestbury; the Norman Chapel was restored by the second Sir William Meredith in 1747. Several members of the family were buried in Prestbury. As a record of the achievements of this family there is a date of 1743 on the Stable Block which has been recently restored by Sebastian de Ferranti.

On 17th Dec. 1779, John Bower Jodrell of Yeardsley (between New Mills and Whaley Bridge) bought the Henbury estate for £24000. The Jodrells were an old Derbyshire family who later settled in High Peak. An early Jodrell, William, served as an archer under Edward, the Black Prince, and held lands in Macclesfield Forest in 1351. His son served under Richard II and at Agincourt in 1415. Frances Jodrell, daughter and heiress,

Henbury Hall

married John Bower in 1776. He later changed his name to Bower-Jodrell. He purchased Henbury Hall in 1779 and it passed to his eldest son Francis Jodrell in 1796. Francis Jodrell sold the Hall to John Ryle for £54000 in 1835.

We have almost no record of the Jodrell stewardship of the estate. We know that John Bower took an interest in the woodlands; in January 1792 he bought 2 bushels of acorns from Caldwells of Knutsford.

The Jodrell family were still in Yeardsley in 1835; there is a record of the sale of 2,064 acres of Taxal Valley in that year to Samuel Grimshawe, who built Errwood Hall on this estate. The Cat and Fiddle Inn, built by John Ryle, was on this estate; presumably Ryle sold it soon after building it.

The Ryle or Royle family settled in Styal and Wilmslow early in the 15th century; they may have been associated before then with Royle Hall, near Burnley, a house acquired by the Townley family in the reign of Henry VIII. Thomas Royle at his marriage in 1744 was described as a dyer, and the family may have had a long association with textiles and dying. An earlier John Ryle was mayor of Macclesfield in 1541-42. By the mid-18th century the Ryles were established in Macclesfield, and John Ryle (b. 1744) was involved in silk weaving in the mill originally known as Daintry and Ryle's, later as Frost's and now as Park Green Mill.

John Ryle (b. 1781), who inherited a large fortune made in the silk industry, purchased Henbury Hall in 1829. He also owned Errwood in the Goyt Valley (before Errwood Hall was built by Samuel Grimshaw in 1840). He was "sturdy of intellect, strong in character and mind and limb", and was evidently a flamboyant 'whiz kid' of the 1800s.

In 1800 John Ryle founded the Macclesfield and Cheshire Bank, taking over the first bank in Macclesfield from Hawkins, Mill and Co. who went into liquidation. He became the first MP for Macclesfield. In 1841 the bank failed, Ryle became bankrupt, and he had to sell all his assets[8], including the Hall, which was sold to

---

[8] "*A short biography of John Charles Ryle*", Marius L Loane, publ. James Clarke & Co Ltd. 1953. Here you can read of the catastrophic collapse of June 1841: "the household was broken up without delay, and the pleasant estate of a

Henbury

Thomas Marsland in 1842. He repaid all his creditors – an honorable man. His son, John Charles Ryle (1816-1900) had to make a fresh start at the age of 25; he was ordained and became a curate in the New Forest at Edbury, eventually becoming the first Bishop of Liverpool in 1880. This was evidently a versatile family: a direct descendent, Martin Ryle[9] (1918-1984) became the 12th Astronomer Royal in 1972.

John Ryle formerly lived at Park House, Park Lane and financed considerable building development in that part of Macclesfield. He gave his name to Ryles Park. He built the Cat and Fiddle Inn in 1832; there is a Ryle's Arms in Sutton, and the Cock Inn[10] in Henbury was also named Ryle's Arms until about 1860.

The 1841 census, which was done in June, just at the time of the collapse of the Ryle bank, lists John Ryle (50), Susan Ryle (50), Mary Ann Ryle (20) and Caroline Ryle (20). In the 1841 census, ages over 15 are given only in 5 year groups, so Henbury appears to have been full of 20-year-olds. There are also a dozen or so miscellaneous servants at the Hall, including Ellen Kennerly, whose family name is well known locally.

Major John Thomas Marsland, of Milverton, Warwickshire, moved to Henbury Hall from Stockport in 1842. His son and successor, Edward, was senior Captain (1851) and Major (1867) in the Earl of Chester's regiment of Yeomanry Cavalry. Thomas died in 1867, leaving his wife Jane as proprietor until she sold the estate to Thomas Brocklehurst in 1874. Edward is listed in the 1861 census as land proprietor of 190 acres with 14 labourers and a boy (location uncertain). There are exquisite alabaster mural memorials in Henbury Church to Thomas Marsland (died 18 November 1854 aged 77) and Edward Marsland (died 24 December 1867 aged 60). Jane Marsland survived until the age of 83 in 1893.

---

thousand acres was sold as soon as possible…it was in the full charm of its summer beauty..."
[9] Biographical Memoirs of Fellows of the Royal Society, **32**, 497-524, 1986.
[10] See Chapter 7 of this History.

Henbury Hall

Three successive John Brocklehursts (1718-91, 1754-1837, 1788-1870) were key figures in the development of the Macclesfield silk industry[11]. The first joined the button manufacturers Acton and Street in 1748, and became a partner by 1759. The second followed his father, and steered the company, then known as Joseph Street & Co., from buttons to silk. He was a Whig, a supporter of free speech and of the French Revolution. When the third John followed in partnership with his brother Thomas, the business became J & T Brocklehurst. The family connection continued until 1911.

John Brocklehurst and John Ryle were elected the two MPs for Macclesfield in 1832 and were the first two representatives of the Borough at Westminster. John Brocklehurst resigned in 1868, and was followed as MP by his son William Coare Brocklehurst. John's nephew, Thomas Unett Brocklehurst, who bought Henbury estate in 1874, was twice Mayor of Macclesfield and High Sheriff of Cheshire. Among many notable members of the family who were benefactors of Macclesfield are Francis Dicken Brocklehurst (1837-1905), who presented Victoria Park to the public in 1894, land on which had stood his family home, Fence House; and his cousin Marianne (1832-88) who gave West Park Museum, with her collection of Egyptian antiquities, to the people of Macclesfield.

Edward Brocklehurst had a great love for the many varieties of trees in the woods, some of which were quite rare. During the World War II he contracted his large walled garden to a market gardener to avoid it becoming a wilderness. He died in 1957 aged 78. His family crest incorporated three badgers, perhaps chosen because his name when shortened became the country name of Brock, the Badger. ("Brocklehurst" deriving from "badgers' wood"). A datestone (1884) in the stables courtyard shows a badge and crest with four badgers and the motto VERITAS ME DIRIGET.

---

[11] Mary Crozier, *An Old Silk Family* 1745-1945. Aberdeen University Press 1947. See also the library of the Macclesfield Silk Museum.

Henbury

Another local member of the family[12] was Charles Phillips Brocklehurst (1904-1977), who lived at Hare Hill in Over Alderley, and left his house and garden to the National Trust. In the 1930s he travelled widely as a partner at Christie's. During World War II. he served in the Cheshire Yeomanry, taking part in a cavalry action in the Lebanon and in tank warfare against Rommel in the Western Desert. Later he parachuted into Albania as military liaison officer for talks with the Communist ruler, Enver Hoxha. Another Brocklehurst became Sir Philip Brocklehurst of Swythamley, who went to the Antarctic with Shackleton.

Sir Vincent Ziani de Ferranti. The de Ferranti family has a proud history in Italy. The name Ziani can be traced back to the 8th century, and in 1172 Sebastian Ziani was elected Doge of Venice; the inscription on his tomb reads "modest, just, wise and powerful". He was followed as Doge by his son, Peter. The de Ferranti family originated in a branch of the Ziani family who settled in Bologna in the 13th or 14th century.

Starting in 1882, three generations of the de Ferranti family created and ran for 100 years one of the world's most successful electrical engineering firms[13]. The founder of the company was Dr. Sebastian Ziani de Ferranti, who as a young man designed and built the world's first high voltage alternating current power station at Deptford. He was a Fellow of the Royal Society. His son Vincent, born 1893, developed the company to embrace new fields of radar, computers, semiconductors and defence electronics. Vincent served in both World Wars, and was awarded the Military Cross for service in Gallipoli. He lived in Alderley Edge, where his children were brought up, and moved to Henbury in his retirement.

Sir Vincent's son, Sebastian, who built the present Henbury Hall, followed the family traditions of engineering innovation and

---

[12] See entries in Burke's *Landed Gentry*, and Earwaker's *Cheshire*. From the 17th century several generations of the family lived in Gap House, Kettleshulme. Mr Geoffrey Brocklehurst of 26 Thorngrove Drive, Wilmslow has preserved many family records, including a comprehensive family tree.

[13] *Ferranti: A History*. John F. Wilson. Carnegie Publishing Ltd.,2000.

Henbury Hall

Sebastian de Ferranti. Sketch by Pietro Annigoni, 1958.

Naomi de Ferranti, who recreated the gardens of Henbury Hall.

Henbury

public service: he has held the offices of High Sheriff and Deputy Lieutenant of Cheshire. His wife Naomi, whose family origins are in the Greg family (of Styal Mill), was Deputy Lieutenant of Greater Manchester, and Master of the Cheshire Hounds.

Chapter 9

The Birtles Estate and the Birtles Halls.

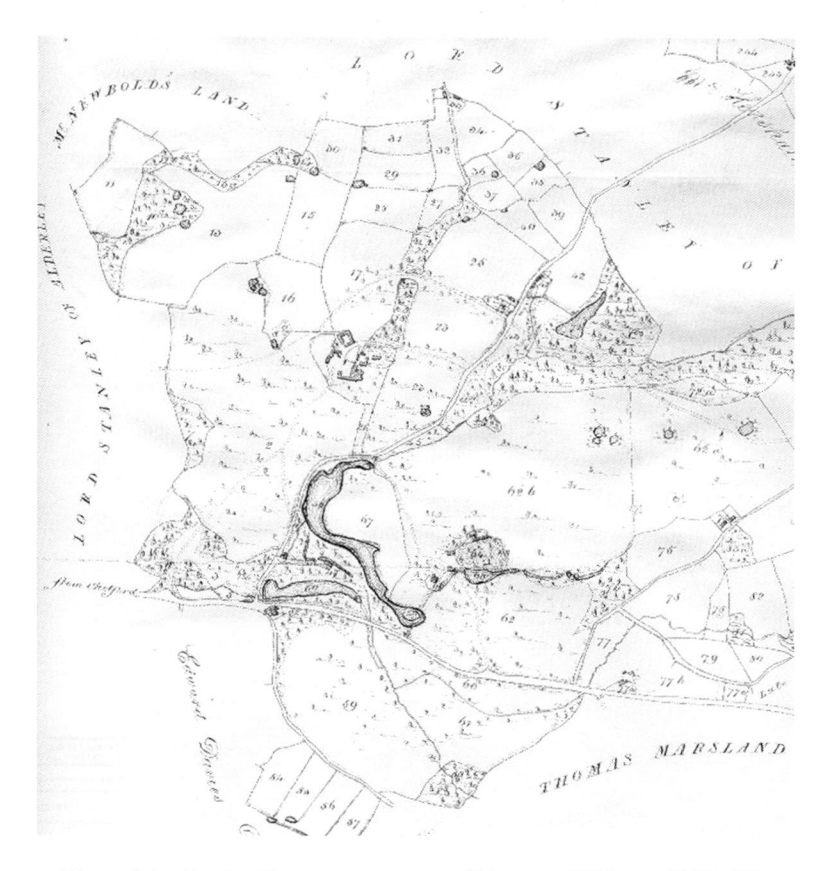

Plan of the Birtles Estates, property of Thomas Hibbert, 1837. The estate extended beyond this map, to Over Alderley and into Henbury, covering much of Birtles Road. The Old Hall is to the east of the lake, and the New Hall to the north.

The manor of Henbury, whose hall and farmlands have long been central to our parish, is neighbour to a group of local manors whose origin dates back at least to the reign of Henry III, two centuries after the Conquest. One of these is Capesthorne, in which the Bromley-Davenport family is linked to the Davenports in the early history of Henbury. Another, Alderley Park, is now the research headquarters of the pharmaceutical firm AstraZeneca.

Henbury

Astle Park[1], in Chelford, was sold in 1833 as a Hall with over 2,600 acres; all that remains today is a park which is occasionally used as a showground. Birtles, which is within our civil parish, continues its existence as several large houses and some smaller houses centred on St. Catherine's Church which is now the Parish Church of Birtles and Over Alderley.

The Birtles Family[2]. About 1260 John de Asthull (Astle) became Lord of the manor of Birtles, and adopted the name of his new manor. As was common in the Middle Ages, the name Birtles was variously spelt. A common variation was "Bircels", pronounced "Birchels". Ormerod's History[3], which is mainly concerned with the landed gentry, gives some glimpses of the family history; for example, in 1289 John was sued by his widowed sister-in-law Christian who claimed to be entitled to rights in part of the manor.

One of the family, Ralph Birchels, served in the cavalry in the army of the Black Prince in Gascony in 1355-57. Had he been at Crecy? Ormerod identified, as a later direct descendant of the 13th century John, Henry de Birthels who was appointed a Justice of Chester in 1397 and Serjeant-at-law for Chester in 1399. Henry de Byrtles occupied the Higher Hall in Over Alderley, which is thought to have been on the site of the present Whirley Hall. This hall was once occupied by the Birtles and afterwards by the Swetenhams. The Swetenham coat of arms used to be displayed on the Whirley Hall stone gateposts.

Thereafter there was direct descent in the male line to John Birtles, born in 1566. He had neither a son nor a brother, but two daughters of whom one, Mary, married Thomas Swetenham, a member of one of the richest families in Cheshire, in 1602. They moved to live at the manor house at Birtles, together with her father John. He died in 1620 and was buried at Prestbury.

---

[1] *Chelford: a Cheshire Village*. Mavis and Keith Plant, Roger Roycroft and Julia Slater, 1999.
[2] Copies of a typescript note of the history of the Birtles family by Terry Birtles, now resident in Australia, are held by Mrs Foschtinsky of Birtles Farm, Hocker Lane, Over Alderley and by Professor McCollum of Birtles Old Hall.
[3] G. Ormerod: A History of Cheshire. 1888.

The manor of Birtles descended in the male line throughout the 17th and 18th centuries, eventually to Thomas Swetenham, Sheriff of Cheshire, who died in 1788 aged 72 without issue. Before his death he had sold the part of the manor which he still owned to Joseph Fowden in 1783. The manor had thus been held by one family, through Mary Swetenham in 1620, for over 600 years.

The division of Birtles. From an early stage - possibly as early as the 14th century, but certainly by the 16th century - the land comprising the manor of Birtles was divided, probably because it was occupied by different members of the family. There were three parts, the main estate, occupying the area from Birtles Old Hall up to where Whirley Hall now stands[4]; the Birtles of the Pale estate, including Pale Farm[5] and a substantial area to the south; and Birtles on the Hill to the south-west, essentially the present farm of that name though somewhat larger. The manor owned by the Swetenham family included the main estate and Birtles of the Pale. The Pale was acquired by Sir William Meredith of Henbury in 1771 and resold by him to John Bower Jodrell in 1796.

Birtles on the Hill has a less straightforward history. In 1701 Thomas Birtles held the fee simple (as we would say, freehold) title in Birtles on the Hill. This presumably means that when Mary née Birtles and her husband Thomas Swetenham inherited the manor of Birtles from her father in 1620 it did not include Birtles on the Hill, which was owned by another member of the Birtles family from whom it descended to Thomas before 1701.

In that year Thomas Birtles became engaged to Elizabeth Bagshaw. In lieu of dower he created a settlement of the Birtles of the Hill estate comprising a manor house and some 88 Cheshire acres (about 220 modern acres), which provided that on his death his widow Elizabeth would inherit one third of the estate, and their oldest son the other two thirds, but with a charge on the estate to provide a sum of £700 to be shared between any other children. Thomas and Elizabeth had seven children, Thomas Jnr., two more sons and four daughters. Thomas Snr. died in 1724.

---

[4] Burdett's map of 1777 shows a village or hamlet of Birtles at the top end of what is now Anderton's Lane, including and near Birch Tree Farm.

[5] The oldest house in Birtles: see Chapter 5.

Henbury

In 1727 Thomas Jnr. and his mother mortgaged the property in order to raise the £700 to pay out the other children. Some time before 1736 Thomas Jnr. borrowed further money on the security of a second mortgage. In 1736 he became engaged to marry Ellen Boulton, and created a settlement for her benefit and that of any children they should have. Obviously the value of this depended on the extent to which the estate was charged with debts. Thomas succeeded in concealing the existence of the second mortgage from his wife and her family. He died in 1754, by which time there was owing on the second mortgage the sum of £1800, together with the £700 on the first mortgage.

Ellen discovered these debts when her husband died. She and her children had to deal with the problem by remortgaging the estate and settling Thomas's debts. It all proved too much for them, and in 1765 they had to sell the estate to the omni-present Sir William Meredith for £4000 to pay off their debts. Sir William in turn mortgaged the estate for £3500 to pay Mrs Birtles. He later resold the property to the Davenport family, and it thus came into the Capesthorne Estate, of which it is still part.

The Hibbert family. In 1791 Joseph Fowden sold the Manor of Birtles to Robert Hibbert, who in 1797 also acquired land in Over Alderley to the west of Birtles called The Pasture, and later re-acquired the Pale Farm house and some adjoining land from the Henbury Estate. With the addition to Robert's estate of The Pasture, and the later construction on it of a new Birtles Hall (see below) the name "Birtles" came to signify both the old manor and a part of Over Alderley.

Robert Hibbert came from a wealthy family, whose fortune had been made in Jamaica, where they owned sugar plantations and slaves. He seems to have lived in Jamaica until shortly before he came to Birtles - his son Thomas was born there in 1790. Robert's wife was a member of another wealthy Jamaican family, the Nembards. Robert Hibbert had an interest in the family merchant business in London, run by his brothers and nephew. He also still owned substantial property in Jamaica. By his last will, made in 1830, he bequeathed to his sons Thomas and John his plantations in Jamaica with their buildings and equipment *"together also with all negro and other slaves upon and belonging to the same plantation"*; slavery was still lawful in Jamaica in 1830. It is ironic that in 1834, a few months before Robert's death, Parliament legislated to abolish slavery in all British colonies. The inevitable and immediate effect was a sharp drop in the profitability and value of plantations worked by slaves.

Despite these substantial interests elsewhere Robert Hibbert became sufficiently immersed in the affairs of his adopted county to be appointed High Sheriff of Cheshire. Robert's son Thomas Hibbert succeeded his father at Birtles. He was in the Army, and served at Waterloo. He also was High Sheriff.

The most renowned member of the family was Thomas's son Hugh. He was born at Birtles Hall on 18 December 1827. He entered the Army in 1847 and served throughout the Crimean campaign, in all the major battles. He was three times wounded and attained the rank of Major in the 7th Royal Fusiliers. On his return home he was treated as a local hero. On 3 January 1856 a great ball in his honour was held at Birtles Hall, and in April of that year in a congratulatory dinner in Macclesfield Town Hall, attended by all the great and the good of the county, he was presented with an engraved sword commemorating his gallantry.

Colonel Hugh, as he became, later served in India and on the Reserve List after his retirement from the Regular Army. After his father's death he lived at Birtles Hall with his family, and also became High Sheriff in 1885. The horse he rode in the Crimea, named "Alma" after the battle, was buried behind the stables at the Hall. In about 1887 Colonel Hugh moved to live near Barnstaple in Devon, where he died in 1895. This ended the permanent connection of the Hibbert family with Birtles, though Hugh's son Admiral Hibbert lived for a time at Birtles Old Hall.

The Birtles houses. Where the original manor house stood is uncertain, but it was probably near the site of the present Birtles Old Hall. There was undoubtedly at an early stage a house called Higher Hall on the site of or near where Whirley Hall now stands.

Birtles Old Hall was built by the Swetenhams between 1700 and 1715. The present owner has placed on the front of the house

Henbury

Birtles New Hall 1890 (courtesy G. Sparrow)

the date 1734, but we believe it was built thirty years earlier. It was a substantial red brick house which became the principal residence on the Estate. In 1819, when Robert Hibbert and his family were living there, it suffered a major fire. A large part of the house was destroyed.

Birtles (New) Hall. Rather than rebuilding the Old Hall, Robert Hibbert built himself a new mansion on the Pasture, west of Birtles Lane in Over Alderley. It has been described as "A severe neo-classical house" with a "top-heavy cornice and balustrade". This became Birtles Hall, and the Hibbert family home from its completion in 1820. In Col. Hugh's time the Hall housed not only his family but 19 indoor servants. The remains of the former Hall, partially repaired, became Birtles Old Hall. During the 19th century this was sometimes used by a member of the family, but more often was tenanted. The last member of the family to live there was Admiral Hibbert, Col. Hugh's son. Pale Farm has already been described in Chapter 5.

Whirley Hall

Whirley Hall. It is believed that a small timber framed building, originally attached to the hall, was built in Tudor times; during extensive alterations carried out by the present owners in the early 1950's a repair stone dated 1599 was found in the roof. One of the former gateposts survives in the garden and has on it the crest of the Fitton family, known locally as 'the monkey in the tree'. The other gatepost had on it the crest of the Swettenham family. The present structure, a handsome brick house with a front of five bays, was restyled in 1670 during the reign of William and Mary and the Dutch influence is apparent in the gables.

Henbury

During the 1745 rebellion some of Bonnie Prince Charlie's officers were quartered at the Hall and according to local legend one was drowned in a nearby pond.

St Catherine's Church. In 1840 Thomas Hibbert, with the assistance of one of his sisters Laetitia, built Birtles Church (St. Catherine's) as a private chapel for the Estate. The Hibbert family had formerly occupied pews in Nether Alderley, but after a quarrel with the Stanleys over a resiting of pews Thomas decided to build his own church. It contains some fine mediaeval glass and a 17th century pulpit and choir stalls, collected from churches and monasteries in Europe in the wake of the Napoleonic wars and has earned a place in "England's thousand best Churches" by Simon Jenkins.

When Col. Hugh Hibbert left Birtles, he decided, probably at the suggestion of his aunt Laetitia, to convey the Church to the Ecclesiastical Commissioners. Laetitia, who died in 1887, left money in her will for an endowment for the new parish, and in 1890 St. Catherine's became the Parish church of the new Parish of Birtles and Over Alderley, carved out of the Parish of Nether Alderley.

The Birtles Estate. In 1857 the Hibberts' Birtles Estate comprised 1038 acres. It included all the old manor of Birtles, except Birtles on the Hill. It also included the land on which Birtles Hall had been constructed, and its surrounding park and farmland. There were about 60 acres of garden and parkland, and about 300 acres of farmland in hand. At Birtles Old Hall the house was tenanted, and there was a farm of about 60 acres with a farmhouse separately let. Pale Farm house and Whirley Hall were also both let with their farmland. In addition there was some land in Henbury and some near Hare Hill in Over Alderley. Almost all the land to the north and west of the Birtles Estate was owned by Lord Stanley of Alderley.

In 1890 the Hibberts sold the Birtles Estate to the Hon. Arthur Lyulph Stanley. It seems that he did not live at Birtles. He served in the Boer War, then became MP for Eddisbury and held minor office in the 1906 Government. He became Governor General of the Australian State of Victoria. In 1925 on the death of his uncle he became 5th Baron Stanley of Alderley, and thus inherited the Alderley Park Estate, to which the Birtles Estate was then added. The 5th Lord Stanley of Alderley died in 1931.

The later history of the Birtles Halls. When Hugh Hibbert left Birtles Hall in the late 1880s he leased it to a family called Close-Brooks. They stayed there after the Estate was sold to the Stanleys and continued to live there until World War I. They were popular tenants, much involved in local life as entries in the Parish Magazine show. There was general disappointment that they did not purchase the Hall. Tragically, their sons Charles and Arthur were both killed in the War.

Birtles Hall was used as a hospital between 1915 and 1918. In 1920 the Hall was purchased by a member of the Haworth family, with its surrounding parkland. Mr. Michael Haworth has recalled his memories of life at Birtles in the 1920s - tennis afternoons, cricket matches, shooting in the winter and occasional dances. Although his parents were Congregationalists, this did not stop them from occupying the squirearchical pew at St. Catherine's. The kitchen gardens were by the Old Hall; all the produce was grown there and transported to the kitchen door in a sort of utility vehicle. The indoor staff included a housekeeper, a cook and four maids.

Mr. A.C.G.Sparrow, father of Col. Geoffrey Sparrow, bought Birtles Old Hall with its land in 1923. He built a small extension at the rear. He and his family lived there until the death of Mrs. Rose Sparrow, who outlived her husband by many years. The Old Hall was then purchased by Mr. Hudson who tried but failed to buy the Lordship of the Manor. After showing a flamboyant interest in the cricket ground, he eventually left the district. The house is now owned by Professor Charles McCollum, who has restored and improved both house and grounds.

In 1937 the burden of meeting death duties twice in six years proved too much for the 6th Lord Stanley of Alderley. He therefore disposed of the whole of his Alderley Estate. Mr. D.O. Norton bought Birtles Hall with its park and farmland. He started to restore it, but only six months later the Hall was virtually destroyed by fire with only the south and east facades and the

Henbury

service quarter remaining. Undeterred, the Nortons engaged Mr Sellars, an architect from Manchester, to rebuild, and the interior of the house included furniture designed by him especially for the rooms.

Again this family maintained a strong local involvement, particularly through Mrs Gwyneth Norton who died in 1993. The Birtles Rose Queen and her entourage were dressed in the Hall and encouraged to walk down the great staircase before being transported in state for the coronation.

After nearly sixty years of occupation by the Norton family, Birtles Hall was sold for development and now contains six apartments, with the stables and out-buildings converted into dwellings. The farm, managed for many years by Ron Williams as a successful dairy farm, closed at this time.

The properties included in the sale of the Alderley Estate in 1937 included Whirley Hall, which was tenanted until after the 1939-45 War, and then bought by Colonel (later Sir) William Mather, who lived there for half a century with his wife and family. Pale Farm was also sold in the 1937 sale. The rest of the farmland in Birtles, such as Rough Heys Farm, was sold either to existing tenants or to new owners. So the Birtles Estate, and the old manor of Birtles, ceased to be one unit.

Chapter 10

Henbury School.

Old School House 2002 (photograph F Graham-Smith)

Before Henbury School opened in 1845 there was little or no education for most of the local population. Although the 1841 census shows a schoolmaster living in Putty Row, the only recorded teaching at this time took place in Sunday School. Even where Sunday School was available, as it was in Broken Cross and on a larger scale in Macclesfield[1], there was criticism of a system which condoned or even encouraged the use of child labour during weekdays. There were however those who argued against education for the poor, on the grounds that it 'gave poor children ideas beyond their station in life, thereby making them discontented with their lot'[2]. Some thought that 'education for the masses would breed vice and discontent among the lower classes, whose continued subservience and honesty - best preserved by ignorance - were essential to the social and economic stability of the nation.'[3] Others more enlightened included Adam Smith, usually known for his economic theory, who argued that 'an

---

[1] Broken Cross Sunday School started in 1828 with 210 pupils. Macclesfield Sunday School was set up by Whitaker in 1796, and the Sunday School building which is now the Heritage Centre was built in 1813.
[2] *An Introductory History of English Education since 1800*, S.J.Curtis & M.E.A. Boultwood. University Tutorial Press, 4th edn. 1966, p3.
[3] De Mandeville 1723.loc cit p 42.

Henbury

educated populace would be capable of recognising mischief-making propaganda and, therefore, would be unlikely to succumb to mass hysteria or to anti-Government agitation'[4].

Henbury School was one of the many National Schools which opened in the mid 19th century, following the lead of the National Society for Promoting the Education of the Poor in the Principles of the Established Church. Several other such 'National Schools' were built in Macclesfield in the 1840s, often attached to Church buildings. Financial help from the Government for building National Schools and British Schools (the Non-conformist equivalent) was available from 1833; a requirement for a building grant was that half the cost must be raised by public subscription (a familiar provision in more recent times!). The intervention of the Government was regarded with some suspicion by the Established Church, although the real tension between Church and State only emerged towards the end of the century, when the Government took responsibility for the whole of education. The distribution of the grant aid was overseen by the Privy Council, through a committee which was the fore-runner of the Department of Education. In 1846 the total grant for the whole country was £100,000, part of which was for running costs, assessed on numbers of pupils and on performance. A charge of a few pence per week was required of each pupil; those who could not pay could only attend a 'ragged school', an option that seems not to have been available in Henbury.

The School was set up through the generosity of Major Marsland soon after he took over at Henbury Hall and at the same time as he financed the building of St. Thomas's Church. The school occupied a large barn[5] or shippon on a farm which was part of the Henbury estate, and a school house for the teacher was added as a new south wing. The school house was small by present standards, but the 1851 census shows it as occupied by John Brindley and his wife Sarah, with their two sons and four

---

[4] Loc cit p 44.
[5] One of two buildings shown on an 1843 map (PC87/5293/1 in the CRO). The farm was known as Hulme's Tenement. From 1806 to 1831 the Land Tax Register shows that it was farmed by Peter Gaskell. See a map in Chapter 6.

The School

daughters. The School and school house were given to a Trust, the first Trustees being A.H.Davenport and Rev. J.Thorneycroft (Rural Dean). The Trustees were to hold the property for a School and for no other purposes whatsoever[6] (a provision which seems to have been conveniently forgotten when the school was eventually sold and converted into a private dwelling!). Endowments of £10 per annum from Marsland, and £5 each from Thorneycroft and Davenport were a charge on their respective estates; they were paid during the whole lifetime of the school.

All classes were taught in the one large school room, which had been the shippon. The 1872 Ordnance Survey map[7] shows the school clearly, with the school house and small outbuildings on the south, without the present-day north wing. The playground is narrow, aligned with the ends of the school room. It appears on the map to be open to the road at that time. It was extended in 1886, when the boundary stones were added. The railings (which still exist) were added in 1901; the story is that Thomas Brocklehurst of Henbury Hall added the railings to protect children from his carriage as it was driven along the lane.

The north wing of the school was added by Brocklehurst in 1884, to provide a classroom for infants. The school could then take up to 130 children, although it usually enrolled only half that number. In 1886 Brocklehurst again contributed land and further funding, and asphalted the playground to the present extent. At the same time the west room of the north wing was converted from an open shed, providing an entrance lobby for the infants and a larger room which was used up to the closure of the school as a kitchen.

In 1895 new 'offices' were built at the north end at a cost of £109, in response to criticism from the Education department. An undated plan of this new lavatory block exists[8], showing the boys' outside urinal (tarred wall which still exists), 3 cubicles for girls and 2 cubicles for boys, access from outside, with a common ashpit in the centre emptied by an access door whose lintel can still be seen in the north end. The need for improvement was never

---

[6] Conveyance 12 Dec 1853.
[7] 1st ed 25"/mile, available in Macclesfield Library.
[8] Chester Record Office ref?

Henbury

met, and contributed to the eventual decision to abandon the school.

The 1910 OS map shows the school buildings essentially as they were when the school closed in 1976.

Henbury School pupils ca 1931. Henry Bayley, later the blacksmith, is at back row left (courtesy Elsie Knight)

Through most of its life the school was providing for between 50 and 70 pupils. Up to 1903, when the Local Education Authority took over, the Manager of the school was the Vicar, who from 1850 to 1886 was Rev R.F.J.Shea. The school log for 1863 to 1913[9] records frequent visits from Rev Shea, mainly to hear the Catechism and rehearse some Bible stories but also to examine the children on reading and dictation. An Inspector appointed by the Education Committee of the Privy Council came every year. His report was usually favourable but often unenthusiastic; for example in 1863 *'Mr Moss works very industriously'* (Moss was Head Teacher from 1861 to 1870). Arithmetic was a weak area: in 1864

---

[9] Library of Macclesfield Museums Trust. There is also a Punishment Book 1913-1920, with 33 named pupils receiving up to four strokes on the hand.

The School

69% of the pupils failed in arithmetic, and the report threatened *'the school will incur a serious forfeiture (of grant) under Article 52a unless H.M.Inspector is able to report more favourably on the arithmetic'*. Some improvement was noted in 1865, but HMI *'urges that Mr Moss needs some help, as all pupils are in one class, contrary to the Ninth Supplementary Rule'*. There were various assistant teachers, but they usually looked after the girls' sewing. The school went through a low period in the 1870s; there were no fewer than seven head teachers between 1870 and 1878.

The Parish Magazine[10] gave occasional reports on the School finances; for example, for the 8 months up to December 1903 the Annual Grant was £78, Fee Grant £23, and the endowment was £15 (£20 in a full year). The Principal Teacher was paid £79, and another teacher £36. The costs of repairs or improvements were met from special local collections; in 1900 the Annual Day School sermons raised £81 for Henbury and Broken Cross Schools. The alterations of 1895, costing £109, were paid for 'by the Managers', apparently under duress from the Education Committee which insisted that they were essential. Funding for local voluntary schools such as Henbury was, however, the subject of several Parliamentary Bills during the 1890s, and increased Government funds were available from 1896 or thereabouts.

The Education Act of 1902 spelled the end of independence for the voluntary schools. Henbury was taken over by the Local Authority, and Cheshire County Education Committee paid some or all of £200 needed for improvements such as a better cloakroom, more windows, better ventilation, hot water heating (from a coke fired boiler), and a playground. The Board of Education had since 1870 been establishing new schools to fill the gaps in local education. Much to the distress of the Church these 'Board Schools' were secular and appeared as a threat to the 'Education of the Poor in the Principles of the Established Church'. The Parish Magazine in 1895 refers damningly to the 'incubus of the Board Schools', and in 1907 the Parochial Church Coucil (PCC) joined the civil Parish Council (PC) in deploring the

---

[10] A complete collection of the Magazine published 1889-1890 and 1894-1911 is in Cheshire Record Office.

Henbury

most recent of the several Education Bills of that era.. The change to more modern education at Henbury School seems, nevertheless, to have been achieved without catastrophe. The final chapter seventy years later, when the Local Authority insisted on closure, was more traumatic.

Many local residents remember the School with affection. Mrs Coleman was the Head Teacher in the 1930s and 1940s. She lived at High Trees in Dark Lane. She is fondly remembered and evidently ran a happy school. Home cooked meals were provided by the caretaker cum cook Mrs Wardle (or Wardell?) who lived with her family in the School House. One famous alumnus is Terry Waite, envoy of the Archbishop of Canterbury; he was the local policeman's son. In its last years the School attained a high standard under its Head Teacher, Mrs Swindells; it had the highest percentage pass rate to grammar school of all Macclesfield primary schools[11].

The School was very much a social centre for the village, especially in the days before television when people made their own entertainment. It was used for dances, whist drives, plays, and meetings of the Brownies, Guides, Cubs and the Youth Club. There were therefore three strands to a tangled but vociferous campaign of objections to a notice of closure which was served on the School in 1961 by the Local Education Authority: the School was much loved[12] both as a successful local primary school and as a social centre, and it was a Church school whose loss would signal the end of conventional religious education.

A Parents' Association was formed, funded by a capitation tax of a few pence per week on pupils at the School, and this Association generated much correspondence in the local press. Both Henbury School and Broken Cross School[13] were to be

---

[11] F.Baker-Brian, chairman of Henbury School Parents Association. Letter to Macclesfield Express 1-2-73.

[12] Tape recorded interviews with several former pupils are preserved in the Henbury archive.

[13] Broken Cross School, which was a Church School within the Parish, was located on the cross roads itself, beside the present newsagents. It closed as a school in 1962.

The School

replaced by an LEA County Primary located in Whirley Road, and the Association was joined by the Parochial Church Council in deploring the loss of the Voluntary Schools. The PCC proposed that the function of the School as a meeting place should be replaced by a new Church Hall; this provoked a reaction from the non-churchgoers, who were worried that this would not be adequate to provide for all the social needs of the village. This secular side was represented by another local organisation, the Henbury Residents' Association, which existed briefly in 1971 and 1972. An added objection to the Whirley Lane location from both Associations was that the journey to the new school would be either across a muddy field path or along a dangerous main road.

The PCC, chaired by the Vicar, Canon Glynn Jones, was determined that the new school should again be a voluntary aided Church school, to be partly funded by the sale of both Broken Cross and Henbury Schools. In 1968 the Vicar and the Wardens of Broken Cross School had already explored the market for Broken Cross, and had received an offer of £12,000. The PCC had also applied successfully to the local planning authorities for permission to build the new Church Hall on Church Lane; again funding would come from the sale of the schools. The PCC, chaired from 1970 by Rev Douglas Evans, then had to take a hard look at the finances; they found, reluctantly, that they could not sustain either the capital or the running costs of the proposed school while also funding the new Church Hall, and withdrew the School proposal in 1971. The end of the argument came in 1973, when the Education Minister (Mrs Thatcher) formally rejected an appeal against the closure of Henbury School, and approved the construction of the County Primary for 280 pupils.

Jackie Booth, who was a teacher at the School from 1972 to 1976, has many happy memories of school life. There were still only two teachers; the Head was Barbara Swindells, and Joan Chadwick came in part-time. Mrs Cook was the cook (!); she was renowned for the excellent meals which everyone took at lunchtime. The school was like a large family, and as such it was a full-time job between 9 am and 3.30 pm. Space for recreation included the field across the road, where earlier there had been two

Henbury

houses (see Chapter 7). Parents would drop in at any time of day, and often there were Barn Dances and other evening parties, some to raise money for children's Christmas parties. Jackie was born in Whirley Lane, and has lived in Holly Bank, Chelford Road since 1974. It is she who appears on the famous Geldart picture of Henbury Church, walking her dog on Church Lane (Chapter 11}.

Henbury School finally closed in July 1976, and was sold by the Trustees for conversion to a private dwelling, now occupied by the editor of this book.

Chapter 11

The Church

St Thomas's Church and the Vicarage (courtesy W. Geldart)

The suffix of a place name *bury* from the Saxon *burh,* often means something more important than the more common *ton* meaning settlement, or *ley* meaning a cleared area of woodland. In a book published in 1993 Higham[1] observed that in Cheshire, *burh* sometimes indicated the site of an early church, probably pre Saxon. The church would attract a settlement around it and take the suffix *bury* into its name.

Within the large area around Macclesfield, which was called the Hamestan Hundred are four *bury* names, Bredbury, Norbury, Prestbury and Henbury. Higham suggests that the mother church in the south of the Hundred may have been Macclesfield, but its parochial area would have been much smaller than the later and very large Prestbury parish. The two *bury* names Henbury and Prestbury so close together in an ancient territory is unusual. Higham's suggestion is that following pre Norman enlargement of the Macclesfield royal estate, Prestbury church became the mother church of the parish succeeding the early minster church of Henbury. If it ever existed it would have been a small timber structure like the church at Marton but smaller. Perhaps some day

---

[1] The Origins of Cheshire. N.J.Higham. Manchester U.P. 1993

Henbury

the remains will be discovered as a mysterious structure - local inhabitants should keep a good look out when digging their gardens or ploughing their fields.

Prestbury Church had a particularly close association with Henbury Hall during the time of the Merediths. Several of the family are buried at Prestbury, and Sir William Meredith restored the 12 th century Norman chapel. Henbury was part of Prestbury parish in the 16 th century; there is a record of a parish levy of five pence on Henbury and Pexhill in 1558.

St Catherine's Church. The parish church of Birtles and Over Alderley was built in 1840 by Thomas Hibbert as a private chapel (see Chapter 9). Pevsner[2] notes some interesting features:

> *With an octagonal SW tower and neo-Henry-VIII windows. Nave and short chancel. With the S porch corresponds the N baptistery. The church is full of WOODWORK and stained glass, all brought in by Thomas Hibbert of Birtles Hall. The W screen e.g. has panels which were stall-backs in the Netherlands and two figured groups of a late date. The elaborate PULPIT is dated 1686. The eagle LECTERN is pre-Reformation and more probably Continental than English. There is also the FAMILY PEW, also with assembled bits and pieces. Most of the STAINED GLASS is Netherlandish too, of the C16 and C17, but the three main figures in the E window, the Virgin, an angel, and St John, are Netherlandish of the early C16 at the latest.*

Some of the same stained glass found its way into Pale Farm (Chapter 5).

St Thomas Church. The Church of St Thomas[3], built by Sir Thomas Marsland in 1843-5 and consecrated on 20 February 1845,

---

[2] N.Pevsner and E.Hubbard. *The Buildings of England: Cheshire*. Penguin Books 1971

[3] A booklet *The Church of St Thomas Henbury*, by Roy Potter, was printed in 1994 to commemorate the 150th anniversary. The Parish magazine, 1889-91 and from 1893 onward, is available in the CRO.

The Church

was the first church in Henbury[4]. Marsland originally proposed a site near the Hall, but others suggested there would be greater benefit from a church built nearer Broken Cross, which was described as "having long borne an evil reputation". Marsland gave the site, £800 for the building fund, the stained glass windows, a clock for the tower and £1000 to endow the living. His wife provided the organ[5].

The architect for the Church was Richard Lane, who also built Stockport Infirmary (1832). Pevsner notes 'the stone lancets and a thin W tower with broach-spire.' The total cost[6] came to about £1600. The Incorporated Church Building Society gave £50, a gift acknowledged by the tablet over the Wardens' pew. Subscriptions and a collection at the consecration provided £600. The bell, which weighs over 7 cwt. and cost £40.8s., came from Aldford Parish Church near Chester where it formed part of a peal given by one of the Earls Grosvenor. Communion Plate was given by Mrs. Thomas Wardle of Macclesfield. There were seats for 270, including 10 paid pews.

Originally there were no choir stalls, the choir being seated in the gallery. In 1893 they moved into the front pews, sitting with their backs to the congregation, until in the following year a Restoration Scheme costing £250 was completed. General repairs, renewals and redecoration were carried out and in addition the present choir stalls were introduced and new seats placed at the west end. To accommodate the choir stalls the front pews were removed. The new seats at the west end are thought to have replaced the six benches for school children, put in when the church was built. The brass lectern was given by Edward Wright of Macclesfield.

Electric lighting was installed in 1928. Originally during the winter, Sunday evening services were held in the two schools. A

---

[4] There is a reference in Ormerod (p 706) to the presentation by Henry VIII of "Dionysius Memo, clerk" to a Henbury church or chapel in 1517. Was this attached to Henbury Hall? No other references are known.

[5] A new organ was installed in 1946; the cost of £1230 was met by a local Centenary Fund.

[6] Churchwardens accounts 1846-1911 are in Chester Record Office.

Henbury

meeting of parishioners during 1889 decided these Services should be transferred to the church and to enable this to be done agreed to install oil lamps[7].

The Ecclesiastical District assigned to the church was taken from the Parish of Prestbury and consisted of the Township of Henbury and that portion of Macclesfield west of the Toll Bar[8] in Broken Cross. The Parish boundary was redefined in 1961, due to the creation of the neighbouring parish of St. John. The Registers[9] for Baptisms and Burials date from 1845, but it was not until 1869 that the church was licensed for Marriages; before then weddings took place at the mother church of Prestbury.

The Parish was formed and the first Vicar, John Hebden, was appointed in October 1845. The other incumbents have been

Robert Francis Jones Shea	1850-1888
William Skinner Farmer	1888-1893
John Howson Wilcockson	1893-1904
Henry.Alfred.Portbury	1905-1935
Albert.Edward Whittingham	1935-1945[10]
Glyn Jones	1946-1968
Douglas Haigh-Evans	1970-1982
Bruce Peel	1983-1995
David Harrison	1996-date

Church Records. The main church records which are deposited in the Diocesan Record Office in Chester are: registers of baptism 1871-1968, marriage 1869-1977, burial 1845-1956, graves 1907, banns 1956-1988, churchwardens' accounts 1846-1911, and PCC minutes 1920-1976. The most recent PCC minutes are kept by the secretary.

---

[7] Until then there had been no general illumination in the church although in 1880 the accounts have an entry "lamps for the choir 18s. and 1s. for oil:"
[8] Toll Bar Road is East of Broken Cross, off Chester road.
[9] Registers of baptism 1871-1968, marriage 1869-1977, burial 1845-1956, graves 1907, banns 1956-1988.
[10] Rev. A.E.Whittingham was called up for war service from 1940 to 1945. Rev. W.D.Thomas acted as Priest in Charge for these years.

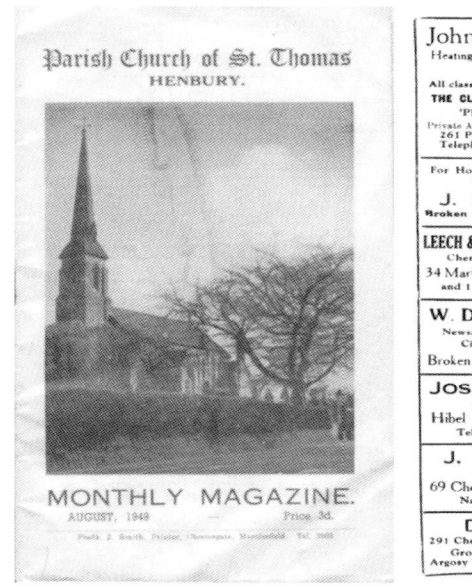

The Church

St Thomas's Parish Magazine: front and back covers, August 1949 (courtesy Elsie Knight)

The Record Office also holds copies of the Parish Magazine published from 1889-1911, which records all baptisms, burials and marriages, and includes many references to the two schools. A recent record of memorial inscriptions from the graveyard is available from the Cheshire Family History Society.

The Parochial Church Council The Churchwardens' Minute Book 1845-1907 gives an account of the financing of the Church in 1845, and the opening of the School on August 31 1846, but there is little more in the record until the PCC Minutes 1920-1976. In a file on School Administration 1897-1951 there is an example of the strong feeling on the management of Henbury School, in a letter from Stanley to Rev J Wilcocks: *'Queen Anne's Bounty accepts my offer of benefaction to Henbury benefice, and has met it with a grant of £200. My share of £6 p.a. goes to the School while it remains C of E, not to encourage the prevalent extravagance in schooling and the exactions of the faddists of the Education Department.'*

Henbury

The PCC met at Broken Cross School until it closed in 1962, and was responsible for the maintainance of both Church schools.

Church Hall or Village Hall? For over 100 years Henbury School was the main centre of local social life. It was not, however, well provided with facilities: in particular the outside toilets were last improved in 1895. The whole future of the School was under discussion from 1945 onwards, and a proposal for a new village hall was put before the PCC in 1946. The new Vicar, Rev Glyn Jones, was in the chair. There was evidently a view that any new hall should be clearly designated as a Church Hall, but Glyn Jones said that he was in favour of a Village Hall and that he would be one of the first to use it. This discussion eventually became part of the heated debate on the future of Broken Cross and Henbury Church Schools (see Chapter 10 on Henbury School), and it was not until 1978 that funding for a Church Hall emerged as part of the proceeds from the sale of the two Schools. The neighbouring house, Beech Cottage, which had been the Verger's house, was sold at the same time. Sufficient funds were then available to build a hall which was adequate for all village meetings, including those of the Henbury Society. The Church Hall, completed in December 1979 and opened by the Bishop of Chester in April 1980, is now the natural venue for all meetings such as those of the civil Parish Council.

The Vicarage is a fine house adjacent to and contemporary with the Church. Pevsner notes the '*two symmetrical gables and a middle porch gable, all three Gothically bargeboarded.*' The turbulent discussions on the future of the Church Hall included briefly a suggestion that the Vicar would find it more convenient to live in a smaller and more modern house, but fortunately this idea was not pursued. During World War II the vicarage was the base for Air Raid Precautions wardens. There was fortunately little action for the ARP wardens in Henbury. Arthur Marshall recalls being on early morning duty at 6 am and encountering the Vicar, Rev Whittingham, returning from a rabbitting expedition, with his overcoat bulging with his catch.

The Rose Queen Fête has been held since 1934, with a gap during the War years. The first Rose Queens were chosen

The Church

alternately from the two schools. The Fête is a distinctly rural occasion, held originally in the Vicarage grounds and more recently on the Millennium Green.

The Brocklehurst Coal Dole. Evidence of the care of Henbury parishioners is found in the bequest by May Vardon Brocklehurst (died 24 April 1914):

> *I bequeath to the vicar and churchwardens for the time being of Saint Thomas Church, Henbury, in and of the fund in connection with that church for the relief of the poor of its parish £200. In addition to the legacy of £200 herein before bequeathed to the vicar and churchwardens for the time being of Saint Thomas Church, Henbury, I bequeath to such vicar and churchwardens the further sum of £300 upon trust that they shall invest the same and shall from time to time at their discretion apply the annual income arising from the said sum of £300 and the investments from the time being representing the same in the purchase of coals for the poor of the parish of Henbury, and I direct that the said fund shall be known as the "May V Brocklehurst Coal Dole"*

The Charity Commissioners ordered that the capital should be put into Dominion of Canada 4% stock and West Australian 4% stock, and left it to the Trustees to define poverty. We have no recent records of disbursements from this charity!

Chapter 12

Pubs, Shops and Roads

Pexhill Post Office and Teashop (Edwardian postcard)

Arthur Marshall has first hand knowledge of the local shops and pubs; he lived at Parkfield House behind the Blacksmith's Arms where his father was landlord. Part of this chapter is based on his notes. Roger Bowling has written about the Blacksmiths Arms and the A537 Chelford Road. His account of the Cock Inn is part of our Chapter 7, on houses. The Cave, in Henbury Park, may also have been a pub some time in the 19th century; it was also reputed to be a centre for cock-fighting, but we have found no records of either activity.

The village shop. Opposite the Blacksmith's Arms on the Chelford Road, there was a farm (Spinks Farm) and two cottages, one standing on the corner of Pepper Street. Spinks Farm now belongs to Bill Geldart, our notable local artist, and there is an extensive display of his work in his gallery. Among the most notable are drawings to be found in this book of the School, the Church, and Ernest Kennerley at work plucking pheasants.

Henbury

Before Bill and his wife Ann lived there, the farmhouse belonged to Mr. Sigley. Alongside the present studio there was a farm track (now the Flora Garden Centre entrance) leading to the rear of the cottages. At the top of this farm track was a reasonably sized wooden shed converted into a shop and run by Mrs. Sigley. She also used an outbuilding at the rear of the house to provide tea and cakes for hungry walkers and cyclists. Cyclists were also catered for, pre-War and in a smaller way, by Mrs Eva Windsor at Lingards Farm. Even earlier, in Edwardian days, there was another teashop at the Pexhill Post Office.

The village shop tried to sell anything from buttons to butter beans, home sweets to pineapple chunks with everything between. It had a very limited trade, but served a need in those days before the war until the 1950's. Coincidentally, the Garden Centre now runs a teashop almost on the same site.

The function of a village shop is now taken over by the local service station, Pexall Garage, run by John Deaville and his family.

The Blacksmith's Arms 1938 (courtesy A. Marshall)

The Blacksmith's Arms. In 1808 just before the main road was constructed Charles Bradbury lived at Park House Farm and owned the adjoining land which would soon front onto the main road. Another Bradbury, John, surely related, lived at Davenport

Pubs, Shops and Roads

Heys and leased out a small piece of land where the Blacksmith's Arms and petrol station now stands. A little later in the 1820s a Charles Bradbury lived with his wife Elizabeth at a small farm and smithy on the same site. It is likely that this Charles was the son of one of the others. Charles the blacksmith, in his wife's opinion was an idle drunkard and a poor breadwinner. She therefore set out to find some more regular source of income. She approached a Macclesfield brewery with the proposition that given one months credit on their products she would start a beerhouse. The brewers agreed and with a new busy main road passing the door she thought she could not fail. In fact she prospered probably beyond her dreams. The pub stayed open sometimes all night, carters with salt from Northwich, lime from Buxton and agricultural produce on its way to Macclesfield all made her business a great success. This was helped by her low prices and good measure (a 'long pull'), which had a bad effect on the takings of the nearby Jodrell's Arms, now the Cock Inn. Soon stabling was erected at the rear of the premises. Because of the past use she named the beerhouse the Blacksmith's Arms, and the first documentary record of this name appears to be the Tithe Apportionment of 1849. The founding of the pub was probably about 1828.

Elizabeth employed her husband Charles in the forge in the day and assisting in the pub at other times. She rationed him to one quart of ale per day. They may have had five children, Rachel, Charles, John, Elizabeth and Isaac. Rachel's great-great-grandson, Edward Barber, contributed much of this family history in correspondence with Roger Bowling. Charles also became a blacksmith and in the 1841 census, aged 20, he was living with the large family of Joseph Lancaster, blacksmith. Charles the elder died in 1848 but Elizabeth carried on, assisted by her daughter also Elizabeth, probably up to her death in 1870. The business was then taken over by son Charles, for in Morris's Directory of 1874 he is listed as blacksmith and beer seller, but in Kelly's Directory of 1892 only as beer retailer.

There is one puzzle in this story: in 1865 Anne Shaw, executor of the long deceased David Willott, leased the Cock Inn to John Bradbury. If this person is, as seems likely, the son of Charles and

Henbury

Elizabeth, then the Bradburys had cornered the market in ale in Henbury.

The Blacksmith's Arms is unusual in that its name really does signify the past use of the building; for fifty years the Blacksmith's Arms was indeed a blacksmith's shop.

Arthur Marshall remembers *'This inn was originally a small farm; the outbuildings were still in evidence when my father became the landlord in the mid-1930s. Until that time it had been a 'free-house' not tied to any brewer. However when the last proprietor, Jesse Banks, died the public house was purchased by Richard Clarke, a Stockport brewer and he set about modernising it by altering the bar area, building a new cellar and connecting to the main water supply.*

In 1874 when Colonel Brocklehurst purchased the Henbury estate, Park House farm was still part of the estate of the late Charles Bradbury. In due course Colonel Brocklehurst purchased Park House farm and a small holding later to become Parkfield farm, the land going to extend Park House farm. The sale of Park House farm did not include the Blacksmith's Arms and an acre of land adjoining the public house. Over the years the pub outgrew the small holding and only the outbuildings were the last vestiges of a holding when we arrived on the scene.

In order to compensate for this loss of earning some enterprising owner of the public house installed three petrol pumps in what is now the car park. They were operated by hand by turning a handle; the petrol was Shell, National Benzol and Cleveland with a variation in price per gallon from one shilling and 4d to one shilling and 6d. Quite a number of these country public houses of that era had a farm attached to them to supplement their beer trade when it dropped in winter months.

The locals in those days were farmers, gamekeepers, gardeners and farm workers all with tales to tell of the good old days. One of the locals had an ARCM in music and on most Saturday nights he would get them all singing as the accompanist. He would always commence his medley of songs with a march "Sons of the Brave".

Pubs, Shops and Roads

Always looking for something new, my father hit upon the idea of holding occasional vegetable shows on a Saturday night judged by the local head gardener. They were a great success and attracted trade from a wide area. Imagine doing that today! I recall the local blacksmith dashing into the pub one night after a Parish Council meeting in the school. He was in a terrible rage, he banged on the bar counter and choked out "The Council have just passed a resolution to have a telephone box on the corner of School Lane and it will put a half penny on the rates!" My father answered "if it saves a life it seems cheap to me" and served him a drink to cool him down.

One of the star turns of the Saturday night sing-alongs was the solo spot by Walter Massey. He was the quintessential country character. No-one could tell a tale with all the actions and different voices as Walter especially when he told tales about the gentry. They were hilarious. His star turns were a couple of songs of which one was about Johnny Bradbury who was Permanent Secretary to the Treasury. The older generation will remember the white £5 notes; they were signed by John Bradbury, Cashier to the Bank of England. In fact the slang term for these notes was 'Bradburys'.

The song had many verses extolling the virtues and advantages of possessing a 'Johnny Bradbury'. He would beat time with a walking stick on a wooden chair during the chorus. How that chair stood up to that punishment I will never know. He was sweating but the pianist was sweating even more.

I tell this tale for two reasons, one to show how we made our own amusement in those days, and thoroughly enjoyed it. Secondly by a strange coincidence I live about a quarter of a mile from John Bradbury's palatial house "Plas Mariandir" near Llandudno. After he died it was converted into a convalescent home. Later one or two wings were added but the main structure of the house remains intact. It is now luxury residential apartments. Very often when I pass it either walking or in the car I think of Walter and his "Good old Johnny Bradbury" and I think of happier times.

Henbury

Roads. The present Chelford Road (A537) and its predecessors, the turnpike through Whirley and Dark Lane, are well documented. Earlier roads are less obvious, and we are left to guess from the old maps such as Meredith's Estate map of 1727. For example, travelling from Capesthorne to Macclesfield seems to have been via the drive across fields (now a public footpath) to Lingards Farm, part of Fanshawe Lane, then through Henbury Park to part of Horseshoe Lane (now School Lane), then on the old road to Broken Cross.

A537 - "one of the great roads" - you may not agree with the above description of the main road through Henbury, but that is how it was described[1] in 1789. For a long time Henbury has stood on the main road westward from Macclesfield, but not the main road we know today; that is a road of more recent construction, 1808 to be precise.

Before the nineteenth century access to and through Henbury was by two roads, both running from Broken Cross to Pale Farm. Broken Cross is a busy road junction and has been so for 1000 years or more. It is the junction of five ancient roads, to Macclesfield, to the saltfields at Middlewich via Siddington and to Knutsford. The north and south roads to Gawsworth and Prestbury were, as long ago as 1270, the western boundary of the medieval Macclesfield Forest. The traffic through the junction accounts for an industry at Broken Cross, still just within living memory, that of basket making, and another activity, counterfeiting, relied on the travellers to disperse the false coinage.

To the west of Broken Cross and along the Whirley Road was Long Moss and Whirley Common. The Common here is low lying and wet, and both roads to Henbury avoided this area, one road to the south, the other to the north. To the south, branching off Pexhill Road at Bromley Road, the road followed the slightly higher ground to the south of the moss, crossing the river to the rear of the Cock Inn, across the front of The Firs and along the

---

[1] Tunnicliff: *Topological Survey*, 1789. Quoted in Harrison W., *Pre-turnpike highways and lanes in Cheshire; J. Lancs and Cheshire Antiquarian Soc.*, **IX** 1891, p101.

hedge by the gardens at Pleasant View to Church Lane. This section of the old road, in 1620 called *"the lane leadinge to Henbury"* can be clearly seen from an aerial photograph and on the ground as a flat ditch and hedge banks. After the modern road was built it rapidly went out of use, but is shown on maps of 1704 and 1720. The road continues along Church Lane and Dark Lane, the only section still a right of way, and at the sharp bend in Dark Lane the old road continued across the fields to join Whirley Lane to the north of Pale Farm. In certain light and with imagination the track of the road may still be seen over the fields. This section probably stayed in use as a field path after the modern road, and is shown on the 1841 OS map. This road was suitable only for foot or packhorse traffic, the river at the back of the Cock Inn being the main obstruction. Two further clues to the antiquity of the road are the names Dark Lane and Pepper Street. Dark Lane is derived from ditch or dyke, meaning a sunken road, one with high banks, the surface having been eroded by traffic and weather for centuries. The wear is of course greater on slopes, such as the east end of Dark Lane. The term "street" in a country area often suggests an old road, sometimes Roman but usually not. But what about Pepper Street? It is certainly not anything to do with the numerous saltways of Cheshire. The best that the experts, learned in the history of road names, can suggest is a derivation from peppercorn, like the gravel that may have surfaced some old roads. Whatever the origin of the name, it usually indicates an ancient road and there are several Pepper Streets elsewhere in Cheshire.

The Old Road and the Turnpike (now A537). In the eighteenth century increasing trade and wheeled vehicles required improved roads. This need was met by the initiative of Turnpike Trusts[2]. We would call this today the privatisation of roads. In return for the making and maintaining of a road suitable for wheeled traffic, the trusts were allowed to collect tolls. In many cases this was not done by the construction of new roads but by the improvement of old roads and in 1769 Whirley Road and Whirley

---

[2] Harrison W. *Trans. Lancs and Cheshire Archaeological Soc.* **4**, 80 1887 gives a list of Cheshire Turnpike Trusts.

Henbury

Lane were turnpiked, being part of the Broken Cross to Tabley Turnpike Trust. It is this road that in 1789 was *"one of the great roads"*. The tolls were collected near Monks Heath and Broken Cross; there was no toll bar in Henbury. No records of traffic or tolls collected survive for this road.

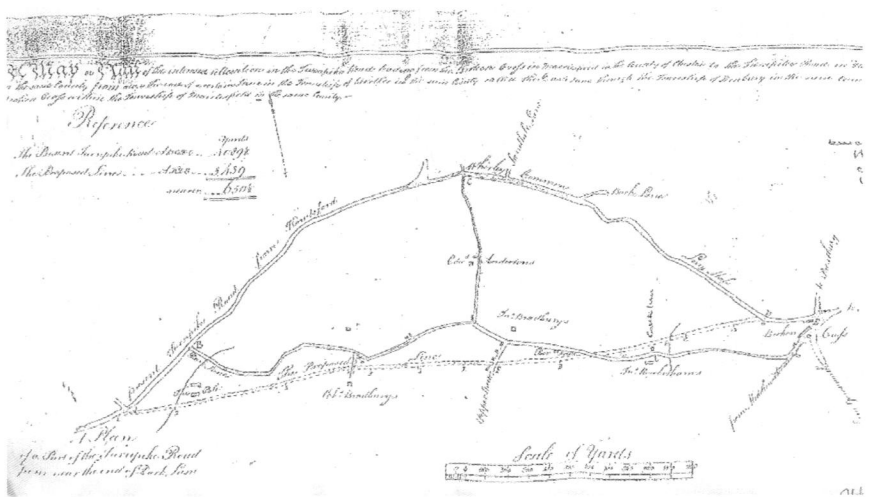

The 1808 Public Undertakings Plan of the intended new turnpike. The 1769 older turnpike is at the top of the plan; it is now Whirley Road and Whirley Lane. The much older earliest track is shown winding its way from Broken Cross to the north of Pale Farm. The planned new turnpike is shown dotted; the numbers at the sides denoting landowners whose livelihood might be affected (CRO)

A turnpike road had to be 60ft wide plus drainage ditches. An old turnpike which had been bypassed and lost its importance, and reverted to a country lane will sometimes reveal its history by the wide grass verges and walls or hedges about 60ft apart. Such is the case between Whirley Hall and Pale Farm. This turnpike did not on any of its course cross Henbury Land, so for carts and carriages the only access to Henbury was by way of Andertons Lane, and the upkeep of this lane would fall on the residents of the township. More likely than not the condition of the lane would be very poor.

Clearly the 1769 turnpike was unsatisfactory, so in 1808 a new section of road was planned, taking a direct line and shortening the distance from Broken Cross to Pale Farm by 650 yards. The

Pubs, Shops and Roads

barrier to this route had previously been the wet ground of Whirley Common, but the new Turnpike Trust successfully did what should have been done 40 years before; maybe the first Trustees thought that upgrading an old road would be more profitable than building a new one. The 1808 plan of the intended route shows all the landowners whose interests may be affected by the new road, so that they could, if they wished, object to the proposal. This foreshadowed a similar proposal in Henbury, also concerning the main road, 182 years later (see Chapter 16). It is believed that in 1808 the construction of the road was held up due to a compensation dispute. Francis Jodrell of the Hall could be a possible objector as he owned several plots of land lying on the route, or maybe John and William Rowbotham of what is now the Cock Inn and The Firs as the new road separated all their land from the farm house and buildings. Crossing the cows over the road four times every day in summer in the nineteenth century was not a problem - in George Dooley's day in the 1980's at Ivydale Farm, next to the Cock Inn, it was sometimes not easy, but today it would be impossible. The 1808 Turnpike Trust was wound up in 1880.

In 1789 the first turnpike was *"one of the great roads"*. This probably means one of the oldest roads, and its origins probably lie in Saxon times. The 1808 turnpike replaced this road but criticism did not cease, especially of the condition at the Birtles bends. When stuck behind a tractor going to Chelford Market you will certainly agree with a description of the road in 1891 - *"Condition poor as formerly"*.

Chapter 13

The Mills at Birtles and Henbury Hall

Two water mills in Henbury! Many of the local inhabitants know little of Birtles Mill, at the extreme west of the parish, and only Arthur Marshall had any idea that another existed at some time on the Henbury Estate. We were able to investigate Birtles in some detail, and a trawl through the archives at the Hall gave us at least a probable site for the other, which had not previously been recorded in local surveys[1]. As if this were not enough, we then found good evidence of a third, probably the oldest of all.

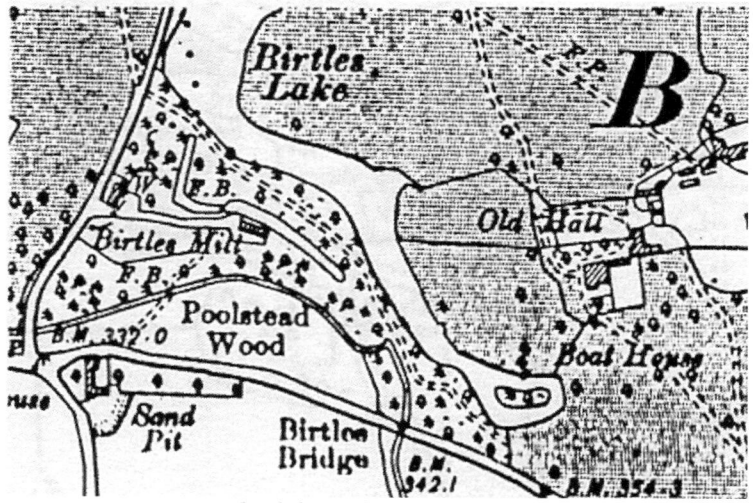

Birtles lake and mill in 1910 (OS)

Birtles Mill. Have you ever wondered when driving along the road from Henbury towards Knutsford, why that dead straight road goes into a series of bends - the notoriously dangerous Birtles bends - before straightening out again for the traffic lights and the road to Chelford? This is actually part of the ancient road, winding between the Bag Brook and the high ground of Birtles Hill Farm. Less obviously, and unknown to many who drive that route every

---

[1] Norris J.H. The Water-Powered Corn Mills of Cheshire. *Trans. Lancs. & Ches. Antiquarian Soc.* **75-76,** 33-71.

Henbury

day, there is an ancient water mill on the Brook, very close to the road but screened from it by a plantation. It was fed by a lake which can be seen from Birtles Lane. Before the damburst of 1872 the lake was supplied by a mill leat from some way up the Bag Brook; the bridge under the Chelford Road had separate arches for the main stream and the leat. The lake is now fed from a smaller stream which forms the Parish boundary.

Our information on the Mill is due both to the local knowledge of Mr Robin West and to the generous response by Mr and Mrs Chris Kershaw to the Henbury Society's questionnaire, asking for information about old Henbury.

Chris and Joan Kershaw fell in love with the Mill site and bought it in 1979. It was by then a romantic ruin surrounded by a tangle of neglected woodland. Only one wall remained standing amid piles of rubble. Beams of wood and stone flags from the roof had been taken away for use elsewhere but much of the machinery was still there. The Kershaws determined to restore the Mill to its former glory.

Restoration was not straightforward. Before they could start, they needed planning permission and there was some local opposition to their proposals. However, after a period of difficulty and inquiry and expense, the courage and vision of Mr and Mrs Kershaw prevailed. In view of the beautiful restoration the Kershaws achieved, the opposition is difficult now to understand.

Mr and Mrs Kershaw rebuilt the Mill to resemble the original 18th century structure and included the massive buttresses and wall plates which were needed in the 19th century to strengthen the walls after more powerful machinery was introduced. The great overshot wheel is preserved within the house. It is in working order again and can be run to the amazement of guests but the wheel is no longer geared up to the mill stones, for that area is now a family room.

Outside the mill pool, the dam and the leats have been restored so that the wheel can function as before. Wild life thrives here too, mallards, coots, waterhens, pheasants and even the kingfisher. The woodland has been managed to look natural yet cared for and in the spring is carpeted with bluebells and wood anemones.

The Water Mills

Birtles Mill 1900 (courtesy Mr & Mrs C Kershaw)

Not far away, on Birtles Lane is the cottage that was formerly the smithy. Here the blacksmith was most conveniently placed to make and repair tools and machinery for the mill as well as for the whole village and to shoe the horses which would have brought the grain to the mill. Across the main road was, until recently, the farm where the miller and his family lived - the original Mill House Farm.

Nothing now remains of Mill House Farm. It was demolished in the 1960s by the Highway Authority prior to their intentions of improving the road; they considered it a hazard, blocking the sight line on a dangerous cross roads. Luckily, we do know a little of its history thanks to the research of Darcy Dobell and Vic Rogers of Victoria, British Columbia, Canada, descendants of William Rogers the 19th century miller.

Henbury

The former Mill House Farm, opposite Birtles Lane (courtesy Mr&Mrs C Kershaw and Darcy Dobell and V Rogers)

In 1997 the Kershaws were visited by Darcy Dobell, the great great granddaughter of William Rogers the miller, and so began a correspondence between them and Vic Rogers, who had also visited Birtles in the 1950s and already knew some family history.

The Rogers family originated in Meerbrook Staffordshire. In 1830, Vic's great grandfather, also called William, moved with his wife Sarah and their two children, the older of whom was called William, to live in North Rode. After farming at North Rode for several years, the Rogers family, now with six children moved to become the tenants at Monks Heath Hall on the Capesthorne estate. By the 1850s the young William Rogers and his wife Mary were living at Mill House Farm, with 14 acres of land, and were running the mill.

William Rogers the younger and his sons ran the mill up to the beginning of the 20th century and it seems that their hard work and diligence brought them prosperity at that time. The Rogers family have given Mr and Mrs Kershaw some wonderful photographs of the mill, Mill House Farm and other scenes in the area. One

The Water Mills

delightful photograph shows William Rogers, tall and lean, and his son Thomas working at the mill while Mrs Rogers and another son wait in a smart little dog cart, perhaps on their way to town. William and Mary died in 1903 and 1904 in Birtles (presumably at Mill House Farm) and were buried at Henbury Church. Joseph, their youngest son, emigrated to Canada in 1899.

How old is the mill? The earliest documentary evidence we have so far, of a mill on the present site is Burdett's 1777 map of Cheshire, but there would certainly have been a corn mill in the manor of Henbury/Birtles much earlier than that. In mediaeval times each manor had to be self-sufficient, primarily because transport was difficult and unreliable. That meant producing all the food they needed within their own settlement. Henbury farmers would all have grown grain for bread, porridge, and animal feed. While the settlement was small they could grind with hand querns and possibly a horse mill, but as the population increased they would need a more efficient method of milling.

The village mill was a very valuable asset and always belonged to the lord of the manor, who rented it out to the miller. Tenants were obliged to use their Lord's mill. The miller was allowed to keep "the sixteenth grain" or thereabouts according to local custom, as his payment or his proportion of the farmer's consignment so he too might prosper (and he sometimes had a reputation for sharp practice). The mill required a great deal of upkeep to keep it in working order; floods, rotten woodwork and the blocking of channels were the major problems and the mill stones were supposed to be re-dressed frequently and replaced when worn out.

The millstones were very costly not least because of the transport costs. Generally the lord of the manor paid for the millstones and others provided the labour. The mill stones for the mill in Macclesfield were probably quarried in the Peak District and maybe those for Birtles originally came from there too; the stones on display, however, are of French origin. Men tenanting land near the mill usually had to help in the upkeep in some way, either with transport for the mill stones or in labour keeping the channels clear. The mill pools may well have been used as a

Henbury

fishery, the lord naturally being the main beneficiary, which would have been a useful source of fresh food in the winter.

The Henbury Mill. The old water corn mill on the Henbury estate has disappeared almost without trace. The earliest record we have found is in 1693, when it was listed in the conveyance of the Henbury estate from Fulk Lucy to Meredith. Our only indication of its site comes from an interesting document of 1745, preserved in the archives at the Hall. This is the record of an agreement between William Meredith of Henbury and John Ward of Capesthorne over the flow of water in streams which crossed the Henbury estate, running from Henbury to Redesmere.

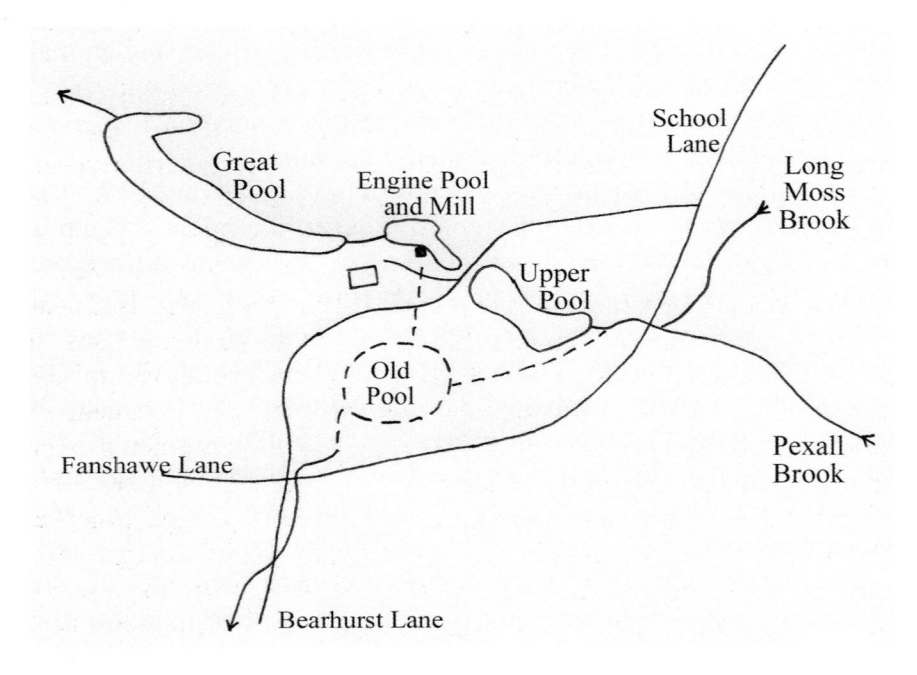

Sketch of the location of the Henbury Mill on the central lake of Henbury Hall, then known as Engine Pool. It was originally fed from an old pool in front of the Hall, and from 1717 it was fed from the Upper Pool.

There is today no such stream across the estate, but before Meredith's time the Long Moss stream (now the Bag Brook), which flows through Cock Wood and under School Lane into the

The Water Mills

Henbury estate, fed a pool[2] to the south of the present top lake. The overflow from this pool found its way south, through Huntley wood to join Fanshawe Brook. The pool also fed a watermill which discharged into the second lake and the lower part of Bag Brook.

Meredith's contribution to the landscape in 1717 was to create the top lake, called Upper Pool in 1842[3], by building a dam, which now carries the main entrance road to the Hall, and by stopping the flow to the south through the estate. He also arranged for the flow from a smaller stream which drained farmlands at Pexhall and High Birch Green to be controlled so that it could either flow across the estate to Fanshawe Brook or be diverted into the new lake (this stream now joins Bag Brook 20 metres to the East of School Lane). Evidently the flow into Fanshawe Brook was considerably reduced, although occasionally there would be an overflow into the old stream. John Ward was complaining that the supply of water for his own mill in Capesthorne had been upset. The dispute seems to have been amicably resolved by an agreement that the smaller Pexhall stream should lead into Fanshawe Brook and not be diverted to join the Long Moss stream.

We believe that the mill for which all this was organised was located at the edge of the middle lake, known as Engine Pool, at the site of a small building which is now a viewing platform for the lake. It has very solid foundations, and there is some 17th century brickwork. A few yards away there is a plinth constructed from masonry blocks, evidently re-used from a previous structure; one of these blocks is a date stone inscribed FL 1666, suggesting that the mill may have been built, or rebuilt, by Fulk Lucy in that year. The existing small building contains a hydraulic ram pump supplying water for the gardens of Henbury Hall. Although there is no other record of the operation of the mill, it is satisfying to realise that the source of 'renewable' power created by Meredith is still being tapped for irrigating the garden.

---

[2] Ormerod III 706 quotes 'the poole head, poole meadow' 1558 ('at Henbyri is a greate poole' c. 1536 Leland).
[3] Conveyance of Henbury estate from Ryle to Marsland. This conveyance includes a map detailing all the fields on the estate.

Henbury

Some support for this identification comes from a Henbury Estate Field Notebook[4] of 1794. On the cover is an engraving depicting a water mill in a location showing a strong resemblance to the Engine Pool, with the bridge carrying the main entrance drive in the background.

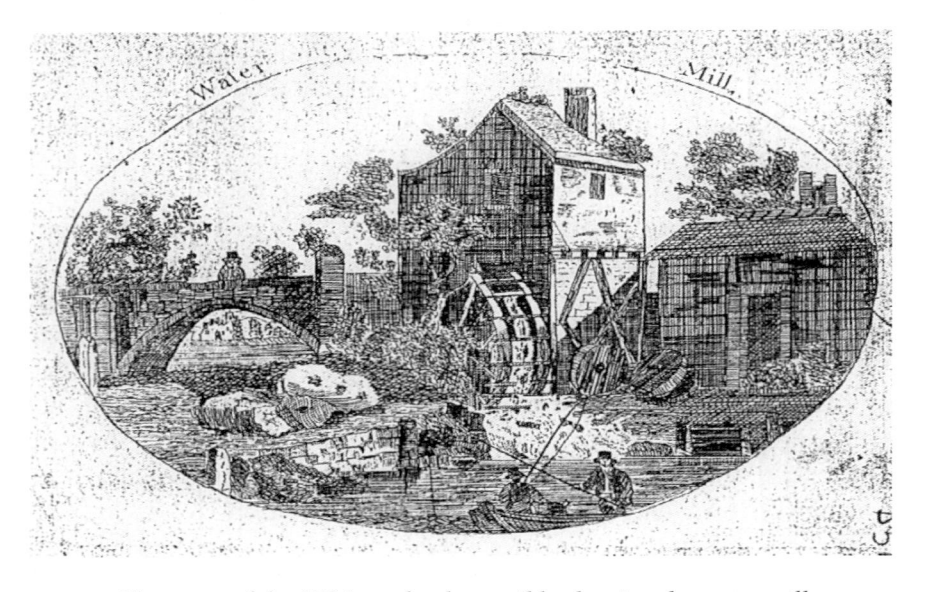

The cover of the 1794 notebook, possibly showing the water mill on the Engine Pool (Cheshire Record Office)

A Third Mill? Two watermills were quite enough to satisfy the history team, but when the earliest map of the Henbury Estate was found in Chester Record Office a probable third showed up. The map was Meredith's estate map of 1727, and it clearly showed the Great Pool on Bag Brook, below the middle pool which we now call Engine Pool. But what was the house shown just below the centre of the dam, with the stream emerging from underneath? The only explanation is that it was another watermill.

---

[4] CRO reference D5678/38

The Water Mills

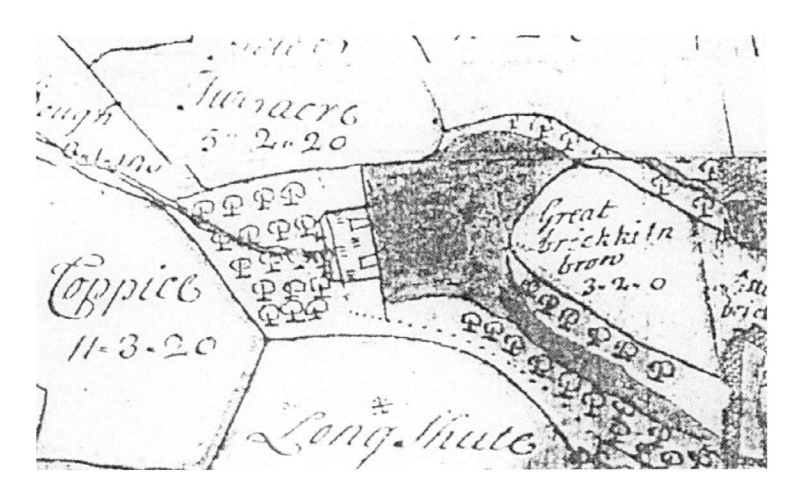

The Mill on the Great Pool, from Meredith's 1727 map of the Henbury Estate (Cheshire Record Office)

There is today little trace of this mill below the dam, which is not surprising as the damburst of 1872 completely swept away a large section of dam at its north end, where the stream now runs (see Chapter 14). No building could possibly have survived there, and even at the centre any building would have collapsed. There would have been no point in reconstruction, as water powered mills were already going out of use in the mid 19th century. However there are in the valley bottom several large broken and tumbled pieces of masonry, whose origin has up to now been a mystery. Among the remains, a few yards downstream from the breach in the dam, are several large pieces of masonry, about 80 cm long, each with one face cut as an arc with radius about 1.5 metres. These were apparently part of a cylindrical "swallow" which was the overflow system for the pool (see the account of the flood in Chapter 14). There is also a stone lined conduit and a small weir in the stream where it emerges from the gap in the dam. Further investigation of the site should reveal foundations of the mill, whose layout would indicate the type of waterwheel that was used.

When were these mills built? The date stone for 1666 preserved close to the Engine Pool may refer to the construction of the upper

Henbury

mill, but a manor like Henbury should have had a mill considerably earlier than that. The nature of the dam on the Great Pool, which is a simple but massive earth bank, suggests that it was mediaeval. The only reference we have found is by Leland in his "Itinerary of England" (1535-1543), who noted that '*at Henbyri is a greate poole*'. If this dam were indeed built for a mill to be used by an early local farming community, the masonry remains must be of later origin, reflecting the technological developments that were a feature of all such mills in the 17th and 18th centuries.

Chapter 14

The Great Damburst

The course of the Bag Brook, showing the three burst dams in Henbury Hall Park, and the four road bridges which were swept away by the torrent on the night of 18/19 June 1872 (map courtesy OS)

The damburst of 1872 has already appeared in our account of Henbury Hall (Chapter 8), and in the discovery of the remains of two water-powered corn mills on the Estate (Chapter 13), but such a cataclysm deserves a chapter on its own. We found a contemporary account in The *Macclesfield Courier and Herald* of June 29, 1872, which gives a more graphic picture than we can construct at this distance of time. We can see from this account how two mills were swept away, and such terrible damage done to the estate, the roads and bridges, and several houses that Mrs Marsland, then owner of Henbury Hall felt compelled to sell up even before the famous ruling that this major disaster should be regarded as an *Act of God* for which she need take no responsibility.

The catastrophe occurred on the night of June 18/19, when 4.75 inches of rain fell in a short time. Damage was reported in other parts of Cheshire, but this was by far the worst.

DEVASTATION AT HENBURY AND BIRTLES. There are certain things which must be seen to be appreciated; the devastation at

Henbury

Henbury and Birtles must be seen to be fully realised. In Mrs Marsland's park at Henbury were a series of large pools or reservoirs, well stocked with fish, and adding greatly by means of waterfalls and rustic bridges to the beauty of the gardens and shrubberies at the rear of the house. The upper pool to the rear of the carriage drive on the approach to the Hall was swollen to an unprecedented extent by the heavy rain. We have been informed, but it seems scarcely credible, that the water was fourteen feet higher in the pool than has been known on any previous occasion.

The extraordinary pressure on the embankment forming the carriage road and upon the bridge which ran under it caused them to give way, and the angry waters, freed from their ordinary limits then commenced a course of havoc and devastation which can be traced as far as the Capesthorne Bridge on the Congleton road and even beyond this point, which is distant four or five miles from the first scene of the disaster. Washing away the carriage way and the greater portion of the brick and stone work which supported it, thereby cutting off communication with the Hall from the ordinary entrance, it swept down through the ornamental grounds, uprooting large trees, sweeping away the stone work of the artificial waterfall, and the light palisaded footbridge below it, which lies overturned amongst the trees and debris which intercepted it. The water made its way to the large pool below the Hall which lies between two high natural embankments to the right and left, extending some hundreds of yards in length and of considerable width, the surplus water being ordinarily taken off by a wide 'swallow' or circular perpendicular tunnel at the lower end of the reservoir, through which it discharged into the stream, which after several winds and turns in the comparatively narrow gorge below the pool, finds its way through the woods to the adjoining estate of T. Hibbert, Esq. of Birtles. The ordinary means of discharge being totally insufficient for the immense volume of water, suddenly let loose from the upper pools, the water swept down the gorge with irresistible force undermining the 'swallow' and partially destroying the culvert. It uprooted large trees which grew on the embankment, tossing them about in wild and picturesque confusion in the bed of the stream where perhaps a

The great damburst

score of 'the monarchs of the woods' may now be seen prostrate. This devastation was more or less continued and repeated throughout the course of the water on the Henbury estate. The fish in the pools, it is needless to say were destroyed, hundreds being left high and dry when the water had receded.

The damage to Mrs Marsland must be very great; we have heard it estimated at £5000 but can only give it as a matter of hearsay, it being manifestly difficult to arrive at an accurate computation in a case of such varied and extensive devastation. On the Birtles estate, and to the county bridges on the highway below Mrs Marsland's estate, the damage has been still more extensive. The damage in county property alone is estimated at £15,000, and that to Mr Hibbert and his tenants will amount to thousands more.

On escaping from the wood, the first damage done upon the Birtles estate was in the Pailfield Farm, occupied by Mr Rathbone, which is perhaps 500 or 600 yards from the 'swallow' above mentioned. Ordinarily there is a small trickling stream running through this field which goes to supply the Birtles mill stream, there being a small sluice in about the centre of the field to take off the waste into the brook below. Here the water spread to the width of forty or fifty yards washing down a cart bridge and gate and gate posts of which not a wrack remains. The width of the water is shown by the fact that the roots of trees are left stranded 50 yards from the level of the brook. For a time the water appears to have been held back by the strong double arched bridge under the high road, the upper part of which, bearing date 1824, was built by Mr Hibbert to carry the mill stream, and the lower part spanning the brook is the property of the county.

The upper part still stands; the lower part is an entire ruin. Before the water swept through it and cut it away however, it had spread to the height of several feet for a considerable distance below it, ploughing up the surface of the roadway between the bridge and Mill Cottage, the residence of Mr Rogers, who occupies the mill. The cottage was flooded to the depth of a foot or eighteen inches, and the water swept past the house like a torrent. The giving way of the bridge diverted the course of the water into the

Henbury

Birtles Mill Pool below. Ordinarily the stream to the right of the bridge is eight or nine feet wide; the course of the destruction which is now to be marked out shows it to have spread 50 or 60 yards.

The bulk of the stonework of the bridge was carried from 40 to 70 yards down the stream by the terrific force of the water, and trees were uprooted and tossed about like corks. A beech tree which is recognised to have grown on the right hand side of the stream now figures on the left and a willow which was on the left has taken the place of the beech on the right; such were the vagaries of the flood in its mad fury. A portion of the byewash from the mill stream shared the fate of the bridge and the stonework now lies in the bed of the stream a considerable distance below. A mass of brickwork, at least two tons in weight, is now sixty yards below the bridge of which it formed a portion, and though the parapet stones were welded together with strong iron clamps let in with lead, they were torn asunder and scattered in all directions.

Further on, one continues to overtake traces of the wreck and debris washed down by the flood. To the right of the beautifully picturesque valley in which lay the Birtles Mill Pool, stands the Corn Mill, the lower room of which was flooded to the ceiling nine feet from the floor. The lower stones were partially submerged.

At the Birtles Smithy, occupied by Hugh Henshaw, the water covered the benches and got into the forge bellows; the adjoining cottage where Henshaw resides was two feet in water. Henshaw was in Macclesfield at the time of the flood; his man finding the water rising dropped out of a window at the back, and ran to the Old Hall to give information to Mr Whitty, the estate agent. The water swept through the Mill lane and over the bottom embankment of the Mill Pool until it was five feet six inches high, as shown by the marks left on the trees. It washed away a portion of the stone wall and swept down the parapet of the township bridge over the Henbury and Birtles streams which unite at this point, and are carried by a culvert under the Mill lane into the Mill croft below.

The great damburst

The culvert stood uninjured, and it is believed that the mill pool embankment would have stood also but for the fact of a large tree growing near being partially uprooted. Even after it had burst, the water in the pool was no more than half a yard below its ordinary level.

In the mill croft below were found pieces of timber brought down from Henbury. Among the debris was a gate washed from Mr Rathbone's field, a considerable distance from Birtles bridge. The water spread in this croft forty yards on each side of the brook, and the water marks on the trees, even on comparatively elevated ground are as much as ten feet high, on one tree it is twelve feet high, the base of the tree being fully six feet above the level of the brook. The water washed down the railings of the adjoining plantation and covered the young trees with debris.

But the scene immediately below, where the carriage drive to Birtles Hall formed a temporary barrier to the course of the waters, is the most imposing evidence of the terrific force which has been exercised. Between the entrance gates to Birtles Park on the Knutsford Road to the Lodge, distant about a hundred yards, there was a strong and deep embankment, bordered on each side with grand trees. The united streams are carried beneath the embankment by a strong culvert which still stands intact; but it was impossible that it could carry off the body of water imprisoned behind the embankment, for nearly the whole width between the lodge and the gates.

Between two and three o'clock, Mrs Worthington who lives at the lodge, found on stepping out of bed that the sleeping room was covered with water. The lodge is only one storey high so that all the rooms are on the same floor. In some alarm, she awoke her husband, who rightly conjecturing, that if the lodge was flooded, the smithy which is the house nearest the bridge must be flooded still worse, set off across the park to assist his neighbour. As he did not return for some time, and the water continued to rise, his wife determined to satisfy herself that he was safe, and left her daughter, a girl of sixteen or seventeen years of age, standing at the door while she ran towards the smithy. At this time the embankment was safe. Suddenly the girl was sensible of a sort of

Henbury

tremor of the earth almost beneath her feet, then there was a slight heave, and the waters rushed through the embankment with a terrific roar, carrying everything before them.

When the poor girl could realise what had happened she found herself within three or four yards of the edge of a deep chasm. The foundations of the cottage were barely left; it is doubtful indeed whether the building has not subsided on the side nearest the opening. At one point the earth is washed away to within seven feet of the walls. The breech torn in the embankment is from 30 to 40 yards across; and it is calculated that 100,000 cubic feet of earth was thus suddenly washed down.

Gigantic trees went with it. Two fine Spanish chestnuts, which stood fifteen yards apart, at the top of the road lie close together sixty yards below: there is probably fifty five feet of timber in each. The bark stripped off one was found suspended on some willows near Lord Stanley's lodge, a good field's length below. Altogether there are nine large trees uprooted at this one spot.

It was shortly before three o'clock that the embankment gave way; it is believed however that the county bridge below, near Lord Stanley's lodge gates, and a short distance from the toll gate had blown up some time previously, as it had gone when the mail cart from Chelford to Macclesfield approached the place, which is supposed to be two o'clock.

Before getting to this bridge, the water would be confined to within a narrower and deeper course, and this with giving way of the timber bridge belonging to Lord Stanley just above the bridge underneath the turnpike road, would account for the concentrated force with which the water swept the latter away, leaving a clear course through the road which might have been hewn out by machinery.

The debris of the bridge is scattered over the field below to a distance of 250 yards; a solid block of stone weighing not less than two tons being traceable most of the distance by the indentations to the earth, where it has been turned over and over by the force of the flood. The bulk of the brick and stonework lies fifty or sixty yards from the site of the bridge in the field below, which belongs to Mr Hixon, a tenant of W.B.Davenport, Esq.

The great damburst

In the hollow between Mr Hibbert's lodge and the bridge, the water, after the embankment burst, spread upwards of a hundred yards wide. It flooded a cottage occupied by a labourer named Leigh under Lord Stanley, where a pig was washed out of the stye. The owner went to its rescue and succeeded in saving it; the instinct of self preservation was shown by the animal swimming towards him.

Below the bridge the water continued to do great damage. It swept through a portion of Mr Bostock's garden at Monks Heath Hall and carried away fruit trees and all that came in its course, and the bridge underneath the Congleton road at Capesthorne was partially destroyed, the crown of the arch being blown out, and the stonework and abutments seriously shaken.

Gangs of men are now at work in providing temporary bridges and by this time probably vehicles can pass between Macclesfield and Chelford, but months must elapse before one tithe of the damage which in a few short hours was occasioned in this district can be anything like repaired.

The *Macclesfield Courier and Herald* also reported widespread damage from the cloudburst in other areas of Cheshire.

An Act of God. Mrs Jane Marsland of Henbury Hall (widow of Major Edward Marsland) was presented with a huge bill by the County Council to meet the cost of repairs to the flood damaged roads and bridges. Four bridges had been swept away, and the Council sued Mrs Marsland for £4000. This was awarded with one reservation: could the flood be regarded as an act of God, a *vis major*? The case was settled by the Court of Exchequer in 1875, and the judgement became a classic referred to for many years as Nichols v. Marsland (1876). Although it was recognised that keeping such a large body of water in artificial lakes presented a danger against which reasonable precautions should be taken, it was considered impracticable to take all possible precautions against every eventuality, and in this case the damage should indeed be classified as a *vis major*. Mrs Marsland was freed of the

Henbury

burden of damages, but she had already sold the Hall to Thomas Brocklehurst in 1874.

Chapter 15

Henbury Parish Council.

The Council of the civil Parish of Henbury came into existence as a result of the Local Government Act 1894. Until that date in places other than boroughs, most of what we now regard as the functions of Local Government - public health, highways, the police, education, together with the relief of poverty which was the beginning of local government - were in the hands of a variety of different bodies or Committees, each of which could levy a separate rate. There had been some rationalisation before 1894 - in 1872 Rural Sanitary Districts, which were responsible for public health in rural areas, were given the same boundaries as the existing Poor Law unions of parishes. The 1894 Act, however, created a new structure. Within counties, for the areas which were not boroughs, Urban and Rural District Councils were established. Rural Districts were in turn divided into civil parishes, with newly created councils. In this way Macclesfield Rural District Council and Henbury Parish Council came into existence.

A minute[1] of the first meeting of the Parish Council reads: *"That the Township of Birtles[2] be grouped with the Township of Henbury for the purposes of the Local Government Act 1894"*. The new council was elected at a meeting of parish electors held in Henbury School for the purpose of electing Parish Councillors and Waywardens (an office which disappeared in the 1930s). Eight Councillors were elected. Mr. W.W.Brocklehurst of Henbury Hall was elected as the first Chairman. Six of the other seven members were farmers, the seventh being the owner of Davenport Heyes. One of the eight was from Birtles.

The first meeting of the new Council was on 14 December 1894. It decided to raise a precept for £12, which was

---

[1] The minutes of the Council.from May 1894 to April 1979 are contained in four minute books which are preserved in the CRO. The fifth and the current Minute books are in the possession of the Clerk to the Parish Council.

[2] See the boundary map in Chapter 2. Birtles is now in the civil parish but not in the ecclesiastical parish.

Henbury

approximately a three farthing rate. Apart from buying some stationery, its expenditure was minimal.

From then onwards the Council met once a quarter but it did practically nothing. From time to time the minutes record that there was no business to transact. During the War of 1914-18 the Council joined the Macclesfield R.D.C. War Relief Committee, and was then involved in fund-raising functions from time to time. In 1917 the Clerk was conscripted into the armed forces, and the Council agreed to his wife taking over his position until he returned. However, he resigned in 1920, and the council had some difficulty in filling the position for some years. The Council marked the end of the war by agreeing in 1919 to pay from the rates the cost to returning servicemen and children at the school of a celebration party.

In the 1930s the Council became more active. Difficulties of water supply and refuse disposal were discussed from time to time, but the most frequent subject of discussion at meetings was bus services and fares. At that time the fare from central Macclesfield to the Cock Inn was 4d., and 5d. to the Blacksmith's Arms.

Contested elections for membership of the Council had, until now, been rare. When they did take place, they were by open vote at a Parish meeting. If a sitting Councillor died or retired, the other members nominated a successor; sometimes son succeeded father. However, in 1934 there was an election at the annual Parish Meeting - 13 candidates contested 7 places. Presumably there was a contentious issue, but the minutes frustratingly do not disclose what it was.

In the 1939-45 War, as in the earlier War, the Parish Council discussed or participated in a variety of fund-raising activities for war charities. There was also a subject of direct relevance to the welfare of the inhabitants. In 1943 the R.D.C. put forward proposals for the construction after the War of council houses in Henbury - until then there were none. The Parish Council expressed its approval and discussed the siting of the houses on Church Lane. The houses were built shortly after the end of the War.

Parish Council

In 1947 Mr. Arthur Marshall was appointed Clerk to the Council, a position he occupied, to the great benefit of the Parish, until his retirement in July 1993. In the late 1940s and the 1950s the range of matters discussed by the Council gradually increased. Bus services continued to be a frequent subject of concern, but other matters which arose were street lighting, to which most members of the Council were opposed as detracting from the rural nature of the village, an electricity supply up Anderton's lane to Whirley Hall, a telephone kiosk and the extension of sewerage to the Vicarage!

In December 1956 the County Council first proposed a "Best-Kept Village" competition. The Parish Council did not support the idea, on the ground that as Henbury was so scattered it would be at disadvantage against other more compact parishes. However, in March 1960 the Council decided to enter the competition and the village has since then been a keen and sometimes successful competitor. We have won the award in our category of 400 to 1000 inhabitants six times in the years 1981, 1983, 1984, 1985, 1988 and 1993, and one year we won the overall prize of all the village categories. In 1992, the Henbury Society was asked by the Henbury Parish Council to take over the responsibility for the BKV, and since then it has entered every year.

The Transformation of Henbury. The construction of the new houses fronting onto Church Lane and Anderton's Lane, and of the estate of new houses to the north and east of these roads (see Chapter 15), was the subject of a series of applications for planning permission, which were decided by the RDC but on which the Parish Council's views were asked. The Council did not oppose any of these applications on principle, but observed that the number of houses proposed in the last and major application was too high. As a result an amended application was made for 54 houses instead of 60, and this was approved in March 1967. The new houses, of course, led to a substantial increase in population. The history of the school and its eventual closure is set out in Chapter 8. The closure was firmly, indeed vehemently, opposed

Henbury

by the Parish Council, but it was the growth in the number of pupils which led to it being deferred by a decade.

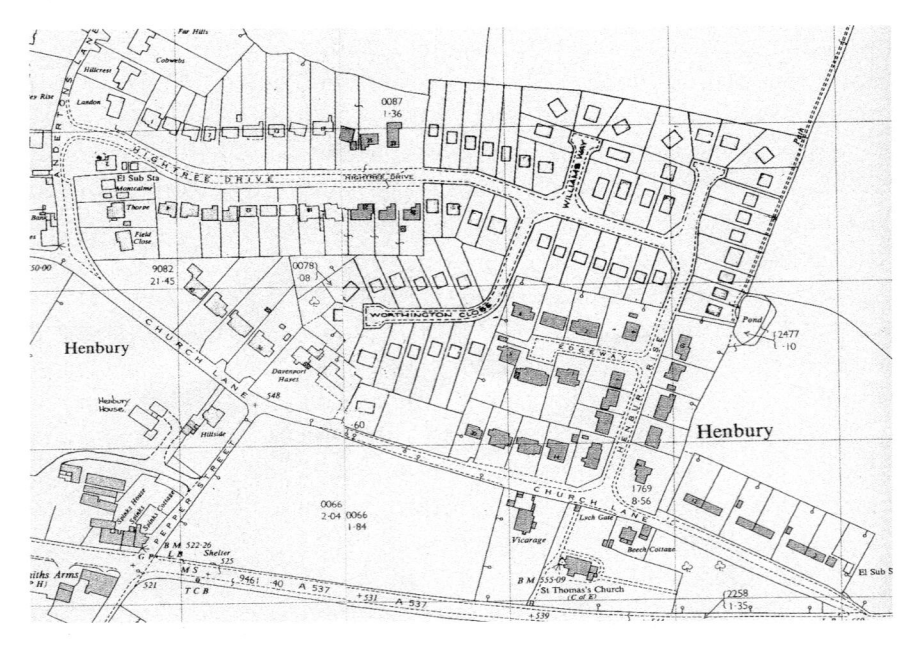

The new houses in Henbury (OS 1990)

In addition to its consideration of planning matters, the Parish Council was active in other ways. Road safety was a recurrent theme at meetings. However, the members of the Council still thought that the installation of street lighting would detract from the rural character of the village, and opposed several attempts to erect lights or install cables.

It seems that until about 1960 the names of many of the existing roads in the parish were not indicated by signs. This led to some confusion. What is now Anderton's Lane, named after a former owner of adjoining land, was so called by many people. Nevertheless in 1961 a sign was erected, presumably by the RDC, which called it Dark Lane. The Parish Council at once realised the error, but it took five years to correct. It was not until March 1966 that the two roads were given their correct names on signs.

Parish Council

From the late 1960s and into the 1970s, the Council was much concerned with, and opposed to, a proposal by (the old) Macclesfield BC for the laying out of an industrial estate between Priory Lane and Sandy Lane. There was an Inquiry in November 1970, at which Henbury and Prestbury Parish Councils joined forces in opposition. I have found no reference in the minutes to the result, but the plan must have been defeated.

Until this time there were still no women members of the Parish Council, although women gained the right to vote a half century earlier. Then, in September 1970 the first woman member, Mrs. P.Coles, joined the Council. She served until June 1972, and was then succeeded by Mrs. F.Davies, who remained a member for 14 years, until June 1986. The next woman member was Mrs. F. Gilliland, who was elected in May 1990 and served until 2002. Mrs. Ann Cousin was elected to the Council in May 1994 and in 1995 became the first woman to be Chairman. In the 1980s and 1990s Borough Councillor Mrs. Di Millett and County Councillor Mrs. Margaret Melrose also attended the Parish Council from time to time by invitation.

To return to the 1970s; in that decade the Flora Garden Centre and Pexall Service Station, two of the three enterprises which with the Blacksmith's Arms form the present commercial centre of the village, were established. Both involved a series of applications for planning permission, which were often supported but sometimes opposed by the Parish Council. Another application which was firmly opposed was for further housing on another 20 acres of land east of Anderton's Lane, for which the RDC refused permission.

On 1st April 1974 the whole structure of local government changed again. Macclesfield RDC ceased to exist, and Macclesfield District and the new Macclesfield Borough Council came into existence. We have found no reference in the Parish Council minutes to this major change taking place, which is surprising. There is an earlier reference to the Parish Councils Association expressing concern that under the new regime Parish Councils might not be consulted about planning applications, a concern which proved groundless. But after that, so far as the

Henbury

minutes are concerned, there is silence. The Parish Council must have noticed some change, if only because Peter Smith, who had been on both the Parish Council and the RDC, did not stand for the Borough Council.

In 1975 the new primary school in Whirley Road was built and in 1976 the old Henbury School was closed. The Parish Council continued to regret this decision, but found it difficult to continue to oppose the closure. The earlier opposition had succeeded in keeping the school open for a further 15 years.

In 1977 an event of less general importance, but of some significance to the Parish Council, occurred; the Council voted to allow its Clerk to spend £44.28 on a second-hand typewriter, provided he used it only for Council business! In fact he continued to write the minutes in his immaculate manuscript.

In or about 1980 Birtles Old Hall was purchased by Mr. Hudson. His arrival was followed after a short time by several activities which caused the Parish Council concern. Mr. Hudson's main enterprise was the establishment of a commercial cricket ground which he called the Birtles Bowl. Some aspects of this required, but did not always obtain, planning permission. By the mid 1980s these and other related matters led to the expression of much indignation at Council meetings. It was a far cry from the somnolence of a century earlier. Matters quietened down when in October 1989 Mr. Hudson sold Birtles Old Hall, and in September 1991 it was reported that he had left the country.

However, this was not the only controversial planning issue. In July 1989 Boddingtons Brewery, the owners of the Blacksmith's Arms, applied for permission to build a 32-bedroom extension at the rear of the public house. This was opposed not only by the Parish Council but by the newly-formed Henbury Society. Permission was refused and Boddingtons appealed. The appeal was heard over several days in October 1990, the Parish Council and the Henbury Society combining to present a case in opposition. In the end the appeal was dismissed, but the Parish Council could not rest on its laurels.

In February 1992 the Draft Macclesfield District Local Plan was published. It contained a proposal to delete from the Green Belt

Parish Council

some 54 acres of open land immediately adjoining the Henbury Parish boundary to the east and to reserve it for future development, together with a new road around the south-western side of this land, emerging onto the A537 Chelford Road opposite Church Lane, Henbury.

The story of how, in collaboration with the Henbury Society, the Parish Council successfully opposed and defeated this major threat to the village is set out in the next Chapter. Fortunately no proposal of such importance has engaged the Council since that time, but it must remain vigilant to preserve the attractions of Henbury.

Chapter 16

The Henbury Society and the Millennium Green

Local Amenity Societies often spring into existence as a response to a perceived threat, such as a planned development or the removal of a communal facility such as a school or post office. A vigorous Parish Council may be able to deal effectively with such matters, but experience in Henbury at the time of threat to the School demonstrates the value of adding an organised local, and often impassioned, voice to the formal proceedings of the Parish Council. The School Parents' Association at least ensured that the proposed closure was properly debated, and was largely responsible for the delay between the original proposal by the Cheshire Local Education Authority in 1961 and the actual closure in 1976. The Residents' Association which had only a brief existence in 1971 and 1972 was concerned with the loss of the School as a meeting place, seeking assurance that a new church hall would be available for use as a village hall. Both these societies had a limited life, each dissolving when its single issue had been resolved.

The Henbury Society was similarly formed in 1989 in response to an individual planning application, but it was realised from the start that there would be other more general and larger scale planning issues that would need to be addressed. Partly because such major planning matters never entirely disappear, but mainly because the experience of working together in a common cause brought an unprecedented sense of unity to the village, the Society flourished, expanded its activities and continued into the 21st century.

From the start the Society worked in close collaboration with the Parish Council. It also affiliated with the Civic Society, who provided a ready-made constitution.

The Society was formed on 21 November 1989 in some urgency to combat the threat of the Boddington's Brewery's plan to expand the Blacksmith's Arms into a 32 bedroom residential hotel, which was widely felt to be most unsuitable for our small

Henbury

village. A committee[1] was charged with preparing an objection to the planning application, and members appeared at a Local Inquiry. The support of the community was realised by the initial membership rapidly growing to more than 170 members by mid January 1990 out of a village population of 669[2]. The planning application was defeated. It was mooted that Boddington's Brewery would reapply with a changed plan but this did not occur. Encouraged by this success, the Society expanded its interests to wider and longer term planning issues. The development of Henbury, as part of Macclesfield Borough, was decided by a long process of consultation which produced a Structure Plan relating to Cheshire, followed by a Macclesfield Local Plan. These plans provided, inter alia, for new houses, responding to the demands of house builders as interpreted by the County and Local Planning Departments. During the evolution of the plans, a new proposal appeared which would designate a large tract of Green Belt land between Henbury and Macclesfield as suitable for building. The Society places great value on the preservation of the Green Belt, which provides a vital buffer between the village and Macclesfield town, and contesting the proposal became the primary activity of the Society.

The Macclesfield Local Plan, as presented in 1994, included a proposal to build a new road from Lyme Green in the south of Macclesfield to the Chelford Road (A537) near Church Lane. This would enclose Green Belt land on the south and west of Macclesfield, on which building would be allowed. As seen by the Society, this proposal would destroy the independent and distinctive character of Henbury, and substantially increase the traffic on the already overburdened A537 road, much of which would decant on to the minor road through the village, used as a short cut to Alderley. The Society noted that a Government Strategic Plan for the region stated that any development should be in the most part to the south side of Macclesfield, not the west, and

---

[1] The founder members were Sir Francis Graham-Smith (President), John Mead (Chairman), John Bruce (Secretary), Brian Barrowclough. (Treasurer,) and Ted Hefford.
[2] From the 1991 census.

The Henbury Society

found good grounds for objecting to the proposal at the Public Inquiry which followed in May 1995.

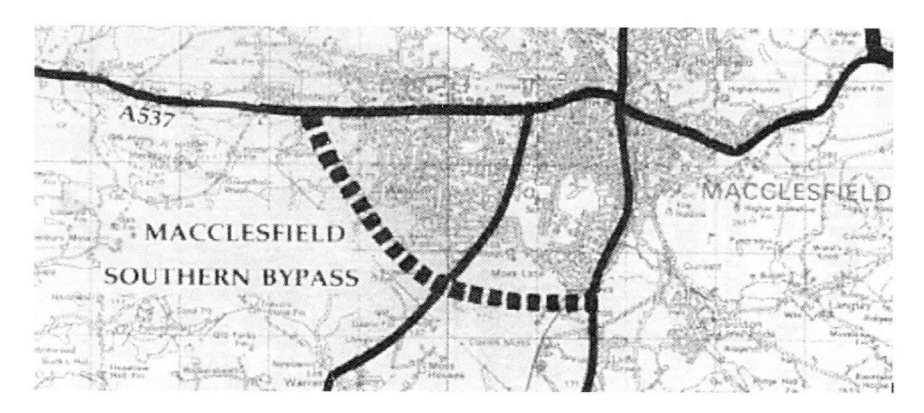

The Proposed Bypass. Macclesfield Borough Council Local Plan 1993

The Parish Council and the Henbury Society submitted their objections to the Inquiry jointly[3]. This was a very detailed presentation, including an analysis of population and housing, traffic and transportation, and the impact on the Henbury community. It also included a new assessment of Cock Wood, which would have been affected by the proposed road; it turned out, to the embarrassment of the local planners, that the wood was a Grade B Site of Biological Importance. At the Inquiry members of the local community found themselves well prepared for the unusual position of amateurs facing a professional Advocate for the local Council.

By this time the Society had learned a great deal in the processes of Local Planning, and had learned the value of presenting a collective view in collaboration with the Parish Council. Planning is a continuous process, and the members of the Society were determined to continue their vigilance into future cycles of planning. Meanwhile the Society had acquired a life independent of the planning controversies, and was enjoying occasional social activities including an annual hot-pot supper and

---

[3] The representations were collected in a substantial volume, with appendices. A copy is in the Henbury Society archives.

Henbury

responsibility for entering Henbury for the county-wide Best Kept Village competition in every year since 1992.

The present History has been compiled by the Henbury Society, and is dedicated to the memory of John Mead, a founder member (d. 21 October 2001) who worked tirelessly for the Society and the village.

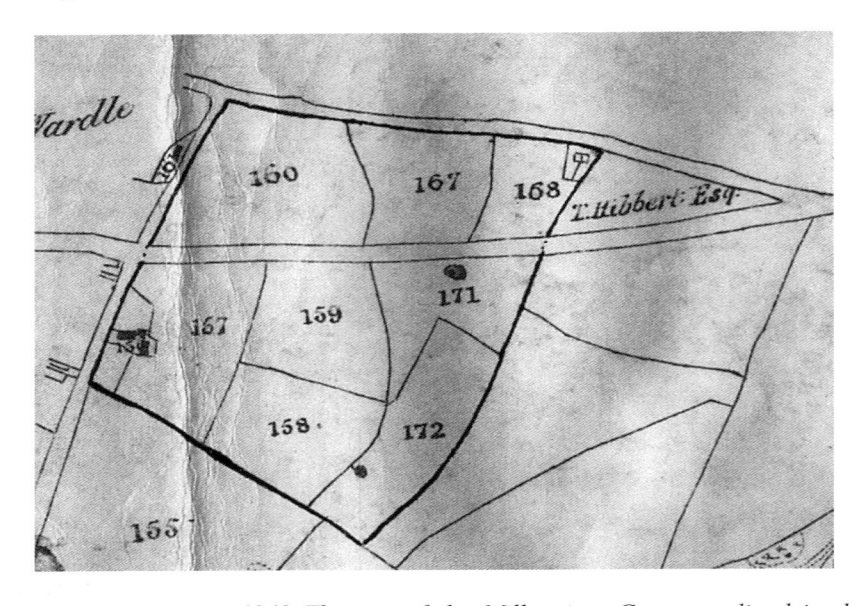

Hulme's Tenement, 1842 *The site of the Millennium Green, outlined in the Conveyance of 1842. The farm was divided by the new road, now the A537. Pepper Street Field (160) and Old Meadow (167) became the Millenium Green; St. Thomas's Church and the Vicarage were built on Little Field (168). The farm buildings were used for the School. 158 and 159 were named Corwood Field, 172 was Cow Meadow (conveyance 1842 from Ryle to Marsland, CRO)*

Henbury Millennium Green. The year 2000 was celebrated as Millennium Year, despite some pedantic claims that 2001 was more correctly two complete millennia after the year 1 AD. A Millennium Commission was set up, funded by the National Lottery, to promote a wide variety of schemes. Among these the Millennium Greens proved to be an outstanding success. The scheme, administered by the Countryside Commission, led to the establishment of some 500 Greens by the end of the Millennium

Year. The Greens were to be open spaces, to be enjoyed by everyone for recreation and play; their best description was "breathing spaces for all, as well as being a place of recreation for young and old throughout the year".

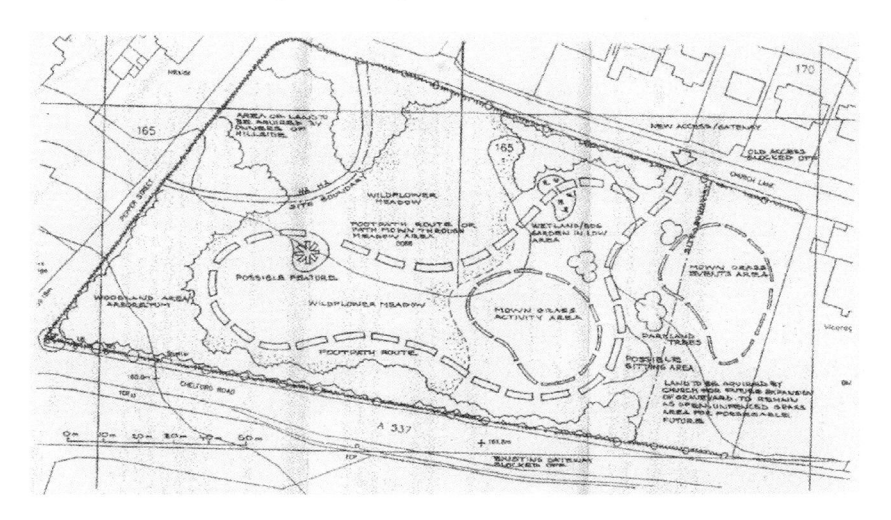

The original plan for the Millennium Green

Henbury Parish Council was one of the first to apply for a preliminary grant for planning such a Green, and the local community gave enthusiastic support. A suitable parcel of land, part of the Henbury Estate, was available for purchase, and Sue Griffiths was appointed as landscape architect to prepare a detailed scheme. Following long established precedent (as for the School in 1845!), half the cost was to be raised locally, and the Chairman of the Parish Council (Ann Cousin) energetically pursued grants, principally from Macclesfield Borough Council, 3C Waste, and Manchester Airport. Donations from local individuals provided a substantial capital fund, whose interest would support maintenance costs. The Countryside Commission agreed and funded the scheme in March 1999. The purchase was made and work began immediately in the same month. The total purchase and establishment cost was estimated to be £55,000, although the final figure did not exceed £47,000. The Green is administered by a

Henbury

Henbury Millennium Green Trust and the land is vested in the Official Custodian for Charities. Of the five Trustees[4], one each is nominated by the Parish Council, the Parochial Church Council, and the Henbury Society.

Part of the field, adjacent to the Vicarage, was purchased by St Thomas's Church. There is no obvious defining boundary, and the whole area is managed as one, but the Church may eventually take over its part as an extension of the churchyard. Most of the total area of over a hectare is mown grass, but part is set aside as a wild flower meadow, depleted of nutrient by removal of topsoil and mown only occasionally. Along the boundaries there are substantial plantations of trees and shrubs, more than 1250 of which were planted in a single session by an enthusiastic team of local residents. The hedges were repaired using traditional mixes of hawthorn, blackthorn and rose, leaving some sections with the existing sycamore; although Church Lane is an old road (see Chapter 10), there seems not to have been any evidence of an ancient well-stocked hedge.

Native trees, such as oak, hornbeam, ash, willow, birch, yew, and holly, were used in the plantations, supplemented by larch to provide early shelter and to encourage upward growth. Some black poplars, raised from local stock, were provided by Cheshire Wildlife. Shrubby thickets used gorse and guelder rose to create a shelter for wildlife. A small group of apple trees, all of which are varieties known to have originated in Cheshire, were provided by the Cheshire Landscape Trust. A boggy area was planted with suitable wet-loving plants, and allowed to develop with minimal attention.

---

[4] The original five Trustees were Roger Cousin, Francis Graham-Smith, John Loring, David Plews and Joanna Robinson.

The Henbury Society

The Henbury Millennium Sundial (courtesy F Graham-Smith)

The Sundial. All Millennium Greens must have a central feature. The Henbury Green has a sundial, whose gnomon is a one-tonne piece of sandstone from Sycamore Quarry at Kerridge. The hours are marked by stones on a circle with a 3 metre radius. Setting up the dial, with a plate engraved to show the relation between sundial time and Greenwich Mean Time, was entrusted to a former Astronomer Royal, Sir Francis Graham-Smith.

The Millennium was duly celebrated on the Green with a torchlight procession on New Year's Eve 1999/2000, an event which received publicity in the BBC news and in the Independent newspaper.

The Green was formally opened by Councillor Caroline Andrew during a week of celebrations in June 2000. The Green is used for traditional annual events such as the Rose Queen festival and Bonfire Night.

Chapter 17

People, places and happenings

The most rewarding task in researching the history of Henbury was to interview many local people whose memories stretched back over the last half century and further back into World War II. The War Memorial in the churchyard records Wilfrith Elstob, a recipient of the Victoria Cross from the 1914-1918 war. His story gives some idea of the contrast between these two wars; both were terrible, but it was the First that had the most impact on Henbury families.

Some individual memories. Many of the people we interviewed had attended Henbury Parish School, and with only one exception regarded their time there as a happy experience. School dinners usually earn a poor reputation; not so at Henbury. Mrs Wardle, the school cook produced meals recalled with pleasure. During wartime in a rural district, rations were sometimes supplemented by local farms, and cooking for small numbers made it easier to provide attractive meals.

One farm ran a flourishing black market in beef. From time to time, the local police felt obliged to respond to what appears to have been a widespread countryside practice, and a raid on this particular farm was planned to recover the buried carcasses of any cattle illegally slaughtered. The daughter of a local policeman (*not* from Henbury) just happened to call at the farm the day before the raid was to take place.

When the police arrived clad in gumboots, the farmer kept insisting that they would *not* find any bones in the midden, a place favoured for the disposal of carcasses, so they began the odiferous task of excavating it from one end to the other. Nothing was found of course, as the bones had been buried elsewhere in one of the meadows.

This illustrates one aspect of country life, a tendency towards equilibrium. The cast in this minor drama had all derived some satisfaction from it: the farmer was not rumbled, the police had a day out in the countryside, nourished by tea and cake from the

Henbury

farmer's wife, and one policeman enjoyed a juicy steak cooked for him by his daughter. In the continuing countryside poacher-gamekeeper manoeuvres, the unforgivable sin was to be found out.

Henbury seems to have been a fairly law-abiding place, apart from incidents originating from one of the two pubs, the Cock and the Blacksmith Arms. During World War II, the local PC, who was the father of the famous emissary of the Archbishop of Canterbury, Terry Waite, lived on Putty Row, and later on the opposite side of Chelford Road, before he was transferred to Styal. Tom Gould reported finding a man loading sacks of his potatoes into a van, before speeding off. He managed to note the number plate. He was later visited by the police asking "Are you the owner of these potatoes Sir ?"

After the mental hospital 'open door' policy in the 1950s, Tom occasionally found patients from Parkside Hospital wandering aimlessly about, but they rarely caused any anxiety. One patient however insisted on entering the farmhouse, but they managed to steer him away from the room in which they kept the telephone, warning him that a fierce dog was kept there. Staff eventually arrived to remove him, and told Jean that he was a 'sex maniac'. She wondered why they took over an hour to get there.

Early in the twentieth century when cars were a rarity, Elsie Knight's grandfather Henry, told her he cycled in great excitement from the smithy up School Lane to the main road to watch the expected arrival of just 6 motor cars. Farmers were able to drive their cattle in complete safety along the lanes to Chelford market, and drovers too made an occasional appearance.

In more recent times, until 1992, George Dooley used to cross a herd of cows over the main road from Broken Cross from Ivydale Farm near the Cock Inn, often assisted by neighbours. Mr Barber used to help by waving a piece of red felt attached to a stick to stop the traffic. It is hard to imagine that this would still be safe or even possible today, given the speed and volume of traffic.

Squirrels: A Big Mistake. 1876 was the year of the first authenticated introduction and release into the wild in this country of the American grey squirrel. To our shame this event occurred in

Estate map 1874 showing enclosures around High Trees, (courtesy Henbury Hall Estate, photo PG Wells)

The Millennium Green, Millennium celebrations, June 2000 (F Graham-Smith)

Lodge Farm 2000 (Mr & Mrs T Hargreaves)

Ernest Kennerley plucking game with his dog "Kennerley" (courtesy Bill Geldart)

Cheshire Hunt meet at Henbury Hall (F Graham-Smith)

Henbury Hall from the west (PG Wells)

Driving in the Park (courtesy W. Geldart)

Henbury Hall, Queen Victoria's Diamond Jubilee, 1897 (courtesy Henbury Hall Estate)

Base of old mill, Henbury Hall (F Graham-Smith)

Henbury Hall Engine Pool with base of old mill (F Graham-Smith)

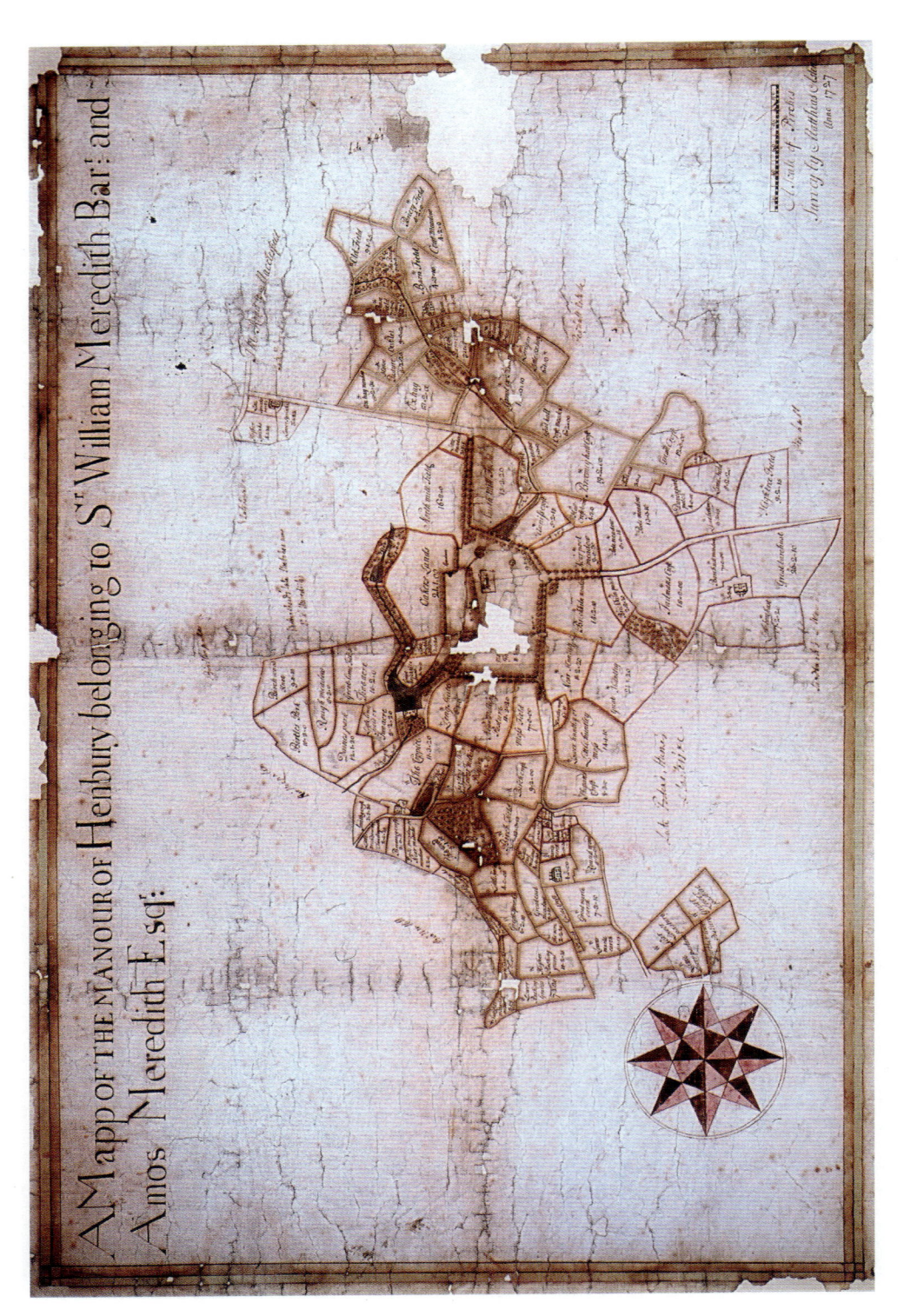

Matthias Aston's Henbury Estate Map of 1727, restored by Cheshire Record Office

People and happenings

Henbury with the release of four animals. Over the next fifty years many more releases in all parts of the country and breeding on some estates, notably Woburn, led to the situation we have today. Whether the Henbury incident was, to use the wrong word, successful, we do not know, but who were the culprits and why did they do it?

The finger must point to the residents of the Hall, the Brocklehursts, newly arrived in Henbury in 1874, the animals introduced probably for the sport on the estate, shooting. In other parts of the world the grey squirrel had for long been a game animal. In this country the red squirrel had been widely hunted throughout the nineteenth century, on account of the damage it caused to gardens, orchards, woods and forests, and because in certain regions it was very abundant. Was it possible that in Henbury few were left and the shooting was poor? Whatever the case, Henbury now has its share of grey squirrels and no red squirrels.

There just may be a brighter side to this story. It is possible the squirrels in your garden that you either feed or shoot are descendants of the original animals, therefore aristocrats of squirrel society, or do you consider them as villains, relatives of the infamous Henbury Four?

Wartime: The Doodlebug. At 6am on Christmas Eve in 1944 the family of Broomfield Farm were gathered in the orchard as a short time ago the siren at Broken Cross had sounded; an air raid was imminent. A plane's engine was heard, then silence as its engine cut out. The farmer told all to get down and seconds later at five past six there was a very loud explosion. It was a flying bomb, VI or doodlebug.

The target was not, of course, Henbury, but Manchester. The Germans were not then able to launch from the ground near enough to the target so used airborne launches, and this was the first raid of its type. Forty five V1s were launched from KG53

Henbury

Heinkels from over the North Sea east of the Humber estuary[1], and thirty one crossed the coast. Six fell in Cheshire. Only half of the Vls fell within 20 miles of the target, and of those that didn't, one fell near Macclesfield Forest, one at Seven Sisters Lane, Ollerton, and the Henbury one in a field at the edge of Bluebell Wood, 500yds from Henbury Hall. Some believed the target to have been the aircraft factory at Woodford, but considering that less than half the bombs launched hit within 20 miles of the centre of Manchester such a hit would have been fortuitous and very unfortunate.

Only minor casualties resulted from these explosions and the Henbury damage was limited to some broken windows in the Hall. More damage may have been prevented by the shelter of the trees in the wood, indeed it is said that the damage to some trees can still be seen.

V1 P.O.W. post

The finder is requested to cut out or copy the letters printed here and to transmit them to the addresses so that they receive them as early as possible. The original letters are being sent through the Red Cross in the usual mail channel.

A leaflet delivered to Henbury by the V1.

Later Joyce Bostock, the daughter of the farm, collected part of the doodlebug nose cone she had picked up at the site of the explosion, with a few fragments of the pamphlets and magazines scattered around which the police had missed. Some of the pamphlets contained supposed letters from allied prisoners in Germany. The German hope was that their relatives would write

---

[1] Peter J.C.Smith. *Flying Bombs over the Pennines*. Privately published, 1988 ISBN 852160292: *Cheshire Life*, December 1984, pp. 40-41,44-45.

People and happenings

to the prisoners revealing useful information to the enemy, where the pamphlet had been found, thus where the bomb had landed. One of these leaflets remains still in Henbury. A few fragments of shrapnel have since been found. One prized souvenir rests on a Henbury mantleshelf, the small aluminium nosecone of the bomb.

The all-clear sounded just after six-thirty, milking could now begin, and the preparations for Christmas continue.

The Bluebell Wood doodlebug is still talked about. Ethel Heathcote of Lodge Farm told us *"it was about half past six on a frosty morning. Whenever the alert went I never used to settle, and they said I'd never die in bed! I got up. There was this bang and dust began to fall down from cracks in the wooden beams. I shot downstairs in my nightie, even though it was frosty, and all I could see was a cloud of smoke beyond the smithy - it wasn't far as the crow flies - and I later moved all the beds from under the beams."*

Walter Hatton of Home Farm reported *"before we went milking, drinking our tea with the door open my father saw something go past. It landed in Bluebell Wood and cracked a few windows"*. The front door of the house on the estate called the Cave was blown up the stairs. Geoffrey Sparrow thought that the explosion lifted the roof of the earlier Henbury Hall, which then neatly fell back into place.

An Oxford two-engined trainer had to make a forced landing during the war in the fields north of Church Lane. The pilot scrambled out unhurt, but had to go to a nearby house to borrow tools to dismantle the plane's armament before returning to base.

Harry Barlow told us that he was cycling from Monks Heath to Henbury and he had just passed Pale Farm when a plane crashed into the hillside near Highlees Farm. This was a Lancaster; the pilot was a local man, Sid Gleave, a test pilot from Woodford. He was killed in the crash. His family used to run a garage in Macclesfield, and Sid used to ride in the Isle of man TT races.

Joan Foschtinsky recounted that a bomb fell on the farmyard at Acton Farm whilst the family were in the kitchen. The room was demolished, killing Mr and Mrs Worth and Mr Worth's brother Israel who was waiting at the back door to collect some milk. The rest of the family escaped. A rescue party, including Jos (Joan's

Henbury

father) were rushed to the scene to help. The farm was rebuilt, and still stands today. Joan recalls visiting the ack ack (anti aircraft) battery on Whirley Lane.

The Plague Stones. One of several persistent stories for which we have found no documentary evidence is based on some large boulders at a gateway to the Henbury Estate , just beyond the Bag Brook culvert. One of these is supposed to have marked the boundary of an infected area, where food and other essentials were left. Money was left, traditionally in a hollow filled with vinegar as a disinfectant. This example of quarantine was supposed to have been organised by Randle Davenport, who was made responsible for controlling the plague in the Macclesfield area in 1602, along with Sir Thomas Stanley and Sir Urian Legh of Adlington. The stones may merely have been markers to the entrance, but we would be glad to hear of any further information.

Life in World War I. Among the names on the war memorial in Henbury churchyard is a Henbury man who was awarded the Victoria Cross in the First World War. This is a time which is moving out of living memory, and we determined to try and find out more about him and what life in the parish must have been like at that time.

The churchyard war memorial records the names of seventeen men of Henbury and Broken Cross who gave their lives in the First World War: significantly there are just four names for World War II which lasted two years longer. Others unnamed now would have returned to the parish, perhaps some to die of their injuries and others to try to forget their experiences. Very little is actually mentioned in the official Parish records of the events of these four years but there can be no doubt that the First World War cast a terrible shadow of grief and anxiety over everyday life. While the pattern of life in the village revolved round the farming year, and Church festivals and the school would have given a sense of purpose and continuity, there must have been much unease, a nervous anticipation of news and a growing feeling that things

People and happenings

would never be the same again. Every family would have been affected in one way or another.

In the beginning many men volunteered eagerly, full of heroic ideals and patriotic enthusiasm but before long the reality of war in the trenches and the appalling losses gave way to a sense of futility and pointless sacrifice. Much of this reality was kept from the civilian population. News and soldiers' letters home were censored: "Look on the bright side" was the order of the day. As a result the civilian population though anxious to help were far less actively involved in this war than they were in the later one.

Edwardian Bible Class (courtesy Elsie Knight)

At home life became more regulated as the government, in their efforts to win the war, strove to take hold of the nation's resources. Henbury farmers, rather sceptically no doubt, would have been aware of the efforts of the "WarAg." to organise food supplies later on and the men who had left to serve in the war would have been replaced by women on the land. Farmers' wives and daughters would have had to "turn to" more than ever in the fields and barns, supported later by the Womens Land Army. The fine gardens at

Henbury

Henbury Hall and Capesthorne would have run down for lack of gardening staff and increasing taxation meant that the lavish life style of the rich in pre-war days was gone for ever. Everyone high and low was affected by rationing. Restrictions in sugar and butchers' meat were felt even in country districts. Income tax increased from one shilling and two pence at the highest rate in 1914 to five shillings in the pound as the standard rate in 1918.

Mrs Elsie Knight who was brought up at Henbury Forge, the younger daughter of the Henbury blacksmith, has lent us a lovely photograph of some young men of the parish in Edwardian dress. We think they are a bible class or confirmation class as several such are mentioned in the pre-war Church magazines (which she also kindly lent us) but we do not know their names and Elsie is not sure now which of the lads was her grandfather. Could some of these young men have been caught up in the war? Perhaps these are some of the faces that go with the war memorial names.

The Henbury V.C. One of the names on the war memorial is that of Wilfrith Elstob V.C., D.S.O., M.C., and we know a great deal about this outstanding man thanks to the researches of Captain Robert Bonner, the historian of the Manchester Regiment, who has kindly allowed us to base the following on the information contained in his biography, "Wilfrith Elstob V.C., D.S.O., M.C." published by Fleur de Lys Publishing Knutsford Cheshire 1998.

Wilfrith Elstob was born on 8th September 1888 in Chichester, Sussex, where his father John was a priest-vicar of the Cathedral. Six weeks later the family moved to Cheshire for John to take up his appointment as vicar of Capesthorne-with-Siddington. The fine old vicarage down by Redesmere where they lived, is in fact situated in the Henbury part of the Capesthorne estate, in Henbury Parish, and this is probably the reason for Wilfrith's inclusion on the Henbury memorial. Wilfrith was educated at the Ryleys School in Alderley Edge, where he found a life long friend in Hubert Worthington, and then at Christ's Hospital in London. In 1905 he went up to Manchester University, gaining his B.A. in 1909 and his teaching diploma in 1910. After two years further

People and happenings

study in France he became senior French master at a prep school in Edinburgh.

A tall and powerful man, he combined great physical strength with seriousness of purpose. He observed to a friend how much he loved his chosen profession of schoolmaster with its immense potential for serving others and the opportunity to use his ability to inspire youth with the desire for higher achievements.

Following the outbreak of war in August 1914 Elstob enlisted on 11 September in the Public Schools Battalion. However, just before setting off to commence training at Epsom, he was offered and accepted a commission in the newly formed 1st Manchester Pals Battalion (later 16th Battalion the Manchester Regiment), second in command to Hubert Worthington. The 16th Battalion was the first of nine Pals Battalions raised to the Manchesters. In Pals battalions in the early days friends and work associates were often placed in the same platoons; later on this idea was dropped as losses could devastate whole communities at a stroke with terrible effects on civilian morale.

Lt Col Wilfrith Elstob

"A GLORIOUS DEATH IS HIS WHO FOR HIS COUNTRY FALLS"

Henbury

Training was in Heaton Park initially and on 31 March 1915 Elstob with the rest of the Pals, 12,000 men in all, paraded through Albert Square, Lord Kitchener taking the salute. Further training at Grantham and Salisbury Plain followed and on 17 November 1915 they arrived in France. Nothing could have prepared them for what lay ahead.

In the spring of 1916, the 16th were engaged in dangerous and unpleasant duties in the trenches; in July they were involved in the great attack on the Somme. During fighting in and around the village of Montauban on 1 July, Elstob was slightly wounded. Other officers of the 16th were not so lucky. Captain Walker lost both his eyes, Captain Johnson was killed. Lieutenant Allen was killed whilst trying to rescue Lieutenant Kerry who subsequently died of his wounds. Hubert Worthington was severely wounded and invalided out of the war.

For his leadership at Montauban Captain Elstob was later awarded the Military Cross. Eight days later, on 9 July, the battalion took part in operations around Trones Wood. Elstob was wounded again and the 16th lost 3 officers and 15 other ranks killed, 85 wounded and 85 missing. On 10 July Elstob was appointed Second in Command of the battalion. In the battle for Guillement on 30 July losses were even worse. Officers at this period wore a distinctive uniform and were an obvious target for enemy marksmen: ordinary soldiers were expected to survive around six weeks on average. In October when the Commanding Officer was killed by a shell, Major Elstob took over command of the battalion and was later appointed acting Lieutenant Colonel.

November and December 1916 passed relatively quietly for the 16th with a routine of 5 days in the trenches and 5 days in support or reserve. The early spring of 1917 saw the battalion assisting in railway construction near Arras. The battle of Arras began in atrocious weather on 9 April.

In a letter dated 15th April to his friend Hubert Worthington, Elstob wrote "It is impossible to realise what Destruction means until one has seen the country laid waste by the Boche in his retreat. Every village is blown to bits; every cross roads blown up;

People and happenings

every bridge ditto - there is absolutely nothing except wreckage and desolation."

During this assault Elstob carried out on his own initiative a most dangerous personal reconnaissance. His report, which still exists, describes the deadly and desperate situation - at the close of the action at the end of April, the 16th numbered less than 100 in all ranks.

In a letter to Hubert Worthington dated 6th May 1917: *"Hu, I hardly dare mention the losses, for my heart is full and I know how you will feel. On the battle field as one moved about amongst shells and bullets - Death seemed a very small thing and at times enviable. Here we are English and German - we, or rather those damned Journalists talk about Hate - it seems to me to disappear on the battlefield. People who have not been there talk a lot of damned nonsense. We are all 'blind' as a private soldier on the night after the battle said to me - 'We know it is not their quarrel sir', this spontaneously."*

For his leadership at Ypres in July 1917, Elstob was awarded the D.S.O. During the period between August and December 1917 Elstob temporarily commanded the 90th Brigade. In January 1918 he was on U.K. leave - briefly - for in February he captained a divisional football team against a French eleven in Paris!

In March 1918 he was in action again. The 90th Brigade were sent to the front line at St. Quentin. It was known that a great attack was imminent and they were one of the battalions which would bear the brunt. Their position was Manchester Hill, a small rise which had been captured by the 2nd Manchesters in 1917. Elstob warned his men that they must be ready for a bombardment which might last for several days, they must hold up the enemy advance and not cause other troops to be sacrificed in regaining a lost position. "There is only one degree of resistance, and that is to the last round and the last man. This is the Battalion HQ. Here we fight and here we die."

The morning of the attack, 21 March brought dense fog. This spelt disaster for the men on Manchester Hill for now the enemy could advance unseen. By 11.30 when the fog lifted the German breakthrough was complete and the little garrison faced

Henbury

overwhelming odds against crack German troops. Elstob rallied his men in spite of being wounded himself three times, repulsed an enemy bombing raid single handed and made sorties under severe fire several times to replenish ammunition, but soon the Germans were in the Redoubt and heavy hand to hand fighting decimated the defenders.

By 3.30 there were very few of them alive. One survivor recalled Elstob's last words to him, "Tell the men not to lose heart. Fight on!" He still held on firing from some twenty five to thirty yards up the trench. When the enemy called him to surrender he replied "Never" and was shot dead. He maintained to the end the duty which he impressed on his men, namely, "Here we fight and here we die."

At the end of the war Hubert Worthington went to France to try to find his friend's body, sadly without success, but he determined to ensure that his friend received full recognition for his bravery. He undertook to produce the evidence, collating statements from the survivors of Manchester Hill (2 officers and 15 other ranks) and successfully submitted the case for the award of the V.C.

Wilfrith Elstob's bravery and sacrifice are recalled in memorials in France, Macclesfield, Manchester, Edinburgh, Alderley Edge; in Siddington Church where a fine stained glass window in his memory is to be found, as well as Henbury where perhaps after all his connection was only accidental. We will probably know very little detail of the actions, feelings and experiences of most of the individual men involved in the Great War. Many survivors found it hard to speak of it at all. So perhaps the story of Elstob's courage, fortitude and patriotism as well as his sense of mutual humanity and the grief, pain and pride of his family and friends will serve as an illustration and a memorial to them all[2].

---

[2] The North Cheshire Family History Society has a CD ROM of all the soldiers who died in the Great War 1914-18. A search can be made using name and rank. The information available is birth place: where enlisted; place of residence; number; rank; place, date and cause of death. Roger Cresswell and Peter Wells could provide further details of the Society.

Chapter 18

The population of Henbury: People and Movement

Within the lifetime of many local people, Henbury has changed dramatically from a predominantly rural farming community to a residential area mainly for professional and retired people. Henbury is not alone in seeing such rapid change, but we need to understand what has happened in some detail if we are to take any part in planning the future development of the village. The general picture is of a farming community stable over many centuries, which has shrunk in only half a century by a factor of five, while the total population has more than doubled.

Statistics can make a dull read, particularly if they merely confirm what we already suspect is the case. Occasionally however, they can spring surprises, or interesting trends that invite explanation or further research. Henbury is no exception; its census figures make an interesting study, although the figures sometimes defy a simple explanation.

The censuses cover the population within Henbury township, of which the boundary is largely coterminous with the parish one, except that the latter includes a part of Broken Cross and Whirley, whereas the former northern boundary runs along High Lees Wood, and includes territory on either side of Whirley Lane.

Between 1851 (total population 464) and 1911 (360) there is a decline of 20.4%, whereas previously there had been a slow rise from 1811 (385), the earliest date for which figures for Henbury are available. In 1911 approximately 60% of the population lived south of the Knutsford Road, now the A537.

From 1911, despite the intervening 1914-18 war there followed a gradual increase in the population of the Parish until 1951, when it reached 400. In that period there was very little house-building in Henbury. The only exception of note was that eleven houses were built between the two World Wars on the north side of the A537 at Cock Bank, east of Church lane. We believe that Whirley Rise, on Anderton's lane, was also built at that time. That apart, no other new houses were constructed in the Parish before the end

Henbury

of the War of 1939-45. Thus, apart from Whirley Rise, at that time all the houses on Church Lane, Anderton's Lane and Dark Lane, and south of the A537 had been built before the end of the 19th century.

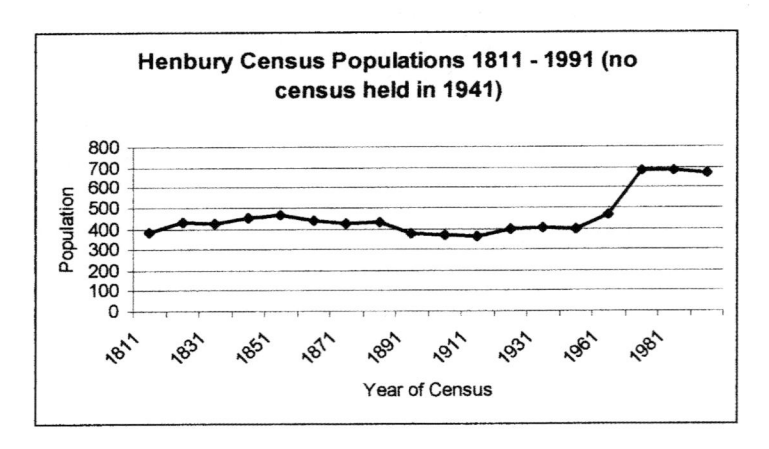

Henbury Census Populations 1811 - 1991 (no census held in 1941)

Shortly after the end of the Second War, from the early 1950s there was a dramatic change. First, the Council houses on the north side of Church Lane, which had been proposed in 1943, were constructed by the RDC. Then individual houses were built on the north side of Church Lane and on the southern part of Anderton's Lane. By 1960 Mr. Bullock, a building contractor, had laid out the southern end of a road leading north from Church lane, with houses on either side. In 1961 this was named Henbury Rise. At about the same time another builder constructed the first part of a road and houses which became Hightree Drive. For a time these separate developments proceeded in stages, but in March 1967 permission was given for the building of a further 54 houses on a layout which linked the two partly built new roads and added the closes off them. Thus much of Henbury as we now know it came into being. As a result there was a large increase in population. From 400 in 1951, it grew to 686 in 1971, an increase of over 70%, and has since remained fairly steady. The substantial majority of the residents now live north of the A537.

What caused the steady decline between 1851 and 1911? The census figures for the age range 0 to 4 may provide a clue. In

Population

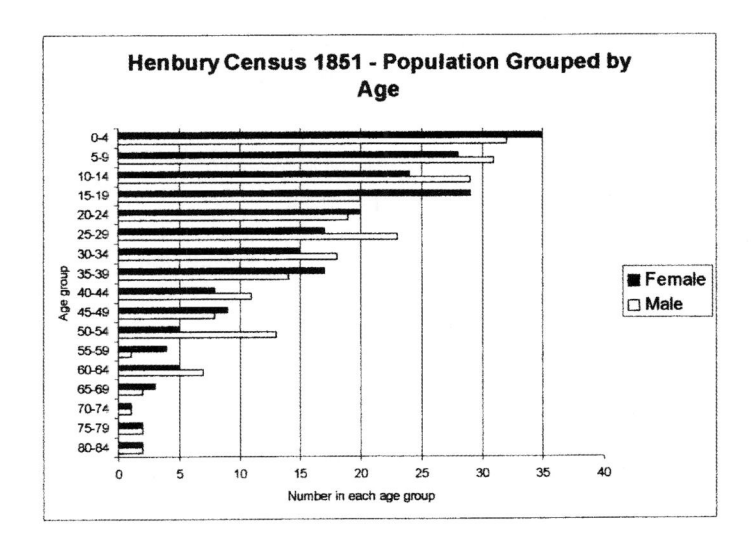

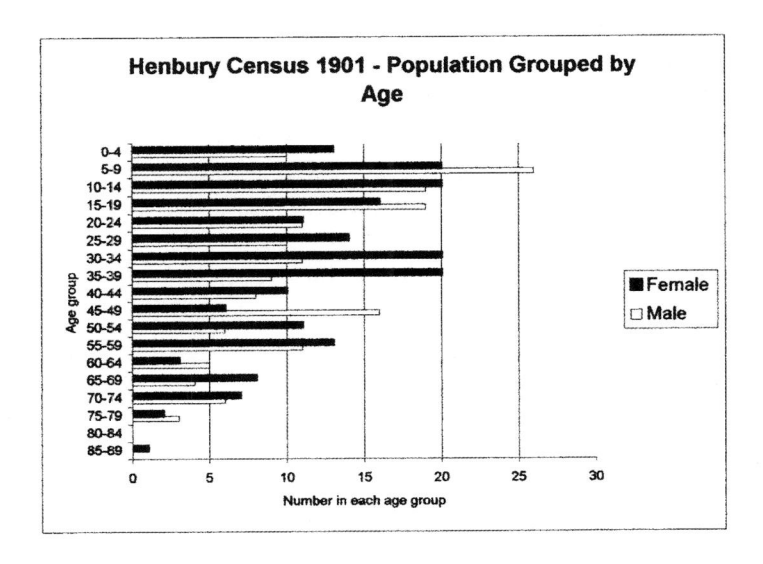

Henbury Census 1851 - Population Grouped by Age

Henbury Census 1901 - Population Grouped by Age

1841, males and females aged 0 to 4 comprised 15.2% of the Henbury population, in 1851 15%, 1861 10.5%, 1881 12.1%, 1891 11.7%, falling in 1901 (6.2%) and 1991 (3.3%). The figures at the turn of the 19th century may reflect a declining birth rate. During

Henbury

the 19th century, there was a tendency to have large families to compensate for the high infant mortality rate and mortality rates during childhood. In 1842 for example, 350 out of every 1000 births died before the age of one year. As chances of survival increased with improved Public Health measures, the need to produce large families diminished. Nevertheless, this cause does not fully explain the fall in Henbury population by a fifth from 1851 until 1911. One plausible explanation may be the opportunities for employment offered in Macclesfield, where late in the 19 century there existed as many as 120 silk mills, requiring a large labour force. Many employees would migrate into town from rural areas, particularly at times of poor harvests, where they were likely to meet partners and marry, and perhaps settle in town rather than in Henbury.

What evidence is there of such a migration? Comparison of figures for Henbury in the 1851 and 1901 censuses show little difference in numbers born in Cheshire as a whole: 84% in 1851 and 77.7% in 1901. There is a considerable difference however in the numbers actually born in Henbury at the times of the two censuses: 41.8% of the Henbury population had been born in Henbury at the time of the 1851 census, but this figure had fallen to 20.6% by 1901. 10.8% of the 1851 population were born in another county, but 20.4%, nearly twice as many, were born in another county in 1901. This suggests a growing mobility of people during the intervening 50 years.

Evidence for a mass migration of Henbury people seeking employment in Macclesfield might be confirmed by examination of the relevant Macclesfield censuses for the numbers of persons born in Henbury. As might be expected, one of the greatest changes is shown by a comparison of occupations listed in the 1851, 1901 and 1991 censuses.

Occupation	1851	1901	1991
Farming and Estate Workers	52	87	20
Skilled and Manual	135	74	50
Professional & Management	6	7	280

Population

Broadly grouped into farming and estate, skilled and manual, and professional and management classes, it is clear that the almost complete loss of the farming community has been more than replaced by those working in a professional or management capacity. A large number of houses were built north of Church Lane after the war to accommodate this new influx.

A further change is indicated by the number of scholars listed in the 1851 and 1891 censuses. 18 scholars listed in 1851 had quadrupled by 1891 (81), the figures affected by the opening of Henbury Parish School in 1846. The Education Act in 1876 made elementary education available to all children, and in 1880 attendance at school became compulsory between the ages of five and ten[1].

Our survey of farms in the district confirms that the patterns in agriculture are rapidly changing, and mirror what is occurring nationally. Of the farms on the Henbury Estate, only two, Sandbach and Broomfield, survive, both now in private ownership. At least 5 farmhousess have been sold in recent times, and are now occupied as private residences, not as farms (Pexhill, Brick Bank, Park House, Bearhurst and Home farm). Of the three Capesthorne Estate farms in Henbury, one, Lodge Farm, has been sold for conversion into a private house. Farms below a certain size are not economically viable and can no longer provide a living.

The land of these ancient farms is still farmed, but under a new system of management in which several may be combined into larger units. Large machines are brought in by contractors as needed to do the work that used to be done by the resident farmer and his men. The scale of this change in agriculture is perhaps not fully appreciated by many of us, and is occurring in Henbury in the context of centuries of a relatively stable farming community.

Some idea of the farming community in the 17th century can be found from the Hearth Tax records. For Henbury in 1663 the records list 53 hearths and 31 owners, and for 1674, 53 hearths and 27 owners. Sir Fulk Lucy of Henbury Hall enjoyed 20 hearths in 1674. By multiplying the number of owners by 4.5 it is possible to

---

[1] The Batsford Companion to Local History. Stephen Friar, Batsford 1991.

Henbury

obtain a very rough approximation of the total population. This gives a population of roughly 139 in 1663. The Hearth Tax record held by Chester Record Office however does not list those who held exemption certificates, or who were too poor to pay the tax - or all those evading the tax. In addition, there would have been a number of employees resident in Henbury Hall. An approximate figure therefore for the mid to late 17th century population of Henbury can be assessed to be around 200 persons, a figure not radically different from that given in the census for Henbury in the early 19th century; this implies an unchanged farming community going back many generations, which has all but disappeared in the last half century.

There is no future in just sitting complacently in the wreckage. We need to plan how to build a future for Henbury which can cherish some of the good things from the past, whilst laying plans for a stable future of this essentially rural environment. This is the subject of the last chapter in this book.

Chapter 19

Looking Ahead

Henbury cum Pexall has always been a small, independent settlement, distinct from Macclesfield and nearby Broken Cross. From time immemorial it has been agricultural in character and is so today. The small mixed farms of fifty years ago have given way to more intensive dairying, many amalgamating into larger units of tenure, but farming remains predominant. Henbury Hall, which has been the focus of much of the development of the village, has long been the home of many prominent and public-spirited men. In the 17th century Sir Fulk Lucy was MP for Chester, and later so was Sir William Meredith. John Brocklehurst and John Ryle were elected the two first MP's for Macclesfield. John Brocklehurst was followed as MP by his son William Coare Brocklehurst. John's nephew, Thomas Unett Brocklehurst, was twice Mayor of Macclesfield and High Sheriff of Cheshire. To Thomas Marsland we owe the School and the Church which have been of such great benefit to the village. Sebastian de Ferranti has continued the tradition with appointments as Deputy Lieutenant and High Sheriff of Cheshire.

The organisation of the village in the 18th and 19th centuries was very much the preserve of the squire and the leading farming families. They now share roles as Parish Councillors and Church Wardens with a more recent group of residents who bring new perspectives and new talents to the village; their background may not be in agriculture but they have the welfare of the village and its way of life very much at heart.

Improvements in roads and communications have enabled the newer villagers to live in the country while finding employment at some distance. This new group have worked with the farming community to bring about many beneficial changes for the village - the Church Hall, awards for the Best Kept Village, the Henbury Society, the Millennium Green with its festivals and festivities - and worked to enliven such activities for old and young alike. All of us are anxious to maintain and increase these blessings, and wish to maintain the separate and proud identity of the village.

Henbury

Progress and change are inevitable, and may be welcome provided that they do not erode the character and quality of village life.

Paradoxically, the roads which have given a renewal of vigour to the life of the village by encouraging the settlement of a new group of people, are now a source of some concern. The main Macclesfield-Chester road A537 is becoming more and more heavily used, primarily by through traffic. It is not so long ago that George Dooley could drive his cows across the road for milking twice a day, but now traffic from the side roads often has to wait many minutes to find a gap in the continuous stream of cars and lorries. Cycling and walking are dangerous; meetings between local inhabitants should be possible without having to drive a car.

As in most of Britain, rapid and large changes are occurring all round us in the countryside. Farming is organised in larger and larger units, and worked more by machines than by human effort. But there have been large changes in farming in the past, and we should not be too sentimental about the passing of the small farms, where the way of life may seem idyllic but could sometimes be grim and gruelling. There is a growing change of attitude to newcomers: the countryside is becoming more welcoming to townsfolk, providing them with relaxation in their leisure time. More access will perhaps be allowed to ramblers, horse riders, cyclists and anglers, who will learn to respond with a sense of responsibility and appreciation. It is some advantage that Cheshire is not a main tourist area, and we are spared the artificiality of so-called attractions and theme parks!

All of us who care about Henbury must take responsibility and be aware that the future is in our hands. We all need to be aware of changes and movements in local government policies, reminding ourselves of our democratic rights. We should welcome benign change, while watching out for and opposing such centralising and doctrinaire diktats as may adversely affect our proud and independent heritage.

Chapter 20

The Henbury Archive

The Hunt for Evidence. During the past three years, the small group researching and producing this book have, like detectives, been out hunting for evidence or any clue that can help to show what has happened in and to Henbury over the last 4000 years. There is a methodical approach to this task, for historical evidence falls into three clear categories, written, spoken and material. The written record is documentary evidence, that which is spoken is the oral evidence, and the third is the history of the landscape, which is the evidence you see on the ground. If these sources are studied as fully as possible, the task has been well done.

The documentary record is vast; even for such a small place as Henbury, a surprisingly large amount of material turned up. The Cheshire County Record Office, was the first port of call, but material was found and studied in eleven record repositories in all, and other material held in private hands in Henbury was loaned to us. Actually finding what records exist is the biggest problem; luck plays a part, and by looking in the right place one member of the group was temporarily overwhelmed by a mountain of paper. Certainly there is material which we have missed, and some which we have not yet been able to study.

The large variety of documents seen includes national and local surveys, maps, photographs, printed material and deeds. The term 'deed' is a cover for many types of documents, which often show ownership of property, whether house, farm or field. They include conveyances, leases, mortgages, court actions and wills. These have been abstracted: not an easy task, for sometimes archaic handwriting and terminology is a problem, and the legal profession hides the information we need, that is who sold what, to whom, when and for how much, in a sea of words. Several hundred deeds and wills have been studied. Not all written evidence is on paper or vellum, some is written on stone. Parts of this story come from gravestones, datestones on houses and the war memorial.

Of equal importance to the documentary evidence are the tape recordings of memories of past and present Henbury people. A good memory, at first hand, can add real and colourful detail to a

Henbury

story, which on paper may appear dull and dusty, rather like making black and white into a colour picture. The changes in Henbury over the time of one memory, say eighty years, were large: changes in agricultural practice, the war and traffic are just a few. The first tractor is remembered, and also the farm horses which it replaced, and the V1 explosion, experienced at very close hand. Without these eye witnesses the story would not be as interesting. What parents and grandparents related, memories at second and third hand, are also here, just as interesting: but beware, memories fade and time flies faster than imagined. Folk tales have also been recorded. Henbury is no exception in having rumours of secret underground passages, and the usual haunted house, but what these stories mean is anyone's guess.

The history of the landscape, the third type of evidence, is there for all to see as we walk around the fields, paths and roads. Every activity of man on the landscape will leave a trace, even long after that activity has ceased. An old road, superseded and not used for centuries, will leave some trace, probably a shallow ditch. Mediaeval ploughing of the same patch of land, which was always in the same direction, for up to several centuries, will leave behind the undulations called ridge and furrow; these persist even after many years of modern ploughing. They cannot be eradicated, except of course by a property developer with a bulldozer, often abetted by an uncaring council. These traces in the fields are all visible, ridges, ditches, humps, lumps and bumps; the question is what do they show; a ditch can be the result of many things, old road, watercourse, defensive structure, or what? Archaeology, in which Henbury is surprisingly rich, and architecture both fall into this category of evidence. The documentary story of a farmhouse can be matched against its architecture.

Occasionally all three types of evidence can be obtained and will tell the same story. This is not common but has happened in this research on Henbury. This is a triumph, and an endorsement of the quality of the work. From a hazy memory, a document turned up, then more documents, one map and then another map. The crowning was two field walks when a few stone remains of a structure were discovered, and possibly even a picture was later found (see Chapter 13). This find was certainly very interesting, and probably important, and it happened in Henbury.

The Archive. This book contains only a selection from the mass of information and material collected by the history group. The whole collection will be indexed and placed in an archive, or rather two versions of an archive, one to be retained in the Church Hall in Henbury, and the other to be given to the Cheshire Record Office. Our archive will contain references to all the material we have seen, whether used for this book or not, abstracts of documents such as the deeds and wills, whether from the record offices or in private hands, copies of documents such as the census returns and land tax assessments, copies of papers lent to us by usually local people, any original papers or printed books, and transcriptions of the tape recorded interviews. There is a good collection of photographs, only a few of which appear here. There are several maps; some of the estate maps are old, coloured, extremely interesting, large and very fragile. Only rough copies and tracings of most of these have so far been made; some have been photographed but they cannot be photocopied in the usual way. The archive given to the CRO will be smaller than that kept in Henbury, since they already hold the originals of deeds which we have copied or abstracted. All new material will be available to their holdings.

Over the centuries many documents have been lost or destroyed. We are trying to prevent more hard won information being lost, and we are hoping to give a good start to any who follow us in the search for Henbury history. We hope you enjoy it as much as we have.

The lists which follow are a sample of the Henbury archive. The Hearth Tax is a useful guide to households in the 17th century. The listed Henbury and Birtles wills date from the 16th to the mid 19th centuries, showing the occupations of a largely rural community. The occupations listed in the 1851 and 1901 censuses show the beginning of the demographic changes which are the subject of Chapter 18.

Henbury

HENBURY HEARTH TAX RETURNS

Name	1663	1664	1673	1674
Thomas ASKEY		1		
John BAYLEY (BALY)	1	1		1
Ralph BIRTLES	2	4		
Roger BIRTLES	1	1		1
Randle BIRTLES			1	
Tho BIRTLES				2
John BRADFORD			1	
Mary BURGESS			1	
Edw BUTLEY				1
Thomas COWPER (COUPER)	1	1		
Tho COOP (Share with Richard HENSHAW)				2
Edw CRAGG				1
John DAVENPORT	1	1	1	1
Edward DAVENPORT (and his mother)	2	1	1	1
Tho DAVENPORT (being dead)	1			
Mr. DAVENPORT				1
Edward DEANE	1	1		1
Roger FINNEY	1	1		
Will FINNEY	1	1		
? FINNEY			1	
Ralph FINNEY				1
Wm FISHER			1	
Laurence HANCOCK	1	1		1
Tho (or John) HARDING			1	
John HARROP	1	1		1
John HEATH	2	1		
Richard HENSHALL (Henshaw in 1664 & 1674. Share with Tho COOP)	1	1		(share with COOP)

The archive

Name	1663	1664	1673	1674
Tho (or John) HUDSON			1	
Wm HOULME	1			
Ellen HOULME	1			1
William HULME	1			
Richard HULME (or HOULME)	1	1		
William HULME		1		
William HOLME				1
John HUNT	1	1		1
Thomas HUNTT	1	1		
William JUDSON				1
William LEE (or LEGH & LEIGH)	3	2		3
Sir Fulk LUCY	18	18		20
William LOWE		2		
Mary MADDOCK(S)	1	1		
Robert MILLET (MILLOTT)	1	1		
John MOTTER(S)HEAD	1	1		1
John MOTTRAM	1	1		1
Peter RIDGWAY	1	1		
Richard SKELHORNE (or SKELLORNE)	1	1		1
Ann WHITWORTH (or WHETTWORTH widow)	1	1		1
Randell WALKER	1	1		1
Widdow WALKER				3
William WALTON	1	1		
Widdow WHALTON				1
Year Totals	**53**	**52**	**9**	**51**

Henbury

HENBURY WILLS (for Ref see p222)

Surname	Christian	Occupation	Year	Ref
Alvison	Samual	Husbandman	1778	2
Anderton	Edward	Yeoman	1728	1,3
Anderton	Edward	Yeoman	1835	1
Anderton	Joseph	Yeo/Bachelor	1843	2
Atkinson	Joseph	Farmer	1825	1
Baguley	Joseph	Yeoman	1824	1
Barnes	Henry	Husbandman	1767	1
Baylie	Lawrence	Webster	1683	1,3
Birtles	John		1666	3
Birtles	John	Tailor	1746	1,3
Birtles	Purnell		1669	1,3
Birtles	Peter	Carpenter	1622	1
Birtles	Ralph	Yeoman	1666	1,3
Bracegirdle	Philip	Farmer	1826	1
Bradburn	Alice		1786	1
Bradbury	Chas.	Gentleman	1810	1
Bradbury	Hannah		1762	2
Bramhall	Sarah		1797	2
Bredbury	Chas.		1737	2,3
Brooke	Margaret	Widow	1827	1,4
Brownhill	Anthony	Weaver	1830	1
Buckley	Thomas	Husbandman	1809	2
Burges	George	Yeoman	1618	1,3
Burgess	Emma	Widow	1631	4
Burgess	Emma	Widow	1632	1,3
Careless	William	Yeoman	1729	1.3
Careless	William	Gentleman	1843	1
Cooper	Abraham	Yeoman	1726	1,3
Cooper	Thomas	Husbandman	1630	1,3
Cowper	Thomas	Husbandman	1684	1,3
Davenport	Elizabeth		1577	1,3
Davenport	John		1556	1
Davenport	Richard		1616	3
Davenport	William	Blacksmith	1768	2

The archive

Davenport	Elizabeth		1577	1,3
Davenport	John		1556	1
Davenport	Richard		1616	3
Davenport	William	Blacksmith	1768	2
Dean	Thorley	Bachelor	1810	2
Dale	Joseph the Elder	Farmer	1833	1
Davenport	William	Esquire	1640	1,3,4
Finney	Joyce		1623	3
Finney	Ralph		1612	1,3
Foden	Thomas	Carpenter	166	1,3
Gibson	Ann	Spinster	1848	1
Goodwin	Martha	Farmer	1826	2
Hall	John	Yeoman	1690	1,3
Hammond	Robert	Yeoman	1818	1
Hancock	Lawrence		1674	3
Harding	Elizabeth	Widow	1683	1,3
Harding	John		1690	2,3
Harding	Mary		1715	2
Harrop	John		1686	3
Harrop	Thomas	Husbandman	1713	1,3
Henshaw	Ann	Yeoman	1686	3
Henshaw	Richard/		1685	3
Hibbert	John	Yeoman	1760	1
Higginbotham	James	Gentleman	1814	1
Higginbotham	Robert	Gentleman	1849	1
Hockenhull	Samual	Publican	1851	1
Hudson	Amos	Tailor	1817	2
Hulme	Ellen	Widow	1677	1,3
Hulme	Thomas	Yeoman	1643	1,3
Hulme	Thomas	Yeoman	1646	1,3
Hulme	William	Webster	1689	2,3
Hulme	William	Yeoman	1699	2,3
Hunt	Ellen	Widow	1679	1,3
Hutton	William	Yeoman	1690	1
Hyde	Joseph	Carpenter	1759	2,3
Jodrell	Francis	Gentleman	1829	1,4

Henbury

Jodrell	John Bower	Esquire	1796	1,4
Johnson	Thomas	Husbandman	1799	1
Lancaster	Joseph	Blacksmith	1841	1
Lancaster	John	Blacksmith	1825	2
Latham	John	Gentleman	1765	1,4
Leigh	Joseph	Joiner	1855	1
Lingrand	John	Yeoman	1737	1,3
Lockitt	William	Victualler	1842	2
Lounds	William		1723	1,3
Lowe	Thomas	Yeoman	1729	2
Maddock	Thomas	Husbandman	1621	1,3
Marsland	Thomas	Esquire	1855	1
Mellor	Isaac	Yeoman	1806	1
Meredith	Amos	Baronet	1670	1,3
Meredith	Amos		1745	1,2
Meredith	Jane	Minor	1710	2
Meredith	Joanna	Widow	1754	2
Meredith	Sir William	Baronet	1752	1,2,4
Meredith	Sir William	Baronet	1807	1,2
Millitt	Thomas	Yeoman	1724	2
Morris	Samual	Labourer	1816	2
Mottershead	Thomas	Yeoman	1743	2,3
Mottram	John	Yeoman	1604	1,3
Mottram	John		1724	1,3
Mottram			1674	3
Pimlot	John	Husbandman	1801	1
Pimlot	Martha	Widow	1821	1
Pimlott	Joseph	Husbandman	1856	1,2
Pimlott	William	Farmer	1798	2
Plant	Justice	Husbandman	1649	1,3
Prestbury	William		1684	3
Priest	Joseph	Labourer	1853	2
Rathbone	Martha		1824	2
Rowbotham	John	Yeoman	1803	1

Rowbotham	William	Yeoman	1773	1
Rowbotham	William	Farmer	1846	1
Royle	Thomas		1664	2
Sandbach	Richard	Tanner	1725	1,3
Shaw	Thomas	Yeoman	1748	1
Siddall	Alice		1614	1,3
Simpson	Isaac	Farmer	1847	1
Simpson	Jacob	Farmer	1838	1
Simpson	Jacob	Labourer	1840	1
Simpson	Sarah	Widow	1841	2
Swettenham	George	Gentleman	1712	2,3
Taylor	James	Farmer	1835	1
Wainwright	Hannah	Widow	1792	1
Wainwright	John	Yeoman	1769	1
Walker	Peter	Yeoman	1783	1
Walker	Randle	Husbandman	1685	2,3
Walley	Nathaniel	Farmer	1834	2
Walley	Peter		1669	3
Warrington	James	Miller	1760	1
Wharmby	John	Husbandman	1721	1,3
Wharmby	William	Yeoman	1730	1,3
Whittingham	Ellen	Widow	1671	3
Whitworth	Randle	Husbandman	1663	2,3
Williams	Jane	Spinster	1831	1
Wood	James	Whitesmith	1730	1,3
Wood	William	Farmer	1829	2
Worthington	Jeremiah	Yeoman	1830	1
Worthington	Sarah	Widow	1760	2
Worthington	Timothy		1757	2
Wright	Randle	Farmer	1773	1

BIRTLES WILLS (for ref see p222)

Bayley	Martha		1855	2
Birtles	Ann	Widow	1627	1,3
Birtles	Edward	Husbandman	1591	1,3
Birtles	John	Gentleman	1622	3

Henbury

Birtles	John	Birtles, the Hill	1664	3
Birtles	John	Husbandman	1712	2,3
Birtles	John	Yeoman	1771	1
Birtles	Roger	Husbandman	1616	1,3
Birtles	William	Yeoman	1623	1,3
Brasier	John	Husbandman	1688	1,3
Broadhurst	Jonathan	Farmer	1765	2,3
Broadhurst	John	Farmer	1827	1,3
Cottrell	Jasper	Miller	1840	2
Daniel	Edward	Yeoman	1748	1
Davenport	John	Chester	1691	1,2,3
Drake	Thomas	Husbandman	1673	1,3
Edwards	Thomas Hough	Labourer	1870	1,2
Fowden	Joseph	Esquire	1808	1
Harding	Nicholas	Husbandman	1683	1,3
Hibbert	Robert	Also of Chalfont Howe, Bucks	1835	1
Howard	Thomas	Farmer	1857	1
Page	Edward	Husbandman	1591	1,3
Percival	Ann	Widow	1722	1,3
Percival	Thomas	Yeoman	1726	1,3
Priest	John	Farmer	1913	1
Reddish	William	Yeoman	1616	1,3
Slater	Cyrus	Farmer	1855	1
Whittacre	John	Yeoman	1707	2,3
Whittaker	Richard		1627	1,3
Witty	John	Farmer	1864	1
Wright	James	Farmer	1832	1

1 A will is available   *2 Letter of Administration*
3 Inventory   *4 Codicil*

Index

Act of God 175
Agriculture, 12
Alderley Park 123
Alderley Park Estate, 34
Anderton, Samuel 101
Anderton's Lane 180, 206
Apostle Cottage 44
Archive 215
Astle Park 124
Bag Brook 159, 164
Barlow, Harry 197
Bayley, Frank 78
Bayley, Harold 26
Bayley, Henry 78
Bearhurst Farm 2, 60, 112
Beech Cottage 102
Best-Kept Village 179, 188
Bethell, David 2
Birch Tree Farm 34
Birtles on the Hill 125
Birtles 110, 177
Birtles & Over Alderley 130
Birtles Bowl 182
Birtles family 124
Birtles Hall 128ff, 131
Birtles houses 127
Birtles Mill 159
Birtles of the Pale 125
Birtles Old Hall 128
Blacksmith 151

Blacksmith's Arms 104, 150, 182, 185
Booth, Jackie 139
Bostock, Joyce 196
Bradbury, Charles 98
Bradbury, Elizabeth 151
Brick Bank Farm 59
Brocklehurst, Edward 119
Brocklehurst, John 119, 211
Brocklehurst, May Vardon 147
Brocklehurst, Thomas 109, 135, 176, 211
Brocklehurst, William Coare 211
Broken Cross Sunday School 133
Broome Cottage 23, 73
Broomfield Farm 22, 40, 54, 209
Broomfield, John 22
Bypass 187
Capesthorne 11, 123, 126
Cave, The 149
Census 40, 205
Cheese making 22, 25
Chelford Road 154
Cheshire Landscape Trust 190
Cheshire Record Office 213, 215

Henbury

Chester road 212
Church Hall 146
Church Lane 206
Clarke, Edward Arthur 91
Cock Bank 205
Cock Inn 81, 86, 151
Cock Wood 187
Coleman, Mrs 138
Coleman, Phillip 23
Cousin, Ann 181, 189
Cyclists 93
Dale, Anthony 36
Damburst 113, 167, 169
Dark Lane 71, 155, 180, 206
Davenport estate, 16
Davenport Hayes 96, 177
de Davenport Sir John 115
de Ferranti family 120
de Ferranti, Sebastian 211
Dobell, Darcy 162
Domesday Book 1, 7
Doodlebug, V1 195
Dooley, George 84, 194, 212
Elstob, Wilfrith V.C, 193, 200
Enclosure 84
Engine Pool 108, 165, 166
Fairhurst, Harry 110
Fanshawe Brook 41
Fanshawe Cottage 44
Field names 18
Firs, The 81
Fletcher, Andrew 38
Fletcher, David ("Jim") 35
Flora Garden Centre 181
Flying bomb, V1 195
Foschtinsky, Joan 29, 197

Gawsworth 18
Geldart, W 149
Glebe Cottage 45
Glynn Jones, Canon 139
Goddard, Walter 93
Gould, Tom 194
Gould, Tom and Jean 23, 26, 28
Graham-Smith, Sir Francis 191
Great Pool 108, 166
Hameteberie 16
Hardings Tenement 81, 89
Hatton, Ralph 25, 28
Hatton, Walter 197
Hearth Tax 40, 209, 215
Heathcote, Ethel 197
Heathcote, George 26
Henbury Hall, Owners 114
Henbury Mill 164
Henbury Millennium Green Trust 190
Henbury Moss 41
Henbury Moss Farm 43
Henbury Poor House 102
Henbury Rise 206
Henbury School 94
Henbury Smithy 78
Henbury Society 185, 211
Hibbert, Robert 126
High Lodge 79
High Trees 71
Hightree Drive 206
Holland, Samuel 93
Home Farm 26, 61
Home Guard 27
Horseshoe Farm 23

Index

House-building 36, 178, 205
Hugh Lupus 11, 105
Hulme's Tenement 22, 188
Ice house 112
Indentures 39
Ivydale Farm 83, 89
Jodrell, John Bower 16, 116
Jodrells Arms 82, 88
John Day charity 72
Kelly, Felix 111
Kennerley, Ernest 28, 149
Kershaw, Chris and Joan 160
Knight, Elsie 28, 78, 194, 200
Knoll Cottage 52
Land tax records 40
Latham's Tenement 101
Lily Cottage 42
Lime Tree Cottage 35, 76
Lingards Farm 20, 24, 48, 150
Lodge Farm 26, 51
Long Moss 154
Lowndes Tenement 76
Lucy, Sir Fulk 50, 98, 115, 209, 211
Macclesfield Local Plan. 186
Manors 11, 16
Marl Heath 63
Marl pits 22
Marshall, Arthur 81, 103, 149
Marsland, Major John 118, 134
Marsland, Mrs Jane 175
Marsland, Sir Thomas 142, 211

Massey family 21
Matthews' Nurseries 110
Meredith, Amos 116
Meredith, Sir William 105, 211
Meredith, Sir William 16
Mill House Farm 161
Moss Cottage 42
Moss Farm 24
Moss Rooms 99
Mottrams Tenement 81, 86
Mount Farm 35
Mount, The 101
National Schools 134
Nichols v Marsland 175
Old Chapter 75
Over Alderley 15
Pale Croft 78
Pale Farm 39, 40, 66, 125, 142
Parish Council 177, 185
Park House Farm 23, 61, 150
Parkfield House 81, 103
Pepper Street. 155
Pexall Service Station 150, 181
Pexhill Farm 28, 57
Place names 141
Plague Stones 198
Pleasant View 155
Population census 205
Potato harvest 27
Prehistoric henge 4
Prestbury Church 141
Putty Row 71, 81, 90, 133
Residents' Association 185
Rhodes, Bernard 96

225

Henbury

Rinderpest 22
Rose Queen festival 191
Rosemary Cottage 76
Rough Heys Farm 33, 132
Rowbotham, Mike 94
Rowley, Gordon 1
Ruewood 21, 63
Ryle, John 117, 211
Ryle's Arms 82, 118
Sandbach Farm 47, 209
Sandbach, John 22
Scragg's Fowd 77
Shea, Rev RFJ 136
Smith, Peter 181
Sparrow, ACG 131
Spinks Farm 20, 49
Springbank Cottage 24, 43
Squirrels 109, 194
St Catherine's Church 130,
St Thomas's Church 142, 190
St Thomas's Parish 15
Stanley, Arthur Lyulph 130
Street lighting 180
Sundial 191
Swindells, Barbara 139
Sycamore Cottage 83, 92
Sycamore Farm 46
Tatton, Jean 30
Thorneycroft Lodge Farm 2
Trussell family 105
Turnpike Trust 156
Upper Pool 113, 165
Vicarage 146
Waite, Terry 138, 194
Wardle, Mrs 193
Water supply 24, 35, 42, 51
Whirley 17
Whirley Common 154
Whirley Hall 124, 129, 132
Whirley Rise 206
Wills 215
Woodhouse Farm 90
World War I 198
Worthington Close 35
Worthington, Ephraim 33
Worthington, John 34
Yew Tree Farm 74